This book is dedicated to my mother,
Frances Spencer Powell.

About the Author

Elizabeth Powell Crowe has been writing for over 25 years. Her previous editions of *Genealogy Online* have sold a combined total of nearly 200,000 copies. Crowe has been a contributing editor for *Computer Currents* magazine and is the author of numerous articles in both popular and technical publications. Her work has appeared in *Civil War Times*, *PC World*, C|Net, and other publications and websites. She has been a guest on WashingtonPost.com's chat with Jacquelin D. Salmon, DearMRYTLE's Family History Internet Radio Show, and other national news programs. Ms. Crowe often makes speeches and conducts workshops on online genealogy, has been a presenter at the Institute of Genealogy and Historical Research at Samford University and at GENTECH, and has edited genealogy publications. She lives in Huntsville, Alabama with her husband, two children, and dog.

Genealogy Online, Seventh Edition

Elizabeth Powell Crowe

McGraw-Hill/Osborne

New York   Chicago   San Francisco
Lisbon   London   Madrid   Mexico City
Milan   New Delhi   San Juan
Seoul   Singapore   Sydney   Toronto

The *McGraw-Hill* Companies

McGraw-Hill/Osborne
2100 Powell Street, 10th Floor
Emeryville, California 94608
U.S.A.

To arrange bulk purchase discounts for sales promotions, premiums, or fund-raisers, please contact **McGraw-Hill**/Osborne at the above address. For information on translations or book distributors outside the U.S.A., please see the International Contact Information page immediately following the index of this book.

Genealogy Online, Seventh Edition

1234567890 FGR FGR 019876543
ISBN 0-07-222978-0

Publisher   Brandon A. Nordin
Vice President & Associate Publisher   Scott Rogers
Acqusition Editor   Marjorie McAneny
Project Editor   Patty Mon
Acquisitions Coordinator   Tana Allen
Technical Editor   Will Kelly
Copy Editor   Bart Reed
Proofreader   Stefany Otis
Indexer   Karin Arrigoni
Composition   Tara A. Davis, Kelly Stanton-Scott
Illustrators   Kathleen Fay Edwards, Lyssa Wald
Series Design   Gary Corrigan
Cover Designer   William Voss

This book was composed with Corel VENTURA™ Publisher.

Contents

PART II
Using the Internet for Genealogy

PART IV
Appendixes

Acknowledgments

As with any book, this one was made possible by the efforts of many people besides the author. First, I'd like to thank each and every person mentioned in this book, as I obviously couldn't have done it without all of you.

Special thanks go to Bill Ammons, Pat Richley, Jeanne Henry, Terry Ann Morgan, Nick Pawluck, Myra Vanderpool Gormley, Dick Eastman, Gale Fuller, Randy Hooser, Liz Kelley Kerstens, Will Kelley, Margie McAneny, and all the staff at McGraw Hill/Osborne. Immense gratitude is due to all my family and friends, who were more than patient with me while I was writing this book.

But most of all I want to thank my mother, Frances Spencer Powell, who urged and encouraged me, proofread and researched for me, traveled and travailed with me throughout the entire process from initial idea to final galleys.

Introduction

"I've gotten more genealogy done in one year on Prodigy than I did in 20 years on my own!" my mother exclaimed. This quote, from a 30-year genealogy veteran, shows how technology has changed even this popular hobby. The mind-boggling deluge of data needed to trace one's family tree has finally found a knife to whittle it down to size: the computer.

The potential for finding clues, data, and other researchers looking for your same family names has increased exponentially since the last edition of this book was published. In the time since the last edition, major genealogy websites, such as Ancestry.com, Genealogy.com, Everton.com, and FamilySearch.org, have all added more data and made their sites more user-friendly. Even if you've never used the Internet before, these sites can help you get started with online genealogy. And, now, more software programs than ever can help you track your genealogy and share it with others, such as the newest version of Personal Ancestral File, which lets you carry your pedigree around with you on your PDA. In short, online genealogy is just getting better, and it's a good time to try your hand at it!

Bill Ammons' Story

Bill Ammons is a friend of mine who used a few hints on online genealogy from me to break down a brick wall in his genealogy research. Here is what he wrote to me about his quest:

> I started my genealogy research 16 months ago with the name of the only grandparent I knew from my childhood. The journey has taken me from knowing a very small family to discovering an enormously large family. I have learned a lot about history, our society, family secrets, and what not to say in e-mails even jokingly to family. I have hit roadblocks and gotten through some, while others are still being researched.
>
> Some roadblocks will never be resolved, as the documents were destroyed because of Civil War or mysterious fires at the courthouses or newspaper offices. However, on your journey, you, too, will become a collector of websites, books on dead people, and American history.
>
> Roadblocks are very interesting challenges in that one must begin to be creative in their research to find clues to get them through the roadblocks. If the information on the Internet leads to roadblocks, then try going to the county historical society office and then to the county courthouse to look for wills, land documents, bible records, newspaper articles, and even personal letters. I have found old bible records at the historical societies that have provided clues to names I was uncertain of and even provided insights into cemetery records.
>
> I started my journey with a simple posting to the Horry County, South Carolina Historic Society homepage, at www.hchsonline.org (see Figure 1).
>
> From a simple posting on the message board of the four family surnames (Ammons, Denton, Martin, and Tompkins), I received a response the next day that solved the Martin branch of my tree to 1810. My cousin is, in fact, one of the contributors of documents to the Horry Historic Society site. Sometimes one can find a new family member and find genealogy at the same time.
>
> The next day brought another surprise when I received an e-mail from a gentleman in Atlanta who provided the Denton branch of my family tree. His mother was my grandmother's sister. I never met my grandmother's sisters. But this posting yielded another new family member and also received information about the Denton family as a bonus. This family member pointed me to documents and newspaper articles available online that

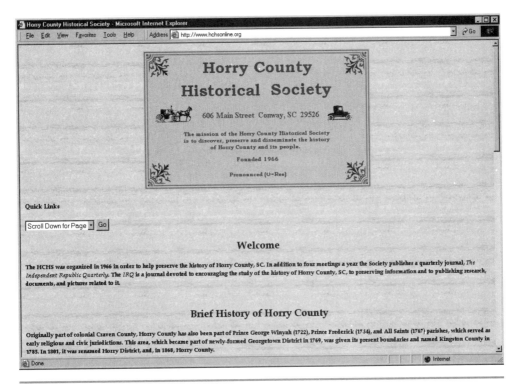

FIGURE 1. *Local organizations can be a big help in online genealogy research.*

provided personal insight as to the possibilities that my grandmother and grandfather were Native Americans.

Then I had to really get into the digging mindset to start finding information and documents on the other surnames. The Ammons surname has taken me from the coast of South Carolina to the Appalachian Mountains and back to Sampson County, North Carolina. I never had any idea that the Ammons family came from North Carolina because I grew up with the understanding that the Ammons were "Black Irish" who migrated to South Carolina. The real surprise has been in the documentation I have obtained that does not support this idea that we were "Black Irish" (see Figure 2).

Census reports from Ancestry.com (www.ancestry.com) have been well worth the monthly cost for the subscription. The census reports are searchable and easily accessed even with a dial-up connection. The census reports provide a roadmap of where the family is migrating or has settled.

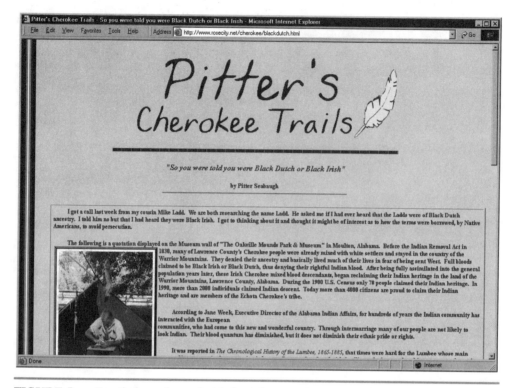

FIGURE 2. *Family legends can hold clues, but you have to research carefully.*

Also, the census reports tell something about the families' living conditions, employment, education, and neighbors. From these documents, I was able to trace my family from 1780 to the 1920s. I found the earliest reference to the Ammons family in Sampson County, North Carolina, then they migrated to Marlboro County, South Carolina after the American Revolution, and the children migrated to Macon and Cherokee Counties of North Carolina.

The documents from the American Revolution were obtained from Wallace State College in Hanceville, Alabama. This community college has a tremendous records area on the American Revolution and the Civil War, as well as access to the 2.5 million microfilm reels from the Genealogical Society of Utah. The college also has courses in family and regional history. I know that the Ammons family received a land grant in Marlboro County because they served in the American Revolution.

I also was able to use Cyndi's List to help search the Native American connections. This can be a very useful page to research roots that are connected to the federally recognized tribes. This issue is a separate and interesting journey, which can involve discovering your genetic markers, such as Asian Shovel Teeth, anatomic knot, and "race" related diseases.

Another helpful resource was the Melungeons page. Some people are really confused about this group of folks who lived in North Carolina. The more I read about the forgotten Portuguese, the more interesting I found this hidden part of America's history.

To date, the journey has brought me to the Waccamaw Indian People of South Carolina and the Croatans of North Carolina. I am a tribal member of the Waccamaw Indian People of South Carolina. The tribal journey has taken me to the Croatan Indians of Sampson County, North Carolina (http://docsouth.dsi.internet2.edu/nc/butler.html), on the University of North Carolina at Chapel Hill Library site (see Figure 3).

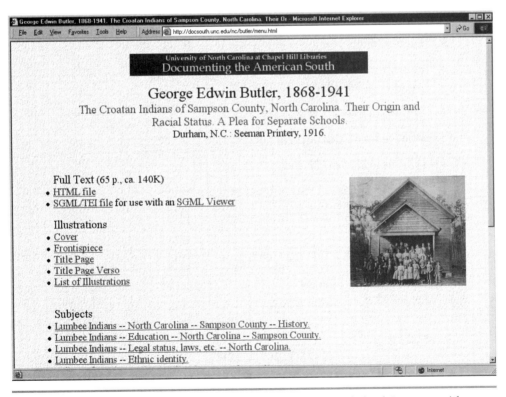

FIGURE 3. *A full-text online book at the NCCH Library site helped Ammons with his genealogy.*

The online book written by George Butler in 1916 was a jewel of a find in this surname search. The book talks to the fact of the Croatans having a connection with the lost colonists of Roanoke. This discovery led to researching the census records. The census places the family in the correct place at the correct time to strengthen the argument of where they originated. Currently, I plan to continue my research focused on the county, state, and federal records of the time. A big plus was the photos in the book with people that resemble family members I know today.

In my research for records, I have been to Raleigh, North Carolina Archives. (A word to the wise: Don't take any ink pens and/or briefcases. You will not be allowed into the records area.) Believe me, it is a tremendous treat to see the historical records that remain. The information you can discover is well worth the frustration.

As you can see, Bill Ammon's journey took him to many different online and offline resources:

- Local college resources for genealogy (Chapter 5)
- Search sites such as Cyndi's List to find online information about Native Americans (Chapter 6)
- Online queries (Chapter 8)
- Vital records from government archives (Chapter 9)
- Online libraries (Chapter 12)
- Ethnic resources online (Chapter 14)
- Ancestry.com (see Chapter 17).

Bill took what he knew from his own immediate family, plus the family legends and gossip, to begin searching for the original records he needed. He went to some resources in person, such as the North Carolina Archives and Wallace State College Library, but only after online research told him that's where he needed to go. This is an excellent example of genealogy online.

Where Computers Come In

Databases, online services, online card catalogs, and bulletin boards are changing the *brick wall syndrome,* that frustrating phase of any lineage search where the information needed seems unavailable. Genealogists who have faced the challenges and triumphed are online, helping others.

State governments and the federal government have recently started to put data, such as death records, veterans' records, and so on, in machine-readable databases that can then be accessible via the Internet. The Bureau of Land Management, the Library of Congress, and the National Archives and Records Administration are just a few examples of government sites that can help the family historian.

The United States alone has numerous genealogical societies that trace people's descendants. Some of these are national, but many more are local or regional, such as the Tennessee Valley Genealogical Society and the New England Historical Society. Others are specific to certain names. Many patriotic organizations, such as the Daughters of the Confederacy, limit membership to descendants of a particular historical group. Many of these groups offer courses in genealogy, which can help you with online and offline research.

A recent cover article in *CompuServe* magazine highlighted the uses of its online forum for genealogy, where forum leader Dick Eastman said thousands of users visit a week. The article then describes how the forum helped one woman find her natural father, how stories about ancestors are swapped, and the sort of informational files uploaded to the library.

There's no denying that the computer has changed nearly everything in our lives, and the avocation and vocation of genealogical research is no exception. Further, a wonderful new resource for computers, the Internet, has come into being and is still developing at a dizzying pace. This book explores many different networks, services, and websites that can help you in your pursuit of your ancestry.

Stories about how online communities have helped people in their genealogical research abound. Here are some examples.

DearMYRTLE Finds a Patriot

DearMYRTLE, a daily genealogy columnist on the Internet (see Chapter 5 or www.dearmyrtle.com), was helping a friend move files, data, and programs from an old computer to a new one. In the course of the conversation, DearMYRTLE's friend wondered aloud what online genealogy could do for him, but expressed doubt anything useful could turn up online.

Then the conversation turned to the first of the new United States quarters, the one with the Delaware patriot Cesar Rodney on the reverse.

"Who was he?" asked DearMYRTLE's friend.

"All right," DearMYRTLE replied, "let's run a test. Your wife here will look up Cesar Rodney in the *Encyclopedia Britannica.* You look him up on your old computer using Microsoft Encarta 97. I'll look him up on the Internet with your new computer."

Faster than the other two could use either a book or a CD-ROM, DearMYRTLE found a transcription of a letter from George Washington to Rodney (see Figure 4).

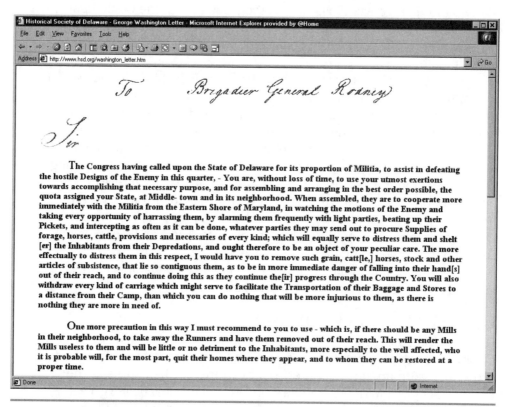

FIGURE 4. *Online research leads to treasures, such as this letter from George Washington to Cesar Rodney.*

Nancy's Story

Nancy is a friend of mine from high school who knows more about computers and the Internet than I do, but not quite so much about genealogy. When her stepmother died recently, Nancy got a large box of her father's memorabilia and photos. She called to ask me about genealogy, and I showed her some good genealogy sites on the Internet on her laptop computer.

I didn't think much more about it until she called me a few weeks later in considerable excitement. She had not only found the USGenWeb (www.usgenweb.org) site for her father's home county in Texas, but also that the moderator of the site had known both her father and her grandfather. She was scanning in the old photos and e-mailing them to the fellow, and he was identifying people in them left and right. One was of Nancy's grandfather as a child. Another showed her father as a teenager. Every day, the USGenWeb moderator was helping her fill in more holes in her family history.

What's a Hoosier? Genealogy Has the Answer

Randy Hooser, of Huntsville, Alabama, has been working on his genealogy for years. One result has been his work with a University of Indiana professor to publish a white paper to prove his family is the origin of the nickname "Hoosier." A fascinating story, the migration of Randy's family involves religious and political movements of this nation's history, which was published and is posted at www.geocities.com/Heartland/Ranch/1226/mmm_intro.html. In it, Randy postulates that his pioneer ancestors, being usually the farthest west of civilization, were the origin of the nickname "Hoosier." Randy has also used the Web to maintain an active e-mail list, organize a family reunion at Pleasant Hill in Kentucky (where an ancestor had been a neighbor to the Shaker religious community), and helped others with their genealogy.

A Quick Look at This Book

This book gives you a basic education in the online world. Nevertheless, please be aware that what is written here was current when written. Since that time, commercial online services and the Internet will have added, expanded, revised, and changed what they offer, as well as how and when they offer it. The only constant in the online world for the last five years has been change, and at an exponential rate. So, be prepared for adventures!

I hope you'll find in this book the tools you need to get started, or continue, pursuing your genealogy with online resources, to share data with other genealogists online, and to participate in the online society in its many facets. Happy hunting!

Part I: The Basics

Chapter 1: Beginning a Genealogy Project   A brief overview of how to do a genealogy project.

Chapter 2: Software You'll Need   From genealogy database programs to CD-ROMs of data, how software can make your search more productive.

Chapter 3: Online Society   The do's and don'ts of getting along online.

Chapter 4: Privacy and Law in Genealogy   Ethical considerations as you pursue your family history.

Part II: Using the Internet for Genealogy

Chapter 5: Genealogy Education   From files to read on the Internet to college credit courses, how to educate yourself on genealogy in general and genealogy online in particular.

Chapter 6: Search Engines   General search tips and genealogy- specific search pages.

Chapter 7: Chat: Hail Thy Fellow Genealogists on the Net!   Instant messaging and traditional IRC can help you connect with other genealogists.

Chapter 8: Genealogy Mail Lists, Newsletters, and Newsgroups
Worldwide, continual discussions on all genealogy topics.

Part III: Specific Online Resources

Chapter 9: Vital Records   How to track down your ancestors' important data.

Chapter 10: The Church of Jesus Christ of Latter-day Saints   How to use the online resources and the Family History Centers.

Chapter 11: Ellis Island Online   An online resource to search for your immigrant ancestors.

Chapter 12: Online Library Card Catalogs   From card catalogs to online books, you can do research in your pajamas!

Chapter 13: International Genealogy Resources   Where to go once you get back to the boat.

Chapter 14: Ethnic Genealogy Resources   Tracking down slave records, Cajun culture, and others.

Chapter 15: The National Genealogical Society   The online site to an important genealogy organization.

Chapter 16: RootsWeb   The oldest volunteer genealogy effort on the Internet.

Chapter 17: The MyFamily.com Network   A network of sites with chats, mail lists, discussion boards, and online data.

Chapter 18: Everton Publishers   A venerable genealogical publisher, with an excellent site.

Chapter 19: Proprietary Content   The major online services, such as AOL and MSN, have genealogy areas.

Chapter 20: Genealogy Database Sites   Where you can search others' GEDCOMs for clues and information.

Chapter 21: Around the Web in 80 (or so) Sites   Sites you shouldn't miss.

Part IV: Appendixes

Appendix A: Genealogical Standards from the National Genealogical Society

Appendix B: Forms of Genealogical Data

Glossary

Part I

The Basics

Chapter 1

Beginning a Genealogy Project

Many folks come to online genealogy after years of doing it the old-fashioned way. They know what they're looking for and simply want to use online tools to help them in their search. However, perhaps you are new to genealogy. In that case, here's some background information before you begin.

Why Genealogy?

My mother and I took a genealogy trip to England in 1989, and one day stopped for lunch in a pub across from St. Mary's Abbey Church in Tewkesbury. St. Mary's has excellent records for a genealogist to search, a beautiful building, and a talented boys' choir, and the town boasts quite a bit of history as well as a first-class golf resort. So, there were many tourists around, British as well as American, and Mother and I had had a grand time poking around in the past.

We were sitting in Miss Marple's Pub enjoying our Ploughman's Lunch when three ladies entered. From their accents and conversation, it was clear they were British and had come for the tour of the abbey. One of them remarked her friend had come earlier in the year to look up her genealogy.

"Why on earth would anybody do that?" she wondered. "Looking up your ancestors. Who cares? They're all dead!"

Mother and I just looked at each other and laughed. The reasons for doing genealogy are almost too many to list for those of us who are practically addicted to it. It can give you a medical history, confirm your rights to an inheritance, qualify your children for specific scholarships, or gain you membership in certain organizations. It gives many people a sense of continuity and belonging. Others get a charge out of the detective-like work that goes into discovering that next generation back.

I asked a few genealogists I know how they got started, what they gain from the hobby, and what they would advise those just getting started.

Curiosity

DearMYRTLE, the genealogy columnist, said, "I want my grandchildren to know who they are, and to have a personal link to some of the events in U.S. history that I missed out on in school. Knowing you had an ancestor who fought in the French and Indian War can make someone pay better attention in class."

What keeps her going, she said, is "insatiable curiosity, and the actual thrill of deductive reasoning when using surviving documents to determine ancestral relationships beyond a reasonable doubt."

DearMYRTLE added, "I've met a lot of cousins, but most importantly, the research I've done with my two closest friends has been incredible. The support we tend to give each other in our work and the fun of helping each other actually find a new ancestor is *great*!"

Jeanne Henry, a certified genealogist in New Market, Alabama, said, "My interest was stimulated as a child by listening to stories told by the old folks around the fireside. I wanted more and more. Then when I saw a tombstone in Newton County, Mississippi that stated a great-grandfather was born in Derry County, Ireland, I really became dedicated to pursue this subject. My advice to a beginner is while conducting your research/investigation, a vital procedure to remember is to record fully who, what, where, when."

Reach Out to Extended Family

Gale Fuller, past president of her local computers-in-genealogy club, said she got hooked on her mother's genealogy files. What keeps her hooked and keeps her going: "The fun people that I meet. I have loved getting to know others who are also related to the same ancestors. And the cousins who are very distant, but we act as if we are next of kin. Discovering about five or six locations of family letters has been a true joy to me. To read the almost 200 letters written as early as 1816 and late as 1890 has told us more about this family than most can ever find.

"If you have the interest, either write or record stories of your youth and what you remember your parents telling you about their youth. Someday this will be so valuable to your grandchildren. Wouldn't you love a diary from your grandparents telling about their life? To me the grandest gift you offer your descendants is the anecdotes of your life. A 'This is my Life' [book] would be wonderful. I am trying to get mine together."

Genealogy Civilized the World

My opinion is that humans became civilized as a result of pedigrees, because when people began to divide themselves into clans based on bloodlines, genealogy begat civilization. To keep track of who belonged in which clan, knowing one's family history was essential. Before people could write down their genealogies, they would pass down family stories to their children by word of mouth. Such storytelling has been important throughout all eras of human history and could even be considered the beginning of all literature. The endurance of this tradition shows we all care who we are and from where our people came.

When clans formed into tribes and tribes formed into nations, genealogy became an essential part of society. Laws were enacted because the division of wealth and power depended largely on inheritance laws, especially regarding thrones and landholdings. Genealogy was used in land transactions, taxation, lawsuits, and not a few feuds and wars. What were the Wars of the Roses about if not genealogy?

Many genealogists see the hobby as a way to understand where they came from and where they're going. This certainly is a fun and interesting way to make history come alive. When you see an account of the Battle of Saratoga, the potato famine in Ireland, or the French Revolution, seeing proof that your ancestors were present makes history much more interesting.

It also proves, of course, that history is all about *you.*

How to Start

Friends often call and ask, "Okay, I want to start my genealogy. What do I do?" The process of genealogy has these basic steps: Look at what you already know, record it, decide what name to pursue next, research and query to track that information, analyze what you have to see what's needed next, and then do it all again.

Collect Information

The number one rule: Begin with yourself. Collect the information you know for certain about yourself, your spouse, and your children. The data you want includes birth, marriage, graduation, and other major life milestones. The documentation would ideally be the original certificates; such documents are considered primary sources. Write down family stories, legends, and events as you remember them; some of this will be considered secondary sources. Photographs, with the people in them identified and the date on back, can also be very valuable. Such documents are considered primary sources because they reflect data recorded close to the time and place of an event.

Note

A primary source is an original piece of information that documents an event: a death certificate, a birth certificate, a marriage license, and so on. A secondary source is a source that may cite an original source but is not the source itself: a newspaper obituary or birth notice, a printed genealogy, a website genealogy, and so on.

Here are some steps you might consider to gather the information:

♦ *Find published genealogies with your surnames.* You can do this with search sites and catalogs such as Cyndi's List (Chapter 6), FamilySearch.com (Chapter 10), RootsWeb (Chapter 16), Ancestry.com (Chapter 17), and genealogy databases (Chapter 20).

♦ *Communicate with other people searching the same family lines as you.* You can do this with the World Wide Web (Chapter 6), through Chat (Chapter 7), mail lists (Chapter 8), RootsWeb and Ancestry, and online services such as AOL (Chapter 19).

♦ *Find original documents or historical information.* Sometimes historical information (such as the fact that mortality schedules are included with some censuses) will help you decide where to look next, whether online of offline. You can do that with the World Wide Web, certain vital records (Chapter 9), Ellis Island Online (Chapter 11), The Library of Congress, the National Archives and Records Administration, and online library catalogs (Chapter 12), international genealogy sites (Chapter 13), ethnic genealogy sites (Chapter 14), Genealogy.com (Chapter 21), and many other sites such as state archives (Chapter 21).

♦ *Learn more about genealogy techniques and practices.* You can do this at the National Genealogical Society site (Chapter 15), RootsWeb, Everton's (Chapter 18), DearMYRTLE's (this chapter and Chapter 19), and through some online courses (Chapter 5).

Sources That Can Help a Genealogical Researcher

- **Vital records**   Birth, death, and marriage records and the Social Security Death Index. Many states did not require these before the twentieth century.

- **Court records**   Wills, adoptions, land and property bills of sale, tax rolls, deeds, naturalization, and even lawsuits.

- **Church records**   Baptisms, marriages, burials, and so on.

- **Newspapers and magazines**   Not only obituaries and marriage and birth notices but also social news (perhaps parents, siblings, or cousins are mentioned).

- **Military records**   Enlistment, commission, muster rolls, and veterans' documentation.

- **Fraternal organizations**   You can sometimes find historical membership lists of organizations, such as the Lions, Optimist, and collegiate organizations, at the national headquarters.

- **Ships' passenger lists**   Not only for immigrants to your country but for travel within. Also, some rivers, such as the Tennessee, were the site of many pioneer marriages.

- **Family History Centers**   FHCs have resources such as the International Genealogical Index, the Ancestral File, and the Old Parochial Register. More about these in Chapter 10!

- **State archives and libraries**   Many are online!

- **Census records**   Not only federal but also state and local.

- **Published genealogies**   Someone may have already researched, and published, a family history for your line. Check out local libraries for such works, but remember they are secondary material.

Keep Track

Now determine how you will keep track of all this. You can fill out family group sheets, pedigree charts, and other forms (see the boxed section titled "A Baker's Dozen of Free Forms"). Many people find an index card system is a good way to keep track and to have a backup to a genealogy program. A sample index card is shown in Figure 1-1.

Most people feel that finding a good genealogy program, which enables them to record sources (as noted in Chapter 2), is the way to go. Paper sources can be scanned into digital form and/or stored in good old-fashioned filing cabinets. Remember to keep a record of all your research findings, even those pieces of information that seem unrelated to your family lines. You never know when you can use such information or pass it on to someone else who needs it.

Even if you decide to do the bulk of your research on a computer, you might still need some paper forms to keep your research organized.

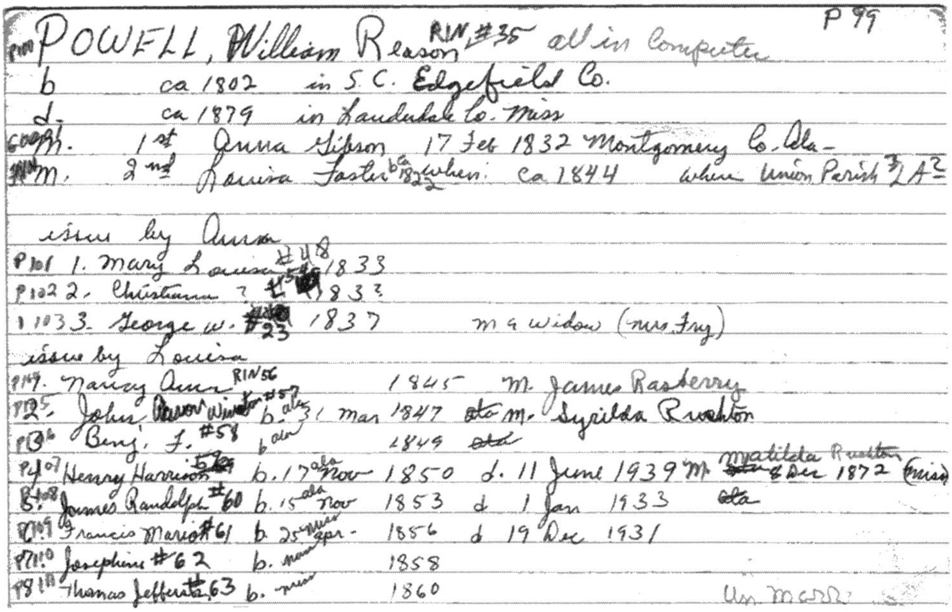

FIGURE 1-1. *An index card can be a useful backup to computer-stored data.*

The following boxed section lists some websites where you can find forms to use as you research censuses and other records, so you can document your findings and sources. There's more about documentation later in this chapter.

A Baker's Dozen of Free Forms

You can find free, downloadable forms to record and track your research. Here are just a few places:

- **Family Search (www.familysearch.org)** Click the Search tab | Research Helps | Sorted by Document Type | Form. You'll find a list of forms from charts to timelines to census worksheets. These files are in PDF format, so you must have Adobe Acrobat to read and print these files.

- **RootsWeb** Several members have posted their most useful forms. At www.rootsweb.org/ ~ ilfrankl, click Research and Resources, for example, and you'll find PDF files of family group sheets and a census summary chart.

- **Ontario GENWEB** A collection of forms useful for recording Canadian research, such as census, vital statistics, and so on, can be found at www.rootsweb.org/ ~ canon/genforms.html.

- **PBS Ancestors Series (www.pbs.org/kbyu/ancestors)** You'll find PDF files for research questions, source notes, and charts. Scroll down the menu at the left and click Charts.

- **Genealogy.com** You can find a chart to keep track of your correspondence at www.genealogy.com/00000007 .html?Welcome = 991338571.

- **Ancestry.com** PDF files of useful forms, such as a research calendar and source summary, can be found at www.ancestry .com/save/charts/ancchart.htm.

- **The Mid-Continent Public Library** This site has a whole section on genealogy and four PDF files to help you record research. Go to www.mcpl.lib.mo.us/ge/forms.

- **The Genealogy Mall**   This site has lots of books and resources for sale, but it also has a set of free forms at www.genealogy-mall.com/freechar.htm. These are HTML files; you can save them to your disk or print them out for copying later. You can also buy sets of these forms from the mall if you find them useful.

- **Mary (Hagstrom) Bailey and Duane A. Bailey**   These two generous genealogists have posted forms they developed for their own use at www.cs.williams.edu/ ~ bailey/genealogy/. They are free for nonprofit use.

- **Judith Haller**   Haller has developed templates for spreadsheets and word processing programs, and she offers them free for personal use at www.io.com/ ~ jhaller/ forms/forms.html.

- **The Genealogical Society of Washtenaw County, Michigan, Inc. (www.hvcn.org/info/gswc/links/ toolforms.htm)**   This site has links to forms and articles discussing how to use them.

- **The National Archives and Records Administration (www.nara.gov/research/ordering/ordrfrms.html)** Here you can find out what forms to use for records. Several are available for printing and downloading.

- **The Roots Forum (CompuServe)**   The Roots Forum offers a set of Genealogy Research Forms in Word for Windows 6.0 and WordPerfect formats. The file for Word is GENERA.ZIP; the one for WordPerfect is WPFRMS.ZIP. These forms were uploaded by Clyde Jones and are free for personal use. Go to www.rootsforum.com, click Genealogy Techniques Forum, and then click Files. Use "forms" in the keyword search, and the files will be in the list. Just right click to download.

Note

A PDF file is an Adobe Portable Document Format file. This is a file with text, and sometimes pictures, saved so that it will be displayed the same no matter what type of computer or operating system you use. With a free program called Adobe Acrobat Reader, you can view and print Adobe PDF files. You can get the reader at www.adobe.com.

Most of the genealogy programs on the market today will print out family group sheets and other report formats and blank forms so you can take them to the library or to a genealogy conference for quick reference, or display them at family reunions. Many can also handle video and sound recordings. Whichever program you choose, be certain you record a source for each fact and keep families together in your system. This is discussed in more detail in Chapter 2.

Pick a Line

The next step is picking a surname to pursue. As soon as you have a system for storing and comparing your research findings, you're ready to begin gathering data on that surname. A good place to begin is interviewing family members—parents, aunts, uncles, cousins, and in-laws. Ask them for stories, names, dates, and places of the people and events in the family. When it's possible, get documents to back up what you're told. Family bibles, newspapers, diaries, wills, and letters can help here.

A good question to ask at this point is whether any genealogy of the family has been published. Understand that such a work is still a secondary source, not a primary source. If published sources have good documentation included, you might find them a great help.

Visit a Family History Center (FHC) and the FamilySearch site (www.familysearch.org), which has indexes to The Church of Jesus Christ of Latter-day Saints' (LDS) genealogy information (see Chapter 10). This includes the following:

♦ **International Genealogical Index (IGI)**   The event-based International Genealogical Index is the largest single database in the world. Use it with care, though, because sometimes mistakes are included.

♦ **Ancestral File (AF)**   A patron-submitted pedigree format genealogy.

♦ **Old Parochial Register (OPR)**   These are indexed and microfilmed vital records for Scotland before 1855. They are far from complete, as registering with a local parish was not required, and cost money, but they are still a valuable resource.

All the previous databases are made up of research done by LDS members, but they might include data on people who aren't members.

Record all you find in your system of choice. This is tedious, but necessary. Get someone to proof your entries (typing 1939 when you meant to type 1993 can easily happen).

Post Queries, Search for Data

When you have enough information, you can begin asking intelligent questions in queries to magazines and mail lists (see Chapter 8). Once you have some solid names, dates, and places, you have enough data to answer questions in chat rooms and Usenet groups (see Chapter 7 and Chapter 8). And most of all, with enough names, dates, and places you can begin using search engines to find World Wide Web and FTP sites.

Note

Do not ever send a letter or query that reads "Send me everything you have on the Jones family" or words to that effect. It is rude and unfair to ask for someone to just hand over years of research. You must have some data to exchange and a specific genealogy goal to fill when you query for information. Also, always offer to pay copying and/or postage costs.

A query, in genealogy, is a request for data or at least a clue to where to find data on a specific person. Queries may be sent to one person in a letter or an electronic mail message. You can also send queries to an online site, a magazine, a mail list, or other forum that reaches many people at one time.

Writing a good query is not hard, but you do have to stick to certain conventions for it to be effective.

Make the query short and to the point. Don't try to solve all your genealogical puzzles in one query; zero in on one task at a time.

You must always list at least one name, at least one date or time period, and at least one location to go with the name. Do not bother sending a query that does not have all three of these elements. No one will be able to help you without a name, date, and place. If you are not certain about one of the elements, follow it with a question mark in parentheses. Here are some points to keep in mind:

♦ Capitalize all surnames, including the maiden name and previous married names of female ancestors. Include all known relatives' names—children, siblings, and so on. Use complete names, including any middle names, if known. Finally, proofread all the names.

♦ Give complete dates as far as you know. Follow the format DD Month YYYY, as in 20 May 1865. If the date is uncertain, use "before" or "about" as appropriate, such as "Born circa 1792" or "Died before October 1850." Proofread all the dates for typos; this is where transpositions can really get you!

♦ Give town, county, and state (or province) for North American locations; town, parish (if known), and county for United Kingdom locations, and so on. In other words, start with the specific and go to the general, including all divisions possible.

♦ Finally, include how you wish to be contacted. For a letter query, or one sent to a print magazine, you will want to include your full mailing address. For online queries, you want to include at least an e-mail address.

Here's a sample query for a print or online venue:

I need proof of the parents of Diadama CRIPPEN born 11 Sept 1794 in (?), NY. I believe her father was Darius CRIPPEN, son of Samuel CRIPPEN, and her mother was Abigail STEVENS CRIPPEN, daughter of Roger STEVENS, both from CT. They lived in Egremont, Berkshire County, MA and Pittsfield, Rutland County, VT before moving to Bastard Township, Ontario, Canada. I will exchange information and copying costs. [Here you would put your regular mail address, e-mail address, or other contact information.]

After posting your queries, the next step is to begin searching the databases and genealogy sites for information on your names, dates, and places, as described in the chapters mentioned earlier.

References to Have at Hand

As you post queries, send and receive messages, read documents online, and look at library card catalogs, you will need some reference books at your fingertips to help understand what you have found and what you are searching for. Besides a good atlas and perhaps a few state or province gazetteers (a geographic dictionary or index), having these books at hand will save you a lot of time in your pursuit of family history:

♦ *The Handybook for Genealogists: United States of America (Ninth Edition)*, by George B. Everton, Editor (ISBN 1890895032).

  DearMYRTLE says she uses this reference about 20 times a week. This book has information such as when counties were formed, what court had jurisdiction where and when, listings of genealogical archives, libraries, societies, and publications, dates for each available census index, and more.

♦ *The Source: A Guidebook of American Genealogy*, by Sandra H. Luebking (Editor) and Loretto D. Szucs (ISBN 0916489671) or *The Researcher's Guide to American Genealogy*, by Val D. Greenwood (ISBN 0806316217).

  These are comprehensive, how-to genealogy books. Greenwood's is a little more accessible to the amateur, whereas Luebking's is aimed at the professional, certified genealogist.

♦ *Cite Your Sources: A Manual for Documenting Family Histories and Genealogical Records*, by Richard S. Lackey (ISBN 0878052860) or *Evidence! Citation & Analysis for the Family Historian*, by Elizabeth Shown Mills (ISBN 0806315431).

  These books help you document what you found, where you found it, and why you believe it. The two books approach the subject differently: The first is more amateur friendly, whereas the second is more professional in approach.

Analyze and Repeat

When you find facts that seem to fit your genealogy, you must analyze them, as noted in the section "How to Judge," later in this chapter. When you are satisfied you have a good fit, record the information and start the process again.

Success Story: A Beginner Tries the Shotgun Approach

Just two months ago, my mother shared some old obits with me that intrigued me enough to send me off on a search for my family's roots. I started at the RootsWeb site with a metasearch, and then I sent e-mails to anyone who had posted the name I was pursuing in the state of origin cited in the obit. This constituted over 50 messages. A real shotgun approach. I received countless replies indicating there was no family connection. Then, one day, I got a response from a man who turned out to be my mother's cousin. He himself had been researching his family line for the last two years. He sent me census and marriage records, even a will from 1843 that gave new direction to my search.

In pursuing information on my father, whom my mother divorced when I was two months old (I never saw him again), I was able to identify his parents' names from an SS 5 application and, subsequently, track down state census listings containing not only their birth dates but also the birth dates of their parents—all of which has aided me invaluably in the search for my family's roots.

Having been researching only a short while, I have found the online genealogy community to be very helpful and am more than willing to share information with newbies like myself. The amount of information online has blown me away.

—Sue Crumpton

Good Practices

As you gather more and more information, you want to check what you find against what's considered good practice for genealogists. The National Genealogical Society (NGS) has a set of standards for research, as shown in Appendix A. You can also find these on the Web at the NGS website (www.ngsgenealogy.org).

Know Your Terms

As soon as you find information, you are going to come across terms and acronyms that make you scratch your head. Sure, it's easy to figure out what a deed is, but what's a cadastre? What do D.S.P. and LDS mean? Is a yeoman a sailor or a farmer?

A cadastre is a survey, a map, or some other public record showing ownership and value of land for tax purposes. D.S.P. is an abbreviation for a phrase that means "died without children." LDS is shorthand for The Church of Jesus Christ of Latter-day Saints, or the Mormons. And finally, a yeoman can designate a farmer, an attendant/guard, or a clerk in the Navy, depending on the time and place. Most of this is second nature to people who have done genealogy for more than a couple of years, but beginners often find themselves completely baffled.

And then there are the calendars—Julian, Gregorian, and French Revolutionary—which mean some records have double dates.

No, wait, don't run screaming into the street! Just try to get a handle on the jargon. I have included a glossary at the end of this book with many expressions. As the book progresses, many words are defined in context. But quickly, here are a few terms you need to know:

- **a. (or c.)** *About* (or *circa*, in Latin). Often used in front of uncertain dates.

- **Ahnentafel** An "ancestor table" that organizes information along a strict numbering scheme. An alternative to the pedigree chart.

- **BCG** Board for Certification of Genealogists.

- **CG** Certified Genealogist, by BCG.

- **CGI** Certified Genealogical Instructor, by BCG.

- **CGL** Certified Genealogical Lecturer, by BCG.

- **CGRS** Certified Genealogical Record Specialist, by BCG.

- **GEDCOM** The standard for computerized genealogical information. It's a combination of tags for data and pointers to related data.

- **Family group sheet** A one-page collection of facts about one family unit—husband, wife, and children—with birth and death dates and places.

- **French Revolutionary calendar** The French Revolutionary calendar (or the Republican calendar) was introduced in France on 24 November 1793 and abolished on 1 January 1806. It was used again briefly during the Paris Commune in 1871.

- **Gregorian calendar** The Gregorian calendar was introduced by Pope Gregory XIII in 1582 and was adopted by England and the colonies in 1752, by which time it was 11 days behind the solar year, causing an adjustment in September 1752.

- **Julian calendar** The Julian calendar was replaced by the Gregorian calendar, which had also fallen behind the solar year.

- **NGS** The National Genealogical Society, U.S.

- **Pedigree chart** The traditional way to display a genealogy—the familiar "family tree," where one person's ancestors are outlined. Other formats are the fan chart, the decendency chart (starts with the ancestor and comes down to the present), and the timeline.

- **Soundex** A filing system, usually for recording surnames, using one letter followed by three numbers. The Soundex system keeps together names of the same and/or similar sounds, but of variant spellings.

- **SSDI** The Social Security Death Index. Details from the SSDI often can be used to further genealogical research by enabling you to locate a death certificate, find an obituary, discover cemetery records, and track down probate records. Several sites offer online searching.

- **Tiny tafel (TT)** A TT provides a standard way of describing a family database so that the information can be scanned visually or by computer. All data fields are of fixed length, with the obvious exceptions of the surnames and optional places. Many TTs are extracted from GEDCOMs.

Beyond these, you'll see many terms abbreviated in queries and messages to save typing. Born, died, and married become b., d., and m., respectively. Great-great-grandmother becomes gggmother. Daughter-in-law will be typed as DIL (and other in-laws similarly abbreviated). You will quickly become acclimated to the shorthand.

Sources and Proof

Most serious genealogists who discuss online sources want to know if they can "trust" what they find on the Internet. Many professional genealogists I know simply don't accept what's found on the Internet as proof of genealogy, period. Their attitude is this: A source isn't a primary source unless you've held the original document in your hand. And a primary source isn't proof unless it's supported by at least one other original document you've held in your hand. To them, seeing a picture of a scanned original on the Internet isn't "proof."

For example, as you can see in Figure 1-2, *The Mayflower* passenger list has been scanned in at Caleb Johnson's site, Mayflower Passenger List (http://members.aol.com/calebj/passenger.html). Would you consider this a primary source? A secondary source? Or simply a good clue?

Some genealogists get annoyed with those who publish their genealogy data on the Internet without citing each source in detail. Once, when I

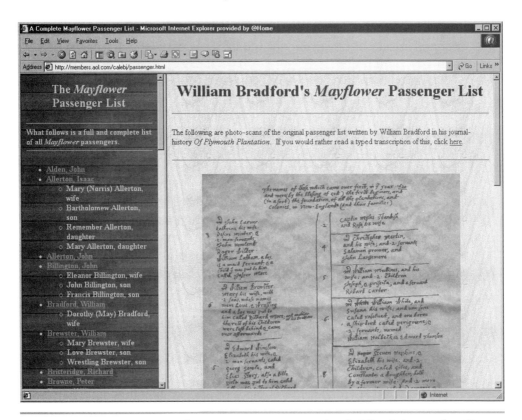

FIGURE 1-2.   *Is a picture of a primary source as good as holding it in your hand?*

was teaching a class on how to publish genealogy on the Internet at a conference, a respected genealogist took me to task over dinner. "Web pages without supporting documentation are lies!" she insisted. "You're telling people to publish lies because if it's not proven by genealogical standards, it might not be true!"

I have to admit I don't see it that way. In my opinion, you must evaluate what you find on the Internet, just as you evaluate what you find in a library, courthouse, or archive. Many a genealogy book has been published with errors, and the same is true of online genealogies. On the Web, no real editors exist. You can find all kinds of information and sources on the Internet—from casual references in messages to documented genealogy to original records transcribed into HTML. The range is astounding. But the same can be true of vanity-published genealogies found in libraries.

You can find some limited primary materials online. People are scanning and transcribing original documents onto the Internet, such as the Library of Virginia and the National Park Service. You can also find online a growing treasure trove of indexes of public vital records, scanned images of Government Land Office land patents (www.glorecords .blm.gov), and more (see Figure 1-3).

Don't be put off by those who sneer at the Internet, saying nothing of genuine value can be found there. This might have been true only a few years ago, but not today. Now you can find scanned images of census records going online at both the Census site (www.census.gov) and volunteer projects such as the USGenWeb Digital Census Project. Looking at these records in HTML is as good as, or better than, looking at them in microfilm or microfiche, in my opinion.

Nevertheless, secondary sources are much easier to find than primary sources. The main value of these secondary sources on the Internet is finding other genealogists who are researching the same lines. Additionally, you might uncover leads to finding primary and secondary sources offline, and, rarely, get a glance at an actual data source, perhaps even a primary source. Simply knowing a source *exists* can be a breakthrough.

Other people are putting their family trees online. Although many of these data files don't have the disk space available to include complete documentation, most people who publish online are willing to provide pertinent details to anyone who has data to exchange with them.

Therefore, I still believe in publishing and exchanging data over the Internet. However, you must use good judgment.

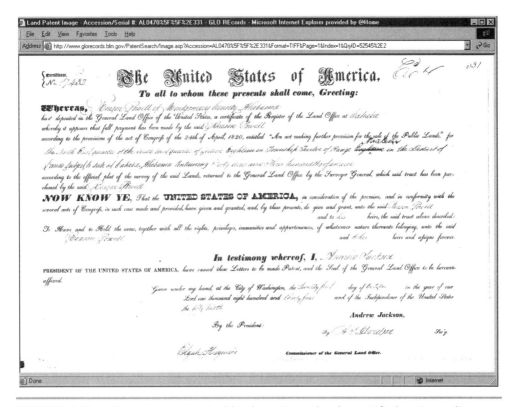

FIGURE 1-3. *You can view original land grants, and order certified copies, online.*

How to Judge

The criteria for the evaluation of resources on the Web must be the same criteria you would use for any other source of information. Be aware that just because something is on a computer, this doesn't make it infallible. Garbage in, garbage out. With this in mind, ask yourself the following questions in evaluating an online genealogy site.

Who Created It?   You can find all kinds of resources on the Internet—from libraries, research institutions, and organizations such as the NGS, to government and university resources. Sources such as these give you more confidence in their data than, say, resources from a hobbyist. Publications and software companies also publish genealogical information, but you must read the site carefully to determine whether they've actually researched this information or simply accepted whatever their customers threw at them. Finally, you can find tons of "family traditions" online. And although traditions usually have a grain of truth to them, they're usually not unvarnished.

How Long Ago Was It Created?   The more often a page is updated, the better you can feel about the data it holds. Of course, a page listing the census for a certain county in 1850 needn't be updated every week, but a pedigree put online should be updated as the author finds more data.

Where Does the Information Come From?   If the page in question doesn't give any sources, you'll want to contact the page author to acquire the necessary information. If sources *do* exist, of course, you must decide if you can trust them—many a genealogical error has been printed in books, magazines, and online.

In What Form Is the Information?   A simple GEDCOM published as a web page can be useful for the beginner, but ideally you want an index to any genealogical resource, regardless of form. If a site has no search function, no table of contents, or not even a *document map* (a graphic leading you to different parts of the site), it is much less useful than it could be.

How Well Does the Author Use and Define Genealogical Terms?   Does the author clearly know the difference between a yeoman farmer and a yeoman sailor? Does the author seem to be knowledgeable about genealogy? Another problem with online pages is whether the author understands the problems of dates—both badly recorded dates and the 1752 calendar change. Certain sites can help you with calendar problems.

Does the Information Make Sense Compared to What I Already Know?   If you have documentary evidence that contradicts what you see on a web page, treat it as you would a mistake in a printed genealogy or magazine: Tell the author about your data and see whether the two versions can be reconciled. This sort of exchange, after all, is what online genealogy is all about!

For example, many online genealogies have a mistake about one of my ancestors because they didn't stop to analyze the data and made erroneous assumptions.

In Figure 1-4, you can see a transcription of the 1850 Census of Lake County, Indiana. The column labeled HN is for household numbered in order of visitation; the column labeled FN is for families numbered in order of visitation. You can see Abraham Spencer (age 58) and his wife Diadama (age 56, her name is misspelled on the census form) have children Stephen through Elisabeth, and underneath are Amanda, age 27, and then three children under the age of 5.

Some assume Amanda and the following children are also offspring of Abraham and Diadama, but if you look at the ages and how the families are listed—with Amanda and the younger children under the youngest of Abraham and Diadama's children—you see this doesn't make sense. If you were to look at the mortality schedule for the county for that year, you would see that Orsemus Spencer (Amanda's husband and Abraham's

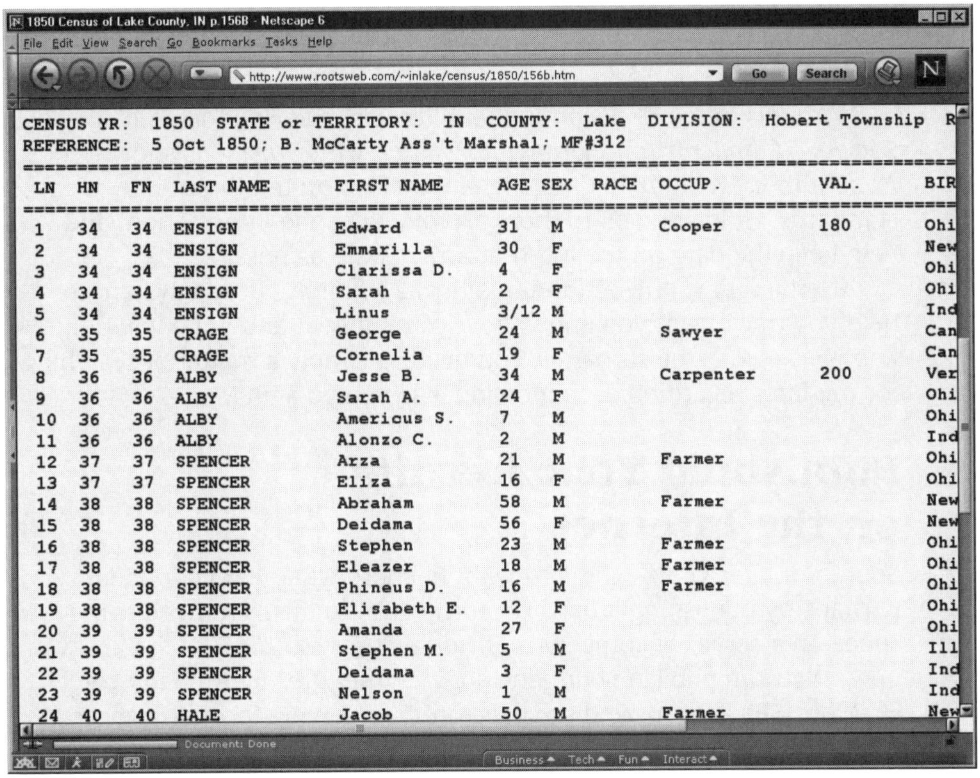

CENSUS YR: 1850 STATE or TERRITORY: IN COUNTY: Lake DIVISION: Hobert Township R
REFERENCE: 5 Oct 1850; B. McCarty Ass't Marshal; MF#312

LN	HN	FN	LAST NAME	FIRST NAME	AGE	SEX	RACE	OCCUP.	VAL.	BIR
1	34	34	ENSIGN	Edward	31	M		Cooper	180	Ohi
2	34	34	ENSIGN	Emmarilla	30	F				New
3	34	34	ENSIGN	Clarissa D.	4	F				Ohi
4	34	34	ENSIGN	Sarah	2	F				Ohi
5	34	34	ENSIGN	Linus	3/12	M				Ind
6	35	35	CRAGE	George	24	M		Sawyer		Can
7	35	35	CRAGE	Cornelia	19	F				Can
8	36	36	ALBY	Jesse B.	34	M		Carpenter	200	Ver
9	36	36	ALBY	Sarah A.	24	F				Ohi
10	36	36	ALBY	Americus S.	7	M				Ohi
11	36	36	ALBY	Alonzo C.	2	M				Ind
12	37	37	SPENCER	Arza	21	M		Farmer		Ohi
13	37	37	SPENCER	Eliza	16	F				Ohi
14	38	38	SPENCER	Abraham	58	M		Farmer		New
15	38	38	SPENCER	Deidama	56	F				New
16	38	38	SPENCER	Stephen	23	M		Farmer		Ohi
17	38	38	SPENCER	Eleazer	18	M		Farmer		Ohi
18	38	38	SPENCER	Phineus D.	16	M		Farmer		Ohi
19	38	38	SPENCER	Elisabeth E.	12	F				Ohi
20	39	39	SPENCER	Amanda	27	F				Ohi
21	39	39	SPENCER	Stephen M.	5	M				Ill
22	39	39	SPENCER	Deidama	3	F				Ind
23	39	39	SPENCER	Nelson	1	M				Ind
24	40	40	HALE	Jacob	50	M		Farmer		New

FIGURE 1-4. *Census records sometimes need careful study and interpretation.*

son) died in February before the census taker arrived in October. Amanda and her children moved in with her in-laws after her husband's death. They are part of the household, but they aren't Abraham Spencer's children.

> ## Note
>
> *A mortality schedule contains data collected during a census about those who died before June in the year of the census. For each person, the following information is listed: name, age, sex, marital status if married or widowed, state or country of birth, month of death, occupation, cause of death, and the length of the final illness. In 1918 and 1919, many of these records were returned to the states; others were given to the Daughters of the American Revolution. Many volunteer-run genealogy websites have posted transcribed mortality schedules for specific counties.*

With this in mind, becoming familiar with the National Genealogical Society's *Standards for Sharing Information with Others*, as shown in Appendix A, would help. Judge what you find on the Internet by these standards. Hold yourself to them as you exchange information, and help keep the data on the Internet as accurate as possible.

After you have these standards firmly in mind, a good system to help you track what you know, how you know it, and what you don't know, as well as the surnames you need, is simply a matter of searching for the facts regarding each individual as you go along.

Publishing Your Results on the Internet

Sooner or later you're going to want to share what you've found, perhaps by publishing it on the Internet. To do this, you need some space on a server of some sort. Fortunately, your choices here are wide open. You can publish your genealogy on the Internet in many places.

Most ISPs allot some disk space on their servers for their users. Check with your ISP to see how much you have. Dozens of sites are out there, offering up to ten megabytes (10MB) of space free, including AOL's Hometown, Yahoo!, Xoom, Angelfire, and more. Most of these are free, as long as you allow them to display an ad on the visitor's screen. Some software programs, as noted in Chapter 2, will put your genealogy database on the software publishers' website, where it can be searched by others. Some websites, such as GENWEB, let you post the GEDCOM of your data for searching in database form instead of HTML. Finally, genealogy-specific sites exist, such as RootsWeb and MyFamily.com, with free space for noncommercial use for HTML format.

In short, publishing on the Internet is very doable, as well as enjoyable.

I should warn you, though, that not everyone may be thrilled to be part of your project. Some people get upset at finding their names published online without their written permission. Some genealogists consider anything published, whether it's online or in hard copy, to be false unless the documentation proving it as true is included in the publication. Still others feel sharing their hard work without getting data and/or payment in return is a bad idea. For these and other reasons, you might want to publish data only on deceased people, or publish only enough data to encourage people to write you with their own data.

In short, be careful about what you post on the Web and how you post it. The National Genealogical Society recently adopted a set of standards for publishing genealogy on the Internet. With their permission, I included these standards in Appendix A.

Almost every good genealogy program now includes a way to publish on the Web. Ultimate Family Tree, Family Origins, Family Tree Maker, The Master Genealogist, Generations Family Tree, and Ancestral Quest are only a few of the programs that can turn your genealogical database into HTML. Most of them simply create a standard tree-branching chart with links to the individuals' data. Others may create a set of family group sheets. Many of them let you have "still living" replace the vital statistics for certain people. In many of these programs, the process is as simple as creating a printed report. You simply choose HTML as the format.

Some of the programs, however, don't give you a choice of where you post your data. Family Tree Maker (FTM), for example, publishes your data on its site. Once there, your data becomes part of the FTM database, which is periodically burned on to CD-ROMs and sold in stores. Simply by posting your data on the site, you give them permission to do this. Quite a bit of discussion and debate is ongoing about this privatization of publicly available data. Some say this will be the end of amateur genealogy, whereas others feel this is a way to preserve data that might be lost to disaster or neglect. Even others say it takes money to store and maintain this data. It's up to you whether you want to post to a site that reuses your data for its own profit.

This is one reason I strongly urge you to visit local genealogy groups that have "show and tell" nights for genealogy software. Try several programs before you buy one. Ask questions about how and where it will publish your work on the Web. Furthermore, some genealogy programs let you record your sources, notes, and anecdotes to go along with your data. This capability to record and cite sources is essential, in my opinion, for any genealogy program. Don't choose one without it. I discuss more about choosing a genealogy program in the next chapter. Think about your goals in genealogy and pick a program that can help you meet them. You'll find more about this topic in Chapter 2.

By publishing at least some of your genealogy on the Internet, you can help others looking for the same lines.

Success Story: Finding Cousins Across the Ocean

After ten years of getting my genealogy onto computer, I finally got the nerve to "browse the Web," and to this day I don't know how I got there, where I was, or how to get back there—but I landed on a website for French genealogists.

I can neither read nor speak French. I bravely wrote a query in English: "I don't read or speak French, but I am looking for living cousins descended from my ancestors ORDENER." I included a short "tree" with some dates and my e-mail address.

Well, within a couple of hours I heard from an ORDENER cousin living in Paris, France. She did not know she had a kin in America and had spent years hunting in genealogy and cemetery records for her great-great-grandfather's siblings! She had no idea they had come to America in the 1700s and settled in Texas before Texas was a state of the union.

So, while I traded her hundreds of names of our American family, she gave me her research back to about 1570 France when the name was ORTNER! About four months later, another French cousin found me from that query on the Web. He did not know his cousin in Paris, so I was able to "introduce" him via e-mail. One of them has already come to Florida to meet us!

What keeps me going? Well, when I reach a brick wall in one family, I turn to another surname. Looking for living cousins is a little more successful than looking for ancestors, but you have to find the ancestors to know how to go "down the line" to the living distant cousins! Genealogy is somewhat like a giant crossword puzzle—each time you solve a name, you have at least two more to hunt! You never run out of avenues of adventure—ever!

—Patijé Weber Mills Styers, Sarasota, Florida

Quick Tips

Experienced genealogists are more than willing to help the beginner. Pat Richley, also known as DearMYRTLE, has a lot of great advice on her site, www.dearmyrtle.com. Here are what she feels are the important points for the beginner:

- ◆ Just take it one step at a time.

- ◆ Devise your own filing system.

- ◆ Don't let the experts overwhelm you.

- ◆ Use the Family History Library's Research Outline for the state/county where your ancestors came from. They get you quickly oriented to what's available and what has survived that might help you out.

- ◆ Don't invent your own genealogy program. You can get Personal Ancestral File (PAF) for free from www.familysearch.org, or you can choose one of the commercially available ones.

- ◆ Only use a GEDCOM-compatible software program because it is the generic way of storing genealogy data. This way, you can import and export to other researchers with common ancestors in the future.

Scams

In the twenty-first century, genealogy is an industry. Entire companies are centered on family history research and resources. Not surprisingly, you will find people willing to take your money and give you little or nothing in return in genealogy, just as in any industry. Many of them started long before online genealogy became popular, and they simply followed when genealogists went online. Halberts of Ohio is one notorious example. Dick Eastman covered this in the March 2001 edition of his online newsletter (see Chapter 8), and it is worth looking up at www.ancestry.com/library/view/columns/eastman/3538.asp.

Books with titles such as *The World Book of [YOUR SURNAME]* and *Three Centuries of [YOUR SURNAME]*, sold via junk mail flyers as well as online, often turn out to be nothing you couldn't find in a telephone book. You have to read such pitches very carefully, and before you send any money, ask on the mail lists, chat rooms, and Usenet groups whether anyone has had experience with the company. Also go online and check the company's name and sales pitch against these sites, which list common genealogy scams:

♦ **Black Sheep (http://blacksheep.rootsweb.org/halberts.htm)** This page describes the Halberts scam and imitators.

♦ **Cyndi's List (http://www.cyndislist.com/myths.htm)** Cyndi Howells keeps on top of myths, lies, and scams in genealogy on this page.

♦ **Ancestor Detective Watchdog (http://www.ancestordetective .com/watchdog.htm)** Liz Kelley Kerstens (CGRS, CGL) investigates reports of genealogy websites with questionable pitches and she posts the results to this page.

Wrapping Up

♦ To begin your genealogy project, start with yourself and your immediate family, documenting what you know.

♦ Look for records for the next generation back by writing for vital records, searching for online records, posting queries, and researching in libraries and courthouses.

♦ Gather the information with documentation on where, when, and how you found it.

♦ Organize what you have and look for what's needed next.

♦ Repeat the cycle.

♦ Beware of scams!

Chapter 2

Software You'll Need

Online genealogy is only different from the old-fashioned kind in the type of tools you use. Instead of using a photocopier, you make copies using your printer. Instead of sending queries in an envelope, you send them by e-mail. Instead of reading an article in a magazine, you read it in a browser. And, instead of going to the library in person, you might visit it by computer connection!

Please understand, I don't mean to imply you won't ever do things the old-fashioned way again. Of course you will! But you'll use these online techniques often, sometimes even before you try to do research the traditional way. These are new tools for age-old genealogical tasks.

You'll need to learn the ins and outs of the Internet, software, and techniques for online information exchange to get the most out of the experience. This chapter covers such considerations and the software you might want to use.

Of course, it's assumed you will need a computer, with some connection to the Internet. If that is by a modem to a phone line, a fax modem will be very useful in asking for vital records from a courthouse miles away. If your connection is via cable or DSL, you will need the processors and connectors that accommodate such high-speed access.

I would say that at a minimum, you should have a Pentium I or equivalent, about 128MB of RAM, and at least 1GB of hard drive space to have a pleasant experience on the Internet today. Newer, faster processors, more RAM, and, of course, a CD-ROM reader and burner will make your experience even better.

For Macintosh users, most ISPs require at least OS 8 for dial-up and OS X for high-speed connections. AOL, as of this writing, has no broadband software for the Mac, but they hope to have it ready in the first quarter of 2004. Other requirements for Mac users: For high-speed connections, you need a network card, at least 80MB of free hard disk space, and at least 128MB RAM; for dial-up, the requirement to get online is less, but to store and manipulate your data, I would recommend you use those same minimums.

Don't forget output. The CD-ROM burner is good for storing and backing up your data, which you *must* do on a regular basis. If you don't use CD-ROMs, use a Zip drive or even floppies. Whatever you have, use it to back up your data. Don't put this off for later. When you are making a lot of progress, back up at least once a month. Once a week is better, because if you lose more than a month's work to a lightning strike or natural disaster, you may be too discouraged to start again.

New Choices

Handheld Internet access devices and wireless phones with e-mail access are popping up all over. The latter can offer you convenience when traveling, but cost will be a big factor.

Personal Digital Assistants

The personal digital assistant (especially those models with Internet connections) has become popular with genealogists. In addition to its usefulness in note-taking, retrieving e-mail, and, if it has the proper port, uploading and downloading information to desktop or laptop computers, some surprisingly functional software for these devices is available. Here are some examples:

- The Personal Ancestral File (PAF) 5.1 from FamilySearch.org has Palm capability, which is handy for storing work until you can upload it to your computer.

- The GedStar (www.gedpalm.com) lets you browse a GEDCOM (see the Glossary) and could be useful for trips to the library (see Figure 2-1). The program even has its own discussion list (http://groups.yahoo.com/group/genpalm/).

- MyRoots (www.tapperware.com/MyRoots) is a genealogical database that can be accessed using a Palm Pilot.

- A list of Palm programs is maintained at Cyndi's List (www.cyndislist.com/software.htm#Palm).

Wireless Phones

Connection to the Internet through a wireless phone is slow, expensive, and hard on the eyes. This isn't something I recommend to genealogists for an everyday Internet connection. Still, if you simply must keep up with a mail list while away from your computer, this is an option.

Choosing an ISP

Just as you do when you choose a mate, you should know what you want before you start looking for an ISP. Your choice isn't final, of course—

FIGURE 2-1. *GedStar from GHCS software keeps your GEDCOMs in a PDA.*

but you don't want to hopscotch from one e-mail address to another, either. So, go into this knowing that Internet providers are as different as dog breeds. All of them will get you on to the Net, but access speeds, services, software, and other goodies vary. Before you put down any cash, ask yourself these basic questions:

- What services do I need?

- How often do I need them?

- How fast do I need them?

- How many hassles will I put up with to save money?

- How much am I willing to pay?

Remember, tradeoffs exist no matter what provider you finally choose. For example, you might find a price break exists for slower and less direct connections, or a premium is necessary to dial in to your account from various places in the country. In addition, you might find companies consider support extremely expensive to provide, so if you sign up with a full-service provider, it can cost a bit more.

You might save money by choosing only what you need. In the end, though, you might find you need the whole shebang. While some users are happy with just electronic mail, to uncover all the genealogical treasures out there, you'll need considerably more features, such as a web browser to fetch sound, pictures, and online animation. Consequently, you'll also need a provider that offers high-speed Internet connections.

When it comes to services, insist on the whole range: e-mail, telnet, Usenet newsgroups, FTP, Gopher, and more—in short, everything the Internet has to offer. Even if the ISP service is basic, it should at least come with a technical support service.

Software

Once you have your hardware in place and you know how you're going to connect, you need to look at your software. As noted before, many ISPs include software as part of the package. AOL, CompuServe, Prodigy, EarthLink, Netcom, and most other national ISPs have front-end software that includes the communications software, browser, FTP, e-mail, and other programs you need.

The programs you use to access the web are often called *clients*. These programs send signals to other computers, called *servers*, instructing them to display files and information to you or to run programs for you. The resulting display might be e-mail, a web page, or a GEDCOM you want to download. The program the clients run might be a browser or a chat room.

Which Browser Should I Use?

I'm often asked, "Which is the best browser?" In my opinion, this is like asking, "Which is the best car?" It all depends on your taste, habits, and budget.

The current leaders in the browser wars are Netscape Navigator and Microsoft Internet Explorer (IE); entire books are devoted to helping you get the most out of these browsers. The major online services and ISPs have lined up with one or the other for their customers to use and install automatically with their software, so you don't have to do any extra work to use it.

Microsoft IE is free, but it makes major changes to your operating system and, therefore, sometimes causes trouble with other programs. Netscape Navigator can also be obtained free of charge, has a nice user interface, and is easy to use.

Other browsers, such as Opera, Mosaic, and Ariadne are less feature-packed, but they're free, easy to use, and sometimes much faster. Some of these programs are a pain for beginners because they're often harder to learn, have some compatibility issues, and don't offer much support. They are fun for experienced users, though. For a comprehensive list, visit www.tucows.com and search for "browser." My advice is to test-drive a few of them (most let you try before you buy) and see which browser suits you best if you don't like the one that comes with your service's software.

Genealogy Programs

Your most important software, however, will be your genealogy program, which is basically a database program. The output can be simply data, whole books with pictures, or wall charts.

In shopping around for the right genealogy program for you, consider these factors:

- ♦ First and foremost, check the program's ability to record your sources. If it doesn't have a way for you to track where and when you found a fact, reject it out of hand. You'll wind up retracing your steps a thousand times without the ability to instantly retrieve the sources you've already used.

- ♦ Second in importance, but only slightly second, is the appearance. This may seem trivial, but it's not. Most genealogy programs have some sort of metaphor: It looks as if you are working on a scrapbook, 3 × 5 cards, or a genealogical chart. Finding one that presents the data in a way that suits *your* methods is important.

- ♦ Third, consider how you output your data. Don't use anything that can't output a good GEDCOM. A *GEDCOM* is a text-only file with the data formatted so that any other program can use it.

This is important for comparing your research to others', but that's not the only output form for your work. For hard-copy output, think about what you want to create. A website? A book? A quilt? A giant mural for the next reunion? Look for a program that fits your output needs.

♦ Fourth, look at the package's support and ask friends what their experience was when they needed support. Read the manual to see how much support is included (and for how long) with the purchase price. Understand that within a year, the software (*any* software) will be upgraded. Find out whether upgrades are free or available for a minimal charge. A really good program may cost from $25 to $50 a year to keep it current; some shareware gives you upgrades for $5 or less. Also, ask at the next meeting of your local genealogy club whether anyone has the program you are interested in and is willing to help you with the learning curve.

♦ Finally, consider the cost. When you find the program you want, can you afford it? If not, see whether the program comes in different versions—some less powerful but also less expensive than others. Sometimes the cost includes CD-ROMs of secondary or primary material, but perhaps some of this material is available at your local library, and you need not buy it.

Brother's Keeper

With Brother's Keeper 6, you can attach sources to any event, person, or family, access a source to view it or modify it separate from data, and print a list of all sources (separate from data). Also, output can be GEDCOMs, a list of people with any fields you want to include, and you can output that list as a text file or as a comma-delimited file. Brother's Keeper 6 is shareware; you try it and then send in the $49 if you decide you like it.

You can also send many reports to a disk file. In the descendant report, group sheets, and custom lists, you set up the report and then pick File | Create Text File. In the Register Book, Indented Book, and Ahnentafel Book, you set up the report and pick File | Create RTF File. Then you load the RTF file into Word or WordPerfect. On the Group Sheet screen, you can also pick File | Create HTML Files.

The program has no real metaphor, unlike most genealogy software, as shown in Figure 2-2. The simple form has blanks to fill in, with tabs

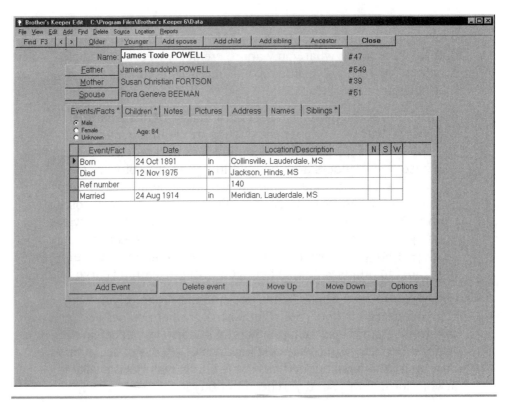

FIGURE 2-2. *Brother's Keeper 6 has a very plain-vanilla interface.*

to click on for entering details. The person's name, father, mother, and spouse are at the top, and in the middle are tabs to hold information for events, children, notes, pictures, additional names for the person, addresses, and siblings.

Brother's Keeper 6 is easy to use, and it prints over 30 different charts and reports. This program has been around for a long time (longer even than Family Tree Maker). Also, the author is open to suggestions from users and will answer requests for help.

Personal Ancestral File (PAF)

Personal Ancestral File is the program that members of The Church of Jesus Christ of Latter-day Saints use. Personal Ancestral File 5 is available on the Internet at www.familysearch.org; click on Order/Download Products, then on Software Downloads. It's free.

PAF 5.2 can produce, either onscreen or on paper, family histories, pedigree charts, family group records, and other reports to help users in their search for missing ancestors. This version includes changes to the individual record to accommodate the wide variety of naming conventions used throughout the world. This version will convert PAF 3.0 and 4.0 data files to its improved file format. PAF 5.2 is available on CD-ROM as well, for a small fee.

PAF has fields that are of use in submitting family members for Temple use that non-Mormons will not use. However, it is designed to be simple, to output in GEDCOM and other formats so you can share your data, and is supported by several forums on the Web.

RootsMagic

This $20 program is what became of Family Origins after some software companies merged and revamped their product lines, eliminating the Family Origins name. If you have an old version of Family Origins, the FormalSoft folks say you can transfer your old databases right into RootsMagic.

There are two main views: Tree View and Family View. You switch between the two views by simply clicking the tab for the desired view. The edit screen allows you to add an unlimited number of facts for every person (birth, death, marriage, occupation, religion, description, and so on). If you want to add a fact type that isn't in the predefined list, you can create your own fact type. GEDCOM import and export, as well as output are supported, and multimedia files can be included.

The program allows notes and unlimited source citations for every fact. You can add, edit, delete, merge, and print the sources of your information. Simply add the source once, then when you add a fact to a person and want to document where that information came from, you simply point to the source in the Source Manager.

Output includes pedigree charts, family group sheets, four types of box charts, six styles of books, 27 different lists, mailing labels, calendars, hourglass trees, graphical timelines, relationship charts, letter-writing templates, individual summaries, five types of photo charts, and seven types of blank charts. Your database can be output into a pedigree chart with HTML links among the individuals in the genealogy.

Family Tree Maker

This program comes in versions from $30 to $100; the more expensive bundles may include a video, subscription to online databases, CD-ROMs, and/or a book.

Genealogy.com, owned by MyFamily.com, distributes Family Tree Maker. The site has subscription databases you can search, as well as the old Family Origins 10 software.

Family Tree Maker's metaphor is a standard pedigree tree, which you fill in by tabbing from branch to branch. Facts and sources are tracked; output can be GEDCOM, HTML, PDF, and other formats. It has all the features you could want, but your output may become part of the Family Tree Maker database, which they will later sell to others.

Family Tree Maker is by far the most popular program because it is easy to use.

The Master Genealogist (TMG)

This program does everything the previously mentioned programs will do, but more—it helps you organize your search. For $40 for the Silver edition and $80 for the Gold, Master Genealogist is not more expensive than the other programs.

Mind you, it has a learning curve, and the program is written with professional genealogical standards in mind. That should not deter you, however. It comes with a tutorial and has much more flexibility than its easy-to-use competitors.

It is this flexibility that makes people feel Master Genealogist is worth the effort to use. The Master Genealogist allows for an unlimited number of people, events per person, names per person, relationships, user-defined events, free-form text, photographs, citations, and repositories. You, not the software, will control the data. There are also features to help you track what you need to find and a to-do list of genealogy chores. You can tie many more facts and historical contexts to your ancestors with TMG, as it is affectionately known, as well as output in almost any format you like.

Referencing source data is TMG's strongest point for the serious genealogist. Each entry provides space for documenting an unlimited number of citations, including a rating scale for their reliability. Newspaper articles, family bibles, and interviews with your relatives all have different reliability, which can be recorded with TMG.

And So On

The short list presented thus far merely scratches the surface of available genealogy programs, by presenting those that are arguably the most popular. Go to Cyndi's List (www.cyndislist.com/software.htm) and poke around a few websites. Go to local meetings of your genealogy club and ask for recommendations. Go through the checklist of programs I gave you and test-drive a few that are shareware. Then you'll be ready to choose.

Additional Programs

There are other programs that are not, strictly speaking, genealogy programs. These include databases, journaling programs, and other, more mundane software such as word processing that can be used to make your quest for family history easier. You may want to consider any combination of these.

Database CD-ROMs

You'll find that many records have been indexed and transcribed or scanned onto CD-ROMs. Some of these you can access at a local library; some you can order with software or by themselves; some are available from the Family History Center.

Census records available on CD-ROM include the U.S. Federal census, various census records from Canada and the U.K., Cherokee and African-American census records, and a few local censuses. Cemetery records and death records from all over North America and the U.K. are available on CD-ROMs; so are parish records.

Check out www.cyndislist.com/cd-roms.htm#Vendors for sources for these CD-ROMs.

Clooz

Clooz is not another genealogy program but instead a database designed in Microsoft Access for systematically organizing and storing all the documents and clues to your ancestry that you have collected over the years. It is an electronic filing cabinet that assists you with search and retrieval of important facts you have found during the ancestor hunt, showing you a complete picture of what you have and what you lack. It has 35 templates for entering genealogical data from myriad document types, and your data can be sorted in dozens of ways.

Once you have imported the individual family members from your genealogy program, you can start to assign documents to each person. Then, a report on a person will show you all the wills, deeds, birth and death certificates, diary entries, or other documents that mention him or her.

Clooz can also help you organize your genealogy to-do list and help you track what needs to be done.

Word Processing

Don't overlook the lowly word processor as one of your genealogy tools. You can use it for journaling your genealogy quest, for creating custom write-ups of your results, and even for creating a book. You can use a word processor to create and track your to-do lists, write letters for vital records, and more.

As with your genealogy program, you need a word processor that can handle all your chores, yet isn't more trouble to use than it's worth.

Notable: A Journaling Program

Notable, available at www.startmyjournal.com, is just one example of a journaling program in which you can record your own life history for future generations. I mention it because it has excellent starter questions, not only for you but also for people you may interview to get genealogy information. Notable is easy to use because it prompts you with ideas and helps you create a life story.

Notable comes in two versions: The LDS edition contains specific topics related to the LDS religion and asks a few more questions that add topics to the user's list that are associated with religion. The regular edition is aimed at non-Mormons but still asks a lot of questions!

The program has no export or import function; it cannot merge, say, GEDCOM data with one of your stories. The Notable output has to be hard copy to accompany any genealogy program output you have. It is also strictly a writing program: No graphics, sound, or animation capabilities are included. However, it is a good way to record family stories—your own or those of your relatives.

These are minor quibbles, however, because the program is intended to be a writing tool, and it's a very good one. The prompts are pertinent, sometimes even surprising or disconcerting, but they certainly get you thinking.

Maps

Sooner or later in tracing your genealogy, you're going to need maps, and not just your handy 2004 road atlas. The boundary lines of cities, counties, states, and even countries have changed over the years; Kentucky used to be part of Virginia after all!

A dictionary or index of place names is called a *gazetteer*. As I mentioned in Chapter 1, a hard copy is a handy thing to have, but you can use software and Internet versions, too. I list several good map and gazetteer sites in Chapter 21. You may also want to have on hand a program such as U.S. Cities Galore, Microsoft Streets, or Pocket Streets to find current places.

Check out Cyndi's List at www.cyndislist.com/maps.htm#Software for the latest in such software.

E-mail

Reading mail is the biggest part of online life. Some of the best information, and even friendships, come through e-mail. If you have an account with an ISP, a mail reader makes your life much easier. The mail readers in browsers tend to have fewer features than the stand-alone mail clients.

To get the most out of electronic mail, you need to get a few things under your belt.

Filters

A *filter* is an action you want the mail program to take when a message matches certain conditions. You can have an e-mail program reply to, copy, move, or destroy a message based on such things as the sender, the subject line, or the words found in the text. You can have the e-mail program do all that before you read your mail or even before the e-mail gets downloaded from the ISP's mail server.

If you've never dealt with e-mail, this might seem like a lot of bells and whistles, but, believe me, when you start getting involved in active mail lists (see Chapter 7), you'll want to sort your mail by geography, surname, and time period, at least!

Furthermore, there'll be some people you don't want to hear from. You can have your mail filters set up to delete mail from those people, which brings up the next important topic: spam protection.

Spam Protection

Long ago (okay, less than ten years ago) only academics and researchers used the Internet, and they liked it that way. They didn't want the general public and, most of all, general businesses to get to play on the Web. Once the Internet was open to the public, they warned, the demons of advertising would hound us. Ads would flood our mailboxes, clog the bandwidth with their shilling and hawking, and make the Internet much less useful and fun. Well, we opened Pandora's box anyway and the result was junk e-mail. The old Netheads were right after all, and the spammers are now on us.

Spammers is Net slang for people who send unsolicited e-mail for the purpose of advertising. Spammers get their name from an old Monty Python skit where people in a restaurant are prevented from having a normal conversation because some folks at the next table insist on loudly praising Spam. The uninvited e-mail advertisements you receive are often called spam because, as in the skit, they rudely interrupt you during more enjoyable activities. The Hormel folks, understandably, don't like the term and prefer the more accurate and official *unsolicited bulk e-mail (UBE)* to describe this annoyance.

UBE could constitute endless messages regarding get-rich-quick ideas, pyramid schemes, vitamins, you name it. Sometimes the pitch is disguised as a newsletter and might include some bogus return address. But, whatever the guise, the purpose is the same: They are using your paid online account for their own advertising.

Why You Get Spam

Any time you post a message to a newsgroup, use a public chat room on America Online, CompuServe, or the Internet, or supply an online service with your profile, the UBE guys are there collecting your e-mail address and any other information they can find. Then they sort the addresses and sell them, causing you to get junk e-mail.

Naturally, they know not everyone is going to be pleased to hear from them, so they disguise themselves with bogus From: and Reply To: lines. You can try to reply and remove or unsubscribe yourself from their lists, but this seldom works. The return addresses either don't exist or aren't designed to receive mail. To reach the culprits and get off their lists, you must do some detective work.

What to Do about Spamming

Frankly, I'm intensely opposed to this noxious form of telemarketing (can you tell?). The first step is for everyone who uses the Internet to write to Congress and have this practice stopped. If Washington can pass a law controlling junk faxes, why can't it do the same for junk e-mail?

Second, learn to protect yourself. One extreme measure would be never to use chat, post to Usenet, use a forum on AOL or CompuServe or a bulletin board on Prodigy, or post your member profile online. But then, online life would be pretty dull, wouldn't it?

A less-harsh solution is to create two e-mail accounts: one public and one private. You use the public one for Usenet, chat, anonymous FTP, and so on. The other you keep hidden like an unlisted phone number, only giving it out to people you truly want to hear from. Then, all you have to do is check your private e-mail box whenever you feel like it and ask your ISP to delete any mail that comes to the public one. (It's more like doing it yourself—highlighting each letter and pressing DELETE before you read it.)

If you use an e-mail program such as Eudora or Pegasus, you can filter out all the junk. Both programs can, based on a message's address, subject line, or body text, drop e-mail into specific folders. Whenever I get junk e-mail, I copy the address, header, and any catch phrase such as "money-making opportunity" to a filter. The next time I get a message from the spammer, it's dumped into my Trash folder and deleted. (In Eudora, for example, select Tools | Filters, enter the e-mail address, check the Transfer To box, and select Trash.) And what about America Online and CompuServe users? AOL can now automatically intercept incoming e-mail from known UBE senders, thanks to a recent court decision. The controls are set by default. To turn them off, use the keyword PREFERRED MAIL. Of course, AOL's action keeps out only so much UBE. If you get junk e-mail from an AOL account, forward it to TOSSPAM. AOL's staff then tells that person to stop sending you e-mail. You can also control what you get by entering the keyword MAIL CONTROLS. Click the icon that reads Set Up Mail Controls and then choose the screen name clicking Edit.

The Mail Controls window gives you several options: Allow All E-mail, Allow E-mail Only from AOL Members, and Block All E-mail are the first three choices. I don't use these because the first is too open, and the second and third are too restrictive. Plus, many UBE senders use AOL screen names.

I use the option Allow E-mail from All AOL Members, and Only from the Listed Internet Domains and Addresses because I need to receive e-mail from AOL's ever-changing public relations staff. Allow E-mail from the Listed AOL Members, Internet Domains and Addresses is the best choice for most people. The drawbacks are you're limited to 100 such names, and this filters out e-mail based on the From: field (not the subject or the text of the message). Still, I find this workable. You can insert a specific address, such as Libbic@prodigy.net in the list. In addition, if you know a certain domain (such as RootsWeb.com or Ancestry.com) will only send you mail you want, you can simply put the part of the address after the @ character, and any mail from that ISP will get through. You can even put in a top-level domain—for example, any address that ends in .gov or .edu is allowed on my list. I figure if I receive any UBE from a government or educational institution, I can quickly report it and have it taken care of!

The last choice, Block E-mail from the Listed AOL Members, Internet Domains, and Addresses is almost useless because of the 100-name limit on the list. Considering hundreds of thousands of UBE senders are out there, this would be like trying to plug a fire hydrant with a golf tee. If you want to block a specific person who is annoying or repeatedly pesters you, you might use this option, as well as report that person to AOL.

CompuServe (CIS) doesn't offer as many options for blocking UBE, but it has always been against the rules for CIS members to send advertising to other CIS members. If you do, CIS can terminate your account. As for non-CIS mail, you can set your e-mail preference never to receive or send any Internet mail, but that's hardly a solution.

File Attachments and Formats

Judging from the comments of my readers, nothing causes more gnashing of teeth to new Internet users than file attachments. You get a message that looks like gobbledygook or has a filename such as foobar.mim, and you don't know what to do with it.

The Internet is so big and powerful, we sometimes lose sight of its limitations. For example, e-mail—the Net's original reason for being—is limited to transmitting the 128 alphanumeric characters (the ones on your keyboard) of the basic ASCII set. Nearly every computer—large and small—uses ASCII, which is why e-mail (and Usenet newsgroups) are limited to these characters.

Yet how does one send the photograph of an ancestor to a newsgroup? The secret has to do with the processes of encoding and decoding. Like Little Orphan Annie's Secret Decoder Ring, *encoding* schemes turn binary files (such as EXE files, graphics, spreadsheets, and formatted documents) into strings of text that, when properly decoded on the other end, resume their original form.

The downside: An encoded file can be 25 to 100 percent larger than the original file.

Many different encoding schemes are used on the Internet. As with FTP, you must know which scheme your correspondent used so you can properly decode the file you received. The key schemes and their file extensions follow (usually your ISP or mail program does the encoding/unencoding for you, so you may never see these in coded form by the time they reach your mailbox):

- UUENCODE (.UUE, .UU) is one such scheme. Its name comes from "UNIX to UNIX Encoding," and it's a common, old method. UUencoded files are deciphered with UUDECODE.

- XXENCODE (.XXE) is a slightly different version of UUENCODE, created for later versions of UNIX.

- BINHEX (.HQX, .HEX) originated on the Mac, but you can now find BINHEX encoders and decoders for the PC.

- MIME (.MME, .MM), or the *Multipurpose Internet Mail Extensions,* specifies the kind of file being sent. This allows many e-mail and web browser programs to recognize what's in a certain MIME file and to display its contents with the appropriate helper application.

If your ISP or your mail program lets a coded file slip through, how do you translate it? If you're using a fairly decent e-mail program, such as Outlook, Pegasus, or Eudora, or you're using AOL and you get a MIME or BINHEX file, you usually don't have to do anything—the software's built-in decoders do the job for you. If you get a file that has been coded with another format, though, you need a third-party program to do the dirty work for you. I note a source later in this section.

"But wait!" you might be saying. "I sometimes get a coded file that has another coded file within in it. In my e-mail program, I see this huge ream of nonsense text. What do I do?" Look closely and you can see instructions in this mess of text—probably the words "copy below this line" and "copy above this line."

Select the text between these lines and paste it into a word processor. Save the file as text only, with the .UUE file extension (because this is a UUencoded file). Then run a UUDECODE program, and the hidden file will emerge.

Which programs decode (and encode) attached files? You can search the shareware sites for the latest offerings. I recommend WinZip (www.winzip.com), which costs $29, but handles many kinds of files, including UUENCODE, and also most compression formats. It's worth the money.

Audio Resources

The Internet has become a broadcast medium, and radio shows originating thousands of miles from you can stream right down to your computer over the Internet. To listen, you need a good media player, whether it is Microsoft's Windows Media Player, RealAudio, or some other version. Most have a free version and are usually easy to set up and use.

Furthermore, most chat programs now allow voice and sound as well as text. AOL Instant Messenger, ICQ, and others have functions to let you speak into a microphone attached to your sound card, sending your voice to your buddy using the same program.

Radio Shows on the Internet

DearMYRTLE's *Family History Hour Internet* radio show can be heard live over the Internet, 9 to 10 P.M. EST several times a week. On Tuesday, Myrtle features genealogy authors, speakers, and publishers. She handles questions e-mailed to her and called into her toll-free line, and she has a weekly list of links for you to surf to. Go to www.dearmyrtle.com/radio.htm to click the button to listen in.

Family History Radio, www.familyhistoryradio.com, features professional genealogist Karen Clifford with host Steve Jensen answering your family history questions as well as updating you on the latest happenings in Family History. Included as a regular feature of this program is the Dick Eastman report, "Genealogy News and Technology with Dick Eastman" (see Figure 2-3). All you need is a regular dial-up Internet connection, speakers, Windows 98 or higher, Internet Explorer, and Windows Media Player.

The Seeker Live is a call-in radio show hosted by Linda Hammer, a former private investigator. Her show airs on Saturdays from 2 to 3 P.M. EST, on WTMY in Sarasota, Florida. The radio station has an Internet broadcast at www.wtmy.com.

Voice Chat

Chat programs such as AOL Instant Messenger, MSN Messenger, and others now allow sound files and streaming audio. Some charge for the

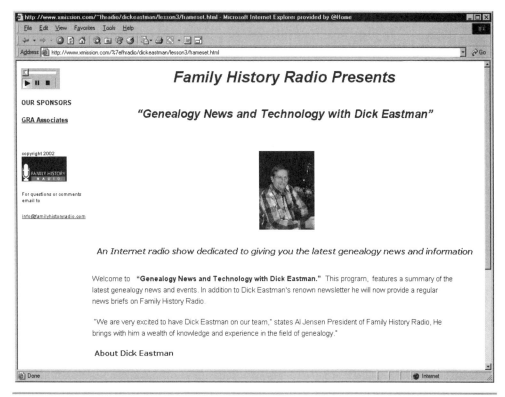

FIGURE 2-3.   *Dick Eastman's "Genealogy News and Technology" can be heard at Family History Radio.com.*

service, some don't, but a voice chat with a genealogy buddy is a fun way to further your research!

Viruses and Worms

No journey is without risk. Whenever you enter the jungle of cyberspace, that dreaded microorganism, the computer virus, might be lurking about. Not only that, but your activities could attract Trojan horses and worms, too, so keep a sharp eye out.

A *virus* is a program hidden on a disk or within a file that can damage your data or computer in some way. Some viruses simply display a message or a joke, while others can wipe out all the information you saved to the hard drive. Therefore, I strongly recommend you inoculate your computer before using any mode of electronic travel.

One breed of computer virus is the Trojan horse. This is a program that seems to be useful and harmless when it first arrives but, secretly, might be destroying data or breaking down the security on your system. The Trojan horse differs from a virus only because it doesn't propagate itself as a virus does.

A *worm* is a program that causes your computer to freeze or crash as it sucks up all your available resources, such as system memory. A worm can make copies of itself and spread through connected systems.

Programs to detect and remove these exotic virtual creatures are available from your local computer store and from various online services. Some are shareware, while others are more costly. But if the program manages to delete a virus before it harms your system, it's worth the price.

The two major virus-protection suites are Norton AntiVirus and McAfee VirusScan, which include one free year of virus updates, available to you once or twice a month. Whatever program you buy, however, be sure to keep it updated.

Even if you have virus-protection software, you need to take precautions. Make a backup of everything important to you—data, letters, and so on—and resave it no less than once a month. The virus-protection software offers to make a recover disk; do so. This can save you much time and trouble later on down the line if your system needs to be restored. Generally, when you download, look for an indication that the files have been checked for viruses. If not, reconsider downloading from that site. If someone mails or hands you a floppy disk with data, always run a virus check on the disk before you do anything else. Once a virus is copied onto your hard disk, removing it can be a major headache. In addition, make sure you run a virus check on your hard drive at least twice a month, just to be certain. This should be part of your regular tune-up and maintenance.

Virus protection is good, but if you opt for a high-speed, continuous connection such as DSL or cable Internet, you also need a firewall to help protect you from crackers, Trojan horses, and worms. A *firewall* is a piece of software, hardware, or combination of both that forms an electronic boundary preventing unauthorized access to a computer or network. It can also be a computer whose sole purpose is to be a buffer between your main computer and the Internet. A firewall controls what goes out and what comes in, according to how the user has set it up. Examples of firewall programs are ZoneAlarm by Zone Labs, BlackICE Defender from NetworkICE, and Internet Security 2000 by Symantec

Corp. A detailed description of how firewalls work can be found on Shields Up, a website devoted to broadband security created by programmer Steve Gibson, head of Gibson Research Corp. (www.grc.com) of Laguna Hills, California. Run the tests. You'll be surprised.

Publishing on the Internet

As I noted in the previous chapter, you can use several free sites to publish as well as search your genealogy. I noted several sites that let you post your facts in HTML; there are other options, as well.

Turning a GEDCOM into HTML

Some programs are available that take a GEDCOM from any program on the market and turn it into HTML. An inexpensive program ($10) such as GedPage (www.frontiernet.net/~rjacob/gedpage.htm, as shown in Figure 2-4) turns GEDCOM files into attractive HTML files. You can choose a version for Macintosh or Windows (3.1 and up). The output is formatted as family group sheets.

Using this program is simplicity itself. First, create a GEDCOM. Then change the files HEADER.HTM and FOOTER.HTM to say what you want, generally your contact information. (You can do this in any text editor. Simply replace the text and leave anything within the < and > brackets alone.) Start GedPage and fill in the blanks for the URL and the e-mail address; then choose colors if you like. Click Create Page. In a few seconds, a set of pages for the database is created. Then you use an FTP program to upload the pages to your site.

This program is only one example; others are out there. Check out Cyndi's List for a current list of programs (www.cyndislist.com/software.htm).

Using an HTML Editor

For the real do-it-yourselfer, HTML editors can help you create your own site from the ground up. Most modern HTML editors work just like word processors; in fact, Word 2000 can save any document file in HTML format, complete with links and graphics. Microsoft IE and Netscape both come with simple, useful HTML editors as part of the package. Microsoft IE can be installed with Front Page Express, and Netscape with the Composer module. Both are fairly easy to use. Once you finish, the programs can post the results for you. Simply choose Publish under the File menu.

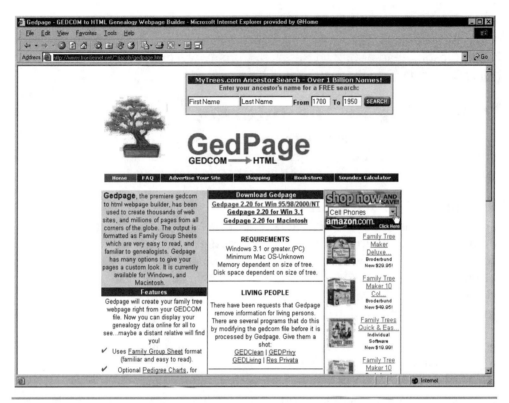

FIGURE 2-4. *GedPage creates family group sheets in HTML for posting to a website.*

Using a Web Site to Publish

MyFamily.com (Chapter 17), RootsWeb (Chapter 16), AOL, and other sites give you an opportunity to publish on the Web. You'll learn how in the chapters that cover these sites.

Blogging

Another way to publish is to keep a "web log" or "blog" at www.blogger.com.

You don't have to learn HTML, FTP, or any other arcane Internet service. You simply log on to Blogger.com and follow several, easy onscreen prompts within your browser to create your "blogspot." The site provides an easy typing or copy/paste data-entry process from then on. You add bold, italics, and underline in the same way you do in e-mail or using your word processing program.

As soon as you click the Publish button, the item is added to www*.yourtitle*.blogspot.com (you can find mine at www.genealogyonline.blogspot.com), no waiting for spiders to find it, and you don't have to worry about the server's capacity or tweaking the code. Just record your family history, anecdotes, recipes, or just keep a journal of your progress. In fact, DearMYRTLE is using hers to preserve stories she told her daughters when they were children (www.dearmyrtle.com).

Wrapping Up

To get online, you need the following:

+ A computer (with lots of hard disk space!)

+ An Internet service provider

+ Software to help you browse, record your findings, and share what you have learned

Chapter 3

Online Society

You've probably heard the Internet described as an online world. This is an apt description, but the differences between the online world and "the real world" have decreased drastically lately. Still, you'll find a set of norms, often termed "netiquette," that holds sway in the online communities. Indeed, Miss Manners herself has laid down a few laws on proper behavior in cyberspace (see *Wired* magazine's interview with Judith Martin, aka Miss Manners, in the following box), and an entire site on the subject can be found at www.albion.com/netiquette.

Genealogy communities also have their own special subset of rules, which this chapter discusses. But first, let's discuss ways to get online besides the traditional home access.

Manners Matter

by Kevin Kelly

Sit up straight, folks—Miss Manners is here. She has mastered her voicemail, got control of her cell phone, and now she's logged on to the Net.

In real life, Miss Manners's true name is Judith Martin. For years she's written about excruciatingly correct behavior for all those moments when the modem is not on; now she has a few interesting things to say about the wired life. For example, people who don't give a hoot about sending thank-you notes are suddenly bent out of shape when they get an e-mail message typed in ALL CAPS. *Wired* spoke to Miss Manners and asked her, very politely, how etiquette is bringing civility to the online frontier.

Wired: What is it about cyberspace that has rekindled interest in etiquette?

Miss Manners: Freedom without rules doesn't work. And communities do not work unless they are regulated by etiquette. It took about three minutes before some of the brighter people discovered this online. We have just as many ways, if not more, to be obnoxious in cyberspace and fewer ways to regulate them. So, posting etiquette rules and looking for ways to ban people who violate them is the way sensible people are attempting to deal with this.

Wired: Do you find online etiquette rules parallel the rules of etiquette offline?

Miss Manners: Yes. Spamming is the equivalent of boring people or mixing in business. Flaming is the equivalent of being insulting. You may not realize how annoying it is when you ask an obvious question to a group that has been meeting for a while. So etiquette refers you to an FAQ file. I'm delighted people are doing a good job on the Net.

Wired: To sort out the correct behavior when corresponding through technology, you suggest the body is more important than any disembodied communication. Somebody sitting in front of you should take precedence over just a voice—like a phone conversation. And a voice takes precedence over a further disembodied e-mail. The more disembodied the communication is, the less precedence it has. Is that fair?

Miss Manners: Yes. And it is disobeyed flagrantly. The interesting thing is why people think that someone who is not present (a phone ringing) is more important than someone who is. Generally it has taken a person a lot more effort to come to see you than to call you on the telephone.

Wired: Let's see. I need some advice. E-mail has an alarming proclivity to be copied. What are the rules for passing on private e-mail?

Miss Manners: For e-mail, the old postcard rule applies. Nobody else is supposed to read your postcards, but you'd be a fool if you wrote anything private on one.

Wired: Most people are not writing their e-mail that way.

Miss Manners: That's their mistake. We're now seeing e-mail that people thought they had deleted showing up as evidence in court. You can't erase e-mail. As that becomes more commonly realized, people will be a little wiser about what they type.

Wired: You're very much of a stickler for keeping one's business life from intruding upon one's social life. That distinction online is becoming more blurred all the time. There seems to be a deliberate attempt to mix these two up—working at home, for example. Is this the end of civilization as we know it?

Miss Manners: Blurring the two is not conducive to a pleasant life, because it means that the joys of being loved for yourself, and not for how high-ranking you are or what you can do for other people, quickly disappear. People who are downsized, for instance, find they've been dropped by everyone they know because they don't have real friends. They only had business acquaintances. One of the big no-nos in cyberspace is that you do not go into a social activity, a chat group or something like that, and start advertising or selling things. This etiquette rule is an attempt to separate one's social life, which should be pure enjoyment and relaxation, from the pressures of work.

Reprinted with permission from *Wired* magazine, November 1997 issue

Alternative Access

I've mentioned this before, but it bears repeating: The fact that you can do lots of genealogy research online does not mean you'll never use the traditional methods again. In fact, online-only researching would be a very shortsighted way to go about it. So, there will be times when you physically go places to track down records. However, that does not mean you have to leave your Internet links behind. You can still check your e-mail for mail lists, and surf to your favorite genealogy how-to site for a quick refresher, even if you aren't at home.

I've already mentioned that it is possible to get Internet features on wireless phones, but that it's expensive and slow, and those tiny buttons are really annoying. You can also use wireless Internet connections on your handheld device, but again, you have to watch the cost as well as put up with slower connection speeds than you are used to at home. Two alternatives: libraries and schools.

Libraries

Most modern libraries have at least a terminal or two dedicated to Internet access. You usually have to sign up for an hour's use at a time, but that's enough to check your e-mail and message boards.

Two things to remember:

♦ Browsers cache all sites visited. Sites deposit cookies, sometimes with passwords. For these reasons, you want to clear the cache and delete new cookies on the browser you use on a library's computer when you are through. Then, for good measure, close the browser so no one can use the Back command to get into your e-mail box or other password-protected site.

♦ Printing out an e-mail message or page will probably cost you a few pennies a sheet.

Schools

Many universities, such as Samford University in Birmingham, Alabama, host genealogy courses, seminars, and workshops, and sometimes grant student privileges to attendees. In that case, you may be able to use the university's terminals to access the Internet.

As with public library access, clear the cache and be sure to pay for printouts.

Civil Discourse

You can converse on the Internet in several ways. Usenet (see Chapter 8) is a fast-paced way of messaging, where you post messages to a newsgroup and usually within a few minutes get a response. This isn't as "instant" as chat (see Chapter 7), but you'll find new postings and responses appear more quickly than on a mail list (see Chapter 8). Online message boards, such as CompuServe's Roots Forum, are somewhat more leisurely: A message might get answered within a week.

 Caution

On Usenet, chat, and in many message boards, it is better to disguise your return address. Type it as something such as "Libbi at Prodigy.net" or "Libbi@nospam.prodigy.net." Real people will know what you mean; address-harvesting programs from spammers will not.

Still, these are all conversations. And, because they are written conversations, with no body language or facial expression to clue the participants, certain rules and standards have developed so that users can understand each other.

Flames

A *flame* is an argument on a message system—a chat, Usenet newsgroup, mail list, or message board—in which people type insults and angry messages back and forth. Often, these arguments are the result of a misunderstanding, where one person misinterprets another, who, in turn, takes offense. Flames accomplish nothing. They never change any minds, and they hurt feelings.

If someone flames you, the best course of action is to a) inform the moderator of the group, list, or chat room that you've been flamed and b) don't respond to the flamer. Indeed, you might even want to set your e-mail program, chat program, or newsreader program to filter out all messages from the flamer. If it happens on a message board, simply stop opening messages from that sender.

The Rules

No, we're not talking about dating, but rather about conversations online. Sometimes you get flamed because you broke a rule—a rule you were probably unaware even existed. The best way to avoid this is to keep yourself informed of the standards and traditions of the group. You can do this in two ways: One way is to lurk until you get the lay of the land, so to speak. To *lurk* is to read the messages without responding or posting any messages yourself. This isn't considered rude. With the exception of chat, most message systems won't alert others to your presence until you post something. Lurking before you leap is completely acceptable in online genealogy.

Another way to familiarize yourself with online rules is to read the rulebook. Almost always, the rules are contained in a Frequently Asked Questions (FAQ) file. On Usenet, almost every newsgroup posts an FAQ at regular intervals. If you joined in the middle of a cycle, you can find most of them at www.faqs.org. The home page of this site has a search box. Type **Genealogy** in the search box, click Search, and you get a list of FAQ files for various groups, as shown in Figure 3-1. You might also want to search the FAQ archive for adoption, family history, and ancestry for related groups.

If you can't find an FAQ message or file for a Usenet newsgroup, make one of your first questions on the group, "Where and when can I get the FAQs for this group?"

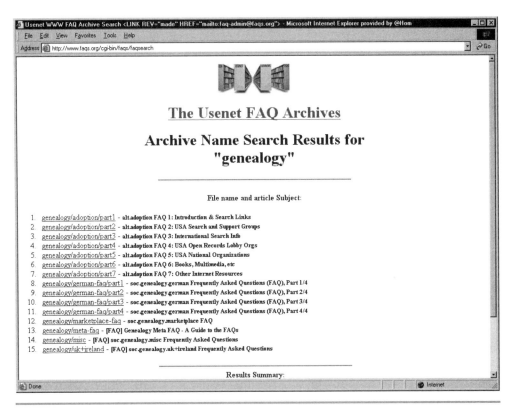

FIGURE 3-1.   *Go to the FAQ Archives to find Frequently Asked Questions (and answers!) about genealogy.*

Mail lists often store their FAQ files on a website and also send it to you as your first message after you subscribe to the list. Save the message as a text or document file for future reference.

An online forum, such as CompuServe's Roots Forum, might have a series of messages or notices that discuss the rules of the forum. When you first join, these are usually shown to you.

Getting Along

Try to stick to the topic being discussed in a chat room, newsgroup, mail list, or message list. Again, the FAQ should list the topics a chat will accept. Ads are usually verboten. A product announcement is typically okay, but an outright sales pitch isn't.

Straying off-topic commonly leads to flames. In general, the following topics are welcome in genealogy newsgroups, mail lists, and chat rooms:

♦ Your family history information and requests for others to help you find additional sources and material. (Tiny tafels, the short, and fixed-length data files are often posted for this.)

♦ Information on upcoming genealogical meetings, workshops, symposia, reunions, and so forth.

♦ Reviews, criticisms, and comments regarding software or hardware you've used in your genealogy/family history efforts.

♦ Names and addresses of bookshops around the world that contain publications or information about genealogy.

♦ Almost any message about genealogy in general.

Remember, what you send is posted exactly as you send it, unless the site, group, or mail list (such as soc.genealogy.surnames) has a moderator who edits all incoming messages. On chat, when you press ENTER, it is sent off—mistakes and all.

Participants in genealogy groups want the topics of discussion to relate directly to genealogy or family history. In some groups, however, the tacit agreement is that anything a subscriber thinks is appropriate *is* appropriate, as long as it relates to genealogy. To discern these tacit rules at a particular site, lurk for a while to discover if it tends to be more lax about off-topic posting.

Assume an attitude of courtesy among subscribers and readers. Remember, your postings and comments might be seen by as many as 20,000 readers on different networks throughout the world.

Read carefully what you receive to make certain you understand the message before replying. Read what you've written carefully to ensure your message won't be misunderstood. As a matter of fact, routinely let a reply sit overnight and then read it again before sending. This can prevent that sinking feeling of regret when you realize what you posted wasn't what you meant to say.

Avoid sarcasm. If humor seems appropriate, clearly label it as such. A smiley face should indicate humor. It is easy to misunderstand what's being said when no tone of voice, facial expression, or body language can guide you. A corollary: Give others the benefit of the doubt. Perhaps what you understood to be rude was meant to be funny. Communicating online is a fine art!

Know your audience and double-check addresses. Make sure the person or list of people you're sending your message to is the appropriate one.

Be tolerant of newcomers, as you expect others to be tolerant of you. No one was born knowing all about the Internet or Usenet. Don't abuse new users of computer networks for their lack of knowledge. As you become more expert, be patient as others first learn to paddle, swim, and then surf the Net, just like you. Be an active participant in teaching newcomers.

Avoid cluttering your messages with excessive emphasis (**, !!, > > > >, and so on). This can make the message hard to follow.

Also, know how your mail program answers messages. Many mail programs default to copying the entire message over again into the reply. When you respond to a message, either include the relevant part of the original message or explicitly refer to the original's contents, but delete the unimportant parts of the original message. People commonly read your reply to the message before they read the original. (Remember the convention to precede each quoted line of the original message you include with the > character.)

In responses, don't quote more than necessary to make your point clear and, please, never quote the entire message. Learn what happens on your particular system when you reply to messages. Is the message sent to the originator of the message or to the list, and when is it sent? When you're responding to another message, your subject line should be the same, with RE: at the beginning.

Always include a precise subject line, with a surname, in your message. This should be something that attracts attention, and the only way to do this is to make sure the subject line describes the main point of your message. Don't put "Looking for…" as the subject line with no surname. People will scroll right past your message and never read it.

If you're seeking information about a family, include the surname in uppercase letters in the message subject. Many readers don't have time to read the contents of all messages.

Here's an example of a bad subject line:

♦   Wondering if anyone is looking for JONES

And here are some examples of good subject lines:

♦   Researching surname ENGLE 1700s

♦   SPENCER: England > MA > NY > OH > IN > MS

- ♦ Delaware BLIZZARDs pre-1845

- ♦ ? Civil War Records

In the good examples, note these conventions: Surnames are in all caps, but nothing else is. A greater than sign (>) is used as an arrow to denote migration from one place to another. A date is always helpful. If your message is a question, indicate this in the subject line. Although passages in all uppercase are considered shouting, the exception to this rule in genealogy is that surnames should be in uppercase, just as in any query.

Limit a message to one subject. This allows readers to quickly decide whether they need to read the message in full. Second subjects within a single message are often missed.

Questions are often the exception to this rule. You might need to post a message that's full of questions on a subject. When you ask a question within such a message, end it with a question mark (?) and press ENTER. This should be the end of that line. This makes it much easier for people to reply, because most newsreaders quote the original message line by line.

Be specific, especially when you ask questions. If you ask about a person, identify when and where the person might have lived. In questions concerning specific genealogical software, make clear what sort of computer (PC/MS-DOS, PC/Windows, Apple Macintosh, and so forth) is involved. The folks reading these newsgroups are helpful, but busy, and are more likely to answer if they don't have to ask what you mean.

A good idea is to put your name in the text of your message, along with your best e-mail address for a reply. You might want to disguise your e-mail address, though, to prevent its being harvested for unsolicited bulk e-mail (see Chapter 2). A good convention is

```
Please reply to libbic "at" prodigy.net.
```

The end of the message is a good place for your name and e-mail address.

Sometimes the message systems get absolutely clogged with messages, such as when, in early 1994, rotten weather, an earthquake, and a national holiday all converged on a certain Monday, and many people were at home online because they were unable or not required to go to work. In this case, you must choose what to read based on the subject line or sender because it is impossible to read everything posted to the group that day. This is when a newsreader that lets you filter the messages for the subject headings is invaluable!

Chat Etiquette

Chat and instant message programs are discussed in detail in Chapter 7. Chat boards might not have formal FAQ files, but the following are some general rules for chat.

Generally, you will find helpful, polite people in genealogy chat rooms in Internet Relay Chat (IRC) and instant message systems such as AOL Instant Messenger (AIM). Often, especially if you have one of the instant message programs such as AIM, you'll be chatting with people you've at least contacted before. And, of course, if you're taking an online course, specific rules are going to be in force as to who can "talk" and when. Nevertheless, in all these scenarios, you must meet certain etiquette standards in chat.

All the etiquette covered earlier in this chapter applies to chat. Using all capital letters, except to mention the surnames you're researching, is considered shouting. Flames are useless and annoying; you should show respect for everyone. And, make certain you aren't taking offense when none was intended.

IRC servers and the instant message programs such as AIM track your connection. Many require you to input an e-mail address and select a "handle." As a security measure, when you choose a nickname or handle to join a chat or use the Internet presence program, you might want to avoid using one that reveals your real name or gender, where you live, and so forth, unless this is a private chat room. Of course, never use offensive handles or nicknames. Chat is extremely public, so be careful about what you reveal in chat rooms.

 Caution

A handle, screen name, or display name is simply the identification that appears to other users about you. It is often best to use something other than your real, full name.

Stay on topic or, if you get sidetracked, create a separate room to follow your tangent.

Lurk before you leap into sending messages: Check out the room and see if the topic is what you're looking for.

Obscenity, cursing, and the like are forbidden on such systems as AOL. You can report people for using them. You can also use the /ignore command in IRC to block all messages from someone who is annoying you. If this becomes persistent, read the Message of the Day (MOTD) to find the name of the system administrator and report the offender.

> ### Note
>
> *The MOTD usually appears right after you sign onto an IRC server. It usually has a greeting, and instructions for how to contact the server's administrator; you can get it to scroll again with the command /motd.*

You can send your e-mail address by private message, but don't post it in the message system, because if you do, the spammers will flood your mailbox. If someone refuses to give you an address, don't be insulted because it is probably just a security measure.

If you want a particular person's attention (for example, to ask or answer a question), precede your message with his or her handle or its abbreviation.

For example, if my screen name is ECWriter, someone with the screen name RootsNewbie might send the following:

```
ECWriter: Where can I buy your book?
```

I could reply as follows:

```
RN: it's a mass market paperback, so it should be in most bookstores! :-).
```

Smileys will be common, as will all sorts of acronyms. Refer to the Glossary for a list of smileys and acronyms used in online chat.

Many IRC servers and most of the instant message programs enable you to send sound files, pictures, and even programs over the chat room. Be wary of this feature for two reasons: First, it represents a security risk to receive files from someone you don't know well; second, this adds to the traffic on the server and slows down everyone's interaction, not only that of the sender and the receiver.

Chat and instant message programs have some limit to the number of characters that can be sent in one chunk. If your thoughts run longer, type the message in parts, each ending in an ellipsis (...) until you finish. Don't be surprised to find that, as you do this, other messages are popping up between your lines. Those paying attention can follow your train of thought better if you take advantage of a feature many programs have: the capability to send your text in a specific color and/or typeface.

Don't ignore people asking polite questions (such as "How are you?"). If someone is being rude, you can use the command /ignore < person's handle > .

Danger: Scams Ahead!

For as long as genealogists have been around, those who would try to rip them off have existed, as mentioned in Chapter 1. Commonly, the scams appear in mail lists, Usenet newsgroups, and chat rooms, disguised as messages from members of the group. One form of scam tries to get money from you for something that is bogus, or available free elsewhere. Another tries to anger, frighten, or otherwise manipulate you with some false story.

Back when my mother started her genealogy in the mid '60s, she quickly came up against bogus offers to "find" her heraldic coat of arms, counterfeit "genealogies," which were nothing but phone directory listings, and so on. Most names *don't* have a coat of arms, but that doesn't stop these companies from inventing them. Check out Chapter 1 for a list of sites that track scams and frauds in genealogy.

Halbert's, one of the longest-running scams, finally folded, but others will of course try to take their place. Morphcorp, GenSeekers (also known as Genealogy-express.com and genlocator.com), and Three Centuries are just a few of the well-documented scams.

The proper online etiquette here: First, do not respond to scams and hoaxes. This only encourages the scoundrels. Second, when you receive e-mail chain letters, virus warnings, and "true stories," don't send them on. That just clogs the bandwidth.

Cyndi's List has a page of scams, as well as debunking misconceptions of the well-intended, at www.cyndislist.com/myths.htm. The "Genealogy Hall of Shame" at http://blacksheep.rootsweb.com/shame/genlocator.htm tries to keep current with genealogy scams, too. A good source for information about other scams (false urban legends, fake virus warnings, and so forth) is the Snopes site at www.snopes.com. This site is regularly updated with the reality behind some of the fantasies that go around the Internet, genealogy-related or not.

You should read the article on the National Genealogical Society's site, "Psst! Wanna Buy Your Name?" at www.ngsgenealogy.org/comconsumerpsst.htm (see Figure 3-2), which lists the most common genealogy scams, and what to do about them.

FIGURE 3-2. *Good advice on avoiding and dealing with scams can be found at the NGS site.*

Wrapping Up

- ◆ To be polite, stay on topic in mail lists, Usenet newsgroups, and chat rooms.

- ◆ Read the FAQ files for any group you participate in.

- ◆ Use filters and chat commands to track the conversations that interest you and ignore those that don't.

- ◆ Use the right formats: Don't use capital letters except for surnames; do use symbols and acronyms to keep things brief.

- ◆ Many scams appear in mail lists, Usenet newsgroups, and chat rooms. Hide your e-mail address, don't respond to spammers, and don't pass suspect messages on!

Chapter 4

Privacy and Law in Genealogy

Genealogy has a long history of legal and ethical connections. From the settling of estates, to the eligibility of soccer players for national teams, to the very course of a nation's history, genealogy has had a role to play. The validation of genealogical information and the publishing of that information, online and otherwise, will also have legal and ethical ramifications. Privacy and copyright are important to consider when you pursue your genealogy. Three genealogy experts will share their views on these topics with you in this chapter.

The National Genealogical Society (NGS) has published a set of standards for sharing information with others, as well as publishing genealogical information on the Web. They appear in Appendix A of this book and are available online at www.ngsgenealogy.org/comstandards.htm (see Figure 4-1). These should be your starting point in ethical and legal considerations in genealogy.

Disclaimer: I am not a lawyer, and this chapter is not meant to be legal advice, but merely information.

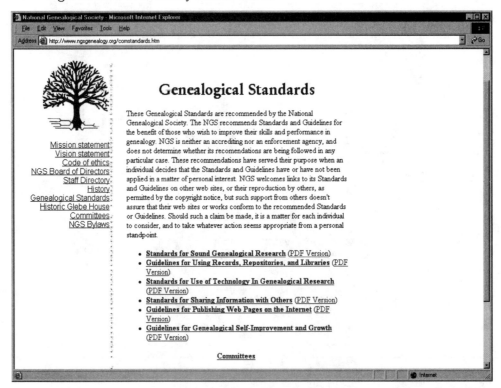

FIGURE 4-1. *The National Genealogical Society has a set of standards for sharing information.*

Legal and Ethical Considerations

You will have two basic issues to confront in genealogy: privacy and copyright. These issues are just as important in the "real world" as they are online. Happily, it isn't very hard to be on the right side of both these issues!

Privacy

"Genealogists are sharing, caring people, and most of us think nothing of handing over all of our genealogical data to distant cousins, even strangers," says Myra Vanderpool Gormley, Certified Genealogist (CG), editor of *RootsWeb Review* and nationally syndicated columnist. Part of being a Certified Genealogist requires adhering to a code of ethics concerning privacy (see Figure 4-2).

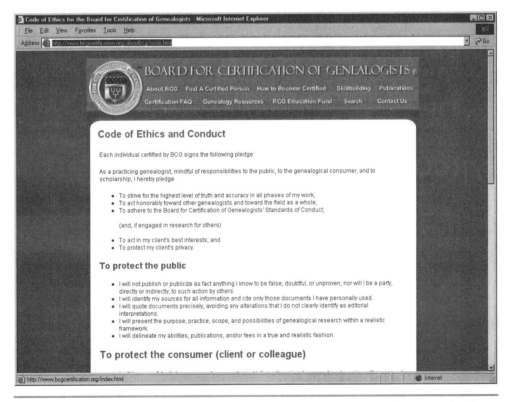

FIGURE 4-2. *The Board for Certification of Genealogists' code of ethics specifically mentions privacy.*

"However, we should start thinking about the ramifications of our actions. The idea of sharing genealogical information is good, and technology has made it easy. However, technology is not an exclusive tool for honest people. If detailed personal information about you and your living relatives is on the Internet, crooks can and do find it, and some scam artist might use it to hoodwink your grandmother into giving out the secrets that will open her bank account. It has happened. If your bank or financial institution still uses your mother's maiden name for a password, change it. Remember that your living relatives have the same rights to privacy that you do, and among these rights are:

♦ The right to be free of unreasonable and highly offensive intrusions into one's seclusion, including the right to be free of highly objectionable disclosure of private information in which the public has no legitimate interest;

♦ Appropriation of one's name or likeness by another without consent; and

♦ False light in the public eye—the right to avoid false attributions of authorship or association.

"Publishing private genealogical information—and the important word here is *private*—about a living person without consent might involve any or all three aspects of their right to privacy. Publishing is more than just printed material or a traditional book. Publication includes websites, GEDCOMs, message boards, mailing lists, and even family group sheets or material that you might share with others via e-mail or traditional mail. They might be able to seek legal relief through a civil lawsuit. It is OK to collect genealogical information about your living relatives, but do not publish it in any form without written permission," Gormley says.

"We should exercise good manners and respect the privacy of our families—those generous relatives who have shared personal information with us or who shared with a cousin of a cousin," Gormley added. "Additionally, there is another and growing problem—identity theft. Why make it easy for cyberthieves to steal yours or a loved one's identity? But, identity theft involves much more than just your name, address, or phone number. This idea that one's name, address, phone number, and vitals fall into the area of privacy laws is a common misconception by many people, for the facts of your existence are a matter of public record in most instances. However, personal information such as health issues, a child born out of wedlock, spouse abuse, how much money you have in the bank, etc.—those are things that are not general public knowledge, and these are personal things that if you publish them about your living relatives, then there could be an invasion of privacy involved (but I'm not a lawyer)," Gormley says.

Note

"When you post public messages (on message boards and mailing lists, for example) about your research, it is sufficient to say you are researching a Jones or a Cynthia Jones line. You don't have to reveal relationship by saying she is your mother or maternal grandmother. In the pursuit of our ancestors, let's not inadvertently hurt our living family members or ourselves. Think twice before you post or share any data about the living."

—Myra Vanderpool Gormley, CG

"The concept is simple, although it is far more complicated in execution. In short, ask yourself repeatedly, 'Is there anyone who will mind if I publish this information?' There are legal issues as well with living individuals and with publishing info about people within the past 72 years in the U.S., 100 years in Canada and the U.K.," says Dick Eastman, the longtime leader of the CompuServe Roots Forum. Eastman's genealogy tips have helped thousands of online genealogists over the last 15 years. His weekly *Eastman's Genealogy Newsletter* has been a treasure trove of news and tips for over 5 years.

"Protecting the privacy of living individuals and the issue of whether or not to publish sensitive family information (such as a great-great-aunt's child born out of wedlock) are big concerns," Eastman says. "Those can become legal issues if a distant (or not-so-distant) relative takes exception to your publishing such information. Lawsuits have been launched because of these things." Indeed, Australia recently amended its privacy laws, and the page in Figure 4-3 notes how it will affect genealogists.

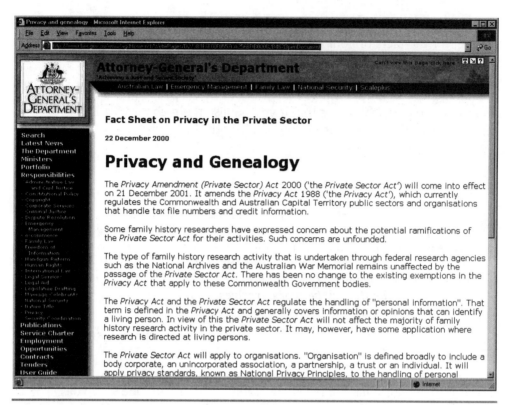

FIGURE 4-3. *The Australian Attorney General has a page explaining privacy and genealogy.*

Copyright

Copyright applies equally to online material and offline material. Just because the material is online changes nothing. Copyright laws are not, however, the same all around the world, and that's where online copyright becomes complicated.

As a genealogist, you should educate yourself about copyright laws (not just U.S. copyright laws) and understand what is "fair use" of other's work and what is copyrightable in the first place. A good start is the publication "Copyright Basics" from the Library of Congress, available online and in hard copy (see Figure 4-4). Be aware that if you take copyrightable material *without* permission, not only are you stealing, but you also may be plagiarizing. In most instances, however, genealogists *will* share some or all of their material with you, if you ask first.

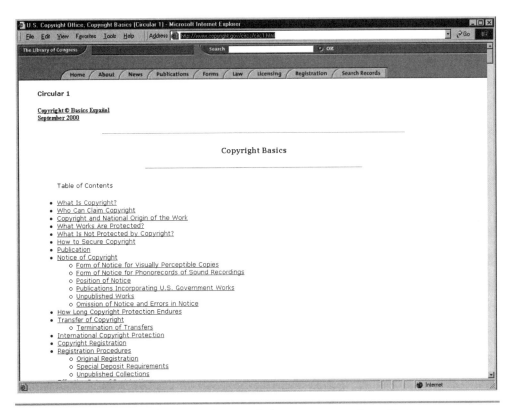

FIGURE 4-4. *"Copyright Basics" is a good place to start on the subject.*

In the U.S., copyright does not extend to the discovery of facts. You cannot copyright the fact that your Jane Smith married John Jones on 3 June 1905 in Paradise Valley, Humboldt County, Nevada, even if you are the one who first "found" the marriage record and spent $300 to drive to the courthouse to get a copy of it. Anyone and everyone can use that marriage fact.

Copyright laws vary by country, but for *most* countries the basic premises are the same:

♦ Facts and data cannot be copyrighted.

♦ Narration, compilations, and creative works can.

In other words, the presentation of facts can be protected by copyright, but not the facts themselves. Therefore, a pedigree chart and GEDCOM file—both common forms of presentation of facts—are not protected by copyright. When you present data in your own distinctive format, such as a book, then that presentation of the material is protected by copyright, even though the facts are not.

Gormley says, "If you do not want to share your genealogical research, that is fine, but you cannot claim copyright to facts, and a great deal of 'online genealogy' is nothing more than compiled facts— although seldom verified or even referenced as to the actual source of the information. If you don't want to be 'ripped off' and if you mean by that that you do not want others to use genealogical facts you have compiled, then don't share your genealogy with anyone—put it in a vault."

DearMYRTLE, the daily genealogy columnist, says, "Fortunately, I know of only one person who has stated she is unwilling to share her compiled genealogy data and documentation with others because she plans to print a book. < sigh > I suspect, though, that the individual in question most certainly benefited from previously compiled research in books, websites and CD databases. It would be impossible to avoid the use of these items as clues leading to the discovery of original documents. For example, one would even have to consider a clerk of the court's marriage indexes as previously compiled research. Such an index is indeed one step removed from the original creation of marriage licenses and marriage returns."

"I wish I knew!" says Dick Eastman when asked how to protect data you have carefully collected. "There is no foolproof method of avoiding being ripped off. Of course, you should always add copyright claims. But that only stops the honest people and maybe a few unknowledgeable ones who never thought about copyrights until they read your claim.

"I used to recommend technical solutions: I recommended Adobe Acrobat PDF files. However, a free program appeared that does a great job of converting PDF files back to useable text, so now even that recommendation has been weakened. I do not know of any other way."

Eastman says there are no easy answers, only guidelines. "The person who is to publish the information needs to ask himself, 'Am I sure that I have a legal right to use this information?' If you have any doubts, don't publish! However, determining whether or not you do have a legal right to publish a piece of information can become very complex. I spent a lot of time discussing this with a lawyer who works for a Boston legal firm that specializes in intellectual properties issues. She is also an experienced genealogist and a member of the advisory board for a prestigious society. The more she talked, the more confused I became. At the end of our conversation, she said, 'Well, there really is no easy way,'" Eastman concluded.

Other Matters

"Traditionally genealogists have been a kindly, sharing group of individuals," says Pat Ritchley, also known online as DearMYRTLE. "After all, no single researcher has every piece of the ancestral puzzle. We need to share research back and forth among those with common ancestors. Successful genealogy research does not exist in a vacuum where one works totally alone. It is then only a matter of common sense to cite the source of each piece of the puzzle, to leave a *wide* audit trail for those that follow, and to give credit where credit is due.

"That wide audit trail is essential for others to be able to evaluate the reliability of our research in our absence. Given such source citations (author, title, call number, microfilm number, publication date, etc.) it would be possible for a great-great-grandchild to obtain photocopies (or whatever they'll be using then) of original documents relating to his family tree. Should additional documentation come to light in the meantime, that distant great-great-grandchild should compare it with our old compiled genealogy, to see if the new information supports or refutes the lineage assumptions we've made.

"Genealogies will improve over time, as one generation takes what others have compiled before and gathers additional documentation— perhaps distinguishing between two John Smiths in an area where it was previously thought there was only one individual by that name. In such a case, it isn't necessary to denigrate the work of the previous researcher. Merely point out the expanded list of documents proving the distinctions and bring the family puzzle into a new light. But in doing so, cite all sources!

"There is also a need for individuals who merely photocopy 25 pages of their personal recollections at the local office supply store and send them in manila envelopes to their distant family members. Wouldn't we each give our eyeteeth to have such a write-up from our Civil War or Revolutionary War ancestor? But as always, family lore must be proved before incorporating it into our pedigree charts. Looking at documents created at the time our ancestors lived are eyewitness accounts of life as they knew it."

For Further Reading, Ritchley recommends *Evidence! Source Citation & Analysis for the Family Historian* by Elizabeth Shown Mills, available at genealogical.com.

Note

"In a perfect world (online or off) everyone would cite their sources properly and give credit to all who have shared research and information with them. Alas, there is no such place—never has been. Evan basic good manners—such as saying "thank you"—are rare. But the genealogist with good manners is far more likely to be rewarded with a wealth of material and help than those without."

—Myra Vanderpool Gormley, CG

Sites about Copyright, Ethics, and Privacy

Here are some good online articles on these topics.

♦ **10 Myths about Copyright Explained**
http://www.templetons.com/brad/copymyths.html

♦ **An Expert in Computer Security Finds His Life Is a Wide-Open Book** http://www.nytimes.com/library/tech/99/12/biztech/articles/13kirk.html (note you will have to finish a (free) registration form to read this article)

♦ **Association of Professional Genealogists' Code of Ethics** http://www.apgen.org/ethics/index.html

- **Australian Attorney General: Privacy and Genealogy**
  http://www.law.gov.au/www/agdHome.nsf/Web + Pages/
  D273B1F8F08F0557CA256BDB000B2B46?OpenDocument

- **Board for Certification of Genealogists' Code of Ethics**
  http://www.bcgcertification.org/aboutbcg/code.html

- **Can You Copyright Your Family Tree?**
  http://genealogy.about.com/library/tips/blcopyright.htm

- **Copyright Resources on the Internet**
  http://www.groton.k12.ct.us/mts/pt2a5.htm

- **"Copyright Basics" from the Library of Congress**
  http://www.copyright.gov/circs/circ1.html

- **Creating Worthwhile Genealogies for Our Families and Descendants** http://www.rootsweb.com/ ~ rwguide/
  lesson12.htm?sourceid = 00392187256799055992

- **Genealogical Standards**
  http://www.ngsgenealogy.org/comstandards.htm

- **Genealogist's Code of Ethics**
  http://www.rootsweb.com/ ~ gasaga/page2.html

- **Nolo.com** http://www.nolo.com/

- **"Privacy and the Web" (article in *Missing Links
  Newsletter* by Myra Vanderpool Gormley)**
  http://www.petuniapress.com/ml/19980605.txt

- **The United States Copyright Office**
  http://lcweb.loc.gov/copyright/

- **U.S. Copyright and Genealogy**
  http://stellar-one.com/copyrightgenealogy/plagiarism.htm

Wrapping Up

- ◆ The first rule: Do not publish anything about living people, on the Web or otherwise. This helps prevent someone from getting a name, birth date, and birth place to create a false identification or to steal an identity.

- ◆ The second rule: Be sensitive about what to publish about those who have passed on. You may find it fascinating that your great-great-grandfather was illegitimate and a horse thief; perhaps your cousins won't be so enthralled.

- ◆ The third rule: Cite your sources, both to protect intellectual property rights and to leave a wide audit trail for future genealogists.

Part II

Using the Internet for Genealogy

Chapter 5

Genealogy
Education

A lot of genealogy is learn-by-doing, but that's no reason to reinvent the wheel. Workshops, seminars, and courses can help you start climbing that family tree efficiently and effectively.

You have lots of choices when it comes to learning about genealogy. You can read books like this one, take college-level courses, or read "how-to" articles on websites. You can learn about one aspect or study to become a Certified Genealogist. You can go to a class or have a class come to you over the Internet. If you decide to go to a class, you can still sign up for it online if you want. It's all up to you!

Online courses allow you to learn at your own pace, create your own experience, and keep the rest of your life going. There are courses that you simply read, and others where you interact with the instructor and/or other students.

"Offline" classes, seminars, and conferences are very worthwhile. Amateurs and professionals, beginners and experts all benefit from them. Most conferences and seminars have tracks for the beginning, intermediate, and advanced levels, and even the most experienced genealogist can learn a thing or two. Plus, there is an indescribable joy in meeting new friends who share your passion (which many family members may not yet understand!).

Most of these require fees—sometimes modest and sometimes more substantial—but if you share travel and lodging with a genealogy buddy, it need not be prohibitively expensive. And, often with a little research, you can find good conferences and classes right in your own backyard!

Note

Institutes are week-long courses of study on a specific area, usually held at the same site every year, with class size ranges from 15–30 students, allowing more personalized instruction. Conference formats are usually speakers and panel discussions over a few days, where attendance for each session can be in the hundreds, and the site usually changes every year. Seminars are somewhere in between in duration and group size.

Online

In some cases you can have the education come to you, that is, learn by independent study. Genealogy societies and even universities have such courses, and in some cases you can take the class over the Internet.

NGS

The National Genealogical Society offers learning resources on its site (see Figure 5-1), both online and offline. The lessons and exercises are read from a password-protected site, and the final exam is a form on the website. The cost varies by course; check the NGS website for the fees.

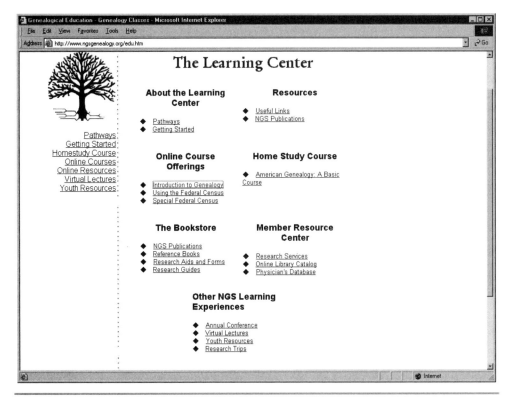

FIGURE 5-1.   *The NGS has a good selection of courses for beginning, intermediate and advanced genealogists.*

Introduction to Genealogy

Introduction to Genealogy is a six-lesson, online course for those who have done little, if any, research on their families, open to anyone who wishes to enroll. Members of the National Genealogical Society (NGS) receive a tuition discount. The six lessons cover genealogy basics, and though online resources may be used as examples, online research is not emphasized. The lessons cover basics such as recording your findings, getting information from published sources and your own family, and getting vital statistics on twentieth-century people.

Federal Population Census Schedules

Using Census Records in Genealogical Research is an online course designed for genealogists who want to learn more about the information that can be found in the federal population census records (1790–1930) and how that information can be used in their genealogical research. It is open to anyone.

The course teaches you to identify the types of information found in the federal population schedules, to interpret and evaluate that information, to use the online census microfilm catalogs, to use the Soundex indexing system, to use online census images, transcriptions, and indexes, and to use proper citations for census records.

Special Federal Census Schedules

Beyond the standard names, ages, and other information, each census has collected special data, and the nature of that data has changed over the years. Special Federal Census Schedules is a three-lesson course that covers the census schedules for special populations, the mortality schedules, and other special schedules. On completion of this course, you will be able to identify the types of information provided in these special schedules, interpret and use that information, identify the availability of the schedules, use National Archives online microfilm catalogs, and write citations for the special schedules.

Audio Teleconferences

NGS offers a sort of class-by-telephone occasionally, called an audio-teleconference. A professional genealogist will discuss a topic such as research techniques. The details are outlined at www.ngsgenealogy .org/audioconference.htm. After you enroll in the audio-teleconference, NGS will send you the course handouts with the audio-teleconference phone number. On the day of the conference, you call this number (which is a toll call) 15 minutes before it starts and then listen in.

DearMYRTLE's Genealogy

DearMYRTLE's daily genealogy column has free news and tips, some of which she has compiled into resources for beginners.

Beginning Genealogy Lessons

DearMYRTLE's Step-by-Step, at www.dearmyrtle.com/stepbystep/index.htm, is a self-paced course on getting started. This series of articles is continually being updated as online resources and technology develop, with links to each individual article from this starting page.

DearMYRTLE's Lessons, at www.dearmyrtle.com/lessons.htm, are 12 how-to articles on specific topics such as keeping dates straight and using government resources.

Finally Get Organized

If you've been at genealogy for more than a year, you are probably feeling a little overwhelmed by what you've collected, what's still on your to-do list, and what to do with both. This list takes you through a checklist for each month of the year, with goals for each week, and tasks to reach each goal.

The page also links to organizations, tips, and articles on other sites.

Kid's Genealogy

This list of links will help you find lesson plans, mailing lists, and school projects to teach young people about genealogy.

Using LDS Family History Centers

Here, DearMYRTLE has compiled her ten-part series on using Family History Centers (FHCs), plus a list of links to LDS resources on using FHCs and the main Family History Library.

Writing Your Personal History

This is a series of 12 articles on recording your life story for future generations, with links to other articles on privacy, taping oral biographies, and other topics.

Success Story

Betty Krohn took one of DearMYRTLE's classes on Internet genealogy research, where it was recommended the students go to Rootsweb.com and check out the message boards. Betty decided her first task was to find information on Robert Suiters, Sr., an uncle of Betty's who had left Ohio in 1929 and lost touch with his family.

"The very first message to pop up when I entered the name of Suiters (my maiden name) was from a person who was looking for any family of Robert Suiters. Until that time I had been unable to locate any trace of Robert Suiters. We knew he existed, but didn't know if he was still alive or where in the world he would be living. So you can imagine my excitement when I read that message," Betty said. "We learned that Robert had gone to Oklahoma, married and had a son, Robert, Jr., but that marriage ended in divorce, and Robert, Sr. left again, leaving the son and never contacting him again." Robert was alive, and he was soon on the phone with Betty's father. Through the message board, Betty was able to reunite much of the family.

Genealogy.com

Genealogy.com has several free, self-paced courses to help you get started in genealogy. Click Learning Center from the home page navigation bar to find them. The Learning Center has the following articles:

- ♦ Begin Your Research at Home
- ♦ What's in a Name?
- ♦ Collaborating with Others
- ♦ Finding Existing Research
- ♦ Outfitting Your Genealogy Toolkit

Beyond that, other courses are available.

Beginning Genealogy

The Beginning Genealogy section has 14 lessons on organizing your search, vital records and civil registration, and more.

Internet Genealogy

Two courses, Beginning and Intermediate, have a total of 31 lessons. Beginning is a basic course on using the Internet and sites that help genealogists. Intermediate covers mechanics such as writing your family history and managing a genealogy mail list.

Tracing Immigrant Origins

Four courses cover tracing immigrants to the U.S., looking for immigrants who arrived after the Civil War, looking for immigrants who arrived between 1820 and 1865, looking for immigrants before 1820, and European sources of immigration data.

Researching with Genealogy.com

This free course covers the ins and outs of using Genealogy.com resources, which will be covered in Chapter 17.

Brigham Young University Certificate Program in Family History

BYU (see Figure 5-2) offers a college-level, 18-credit-hour certificate program in genealogy, which can be taken as an independent study off-campus (what used to be called "correspondence course"), except for a proctored exam. It is not a degree program, but it gives a solid background in fundamental family history research principles, coupled with specialized genealogical training in a particular geographical area.

The required courses are The Family and the Law in American History, English Language Paleography, and Special Topics in Family History Research. In addition, the student chooses two source courses and one elective course from the North American option or the British option.

Details can be found at http://ce.byu.edu/is/site/catalog/certificate.dhtm.

University of Toronto Continuing Education

To support the needs of both amateur family historians and aspiring professional genealogists for reliable and comprehensive education, the University of Toronto and the National Institute for Genealogical Studies

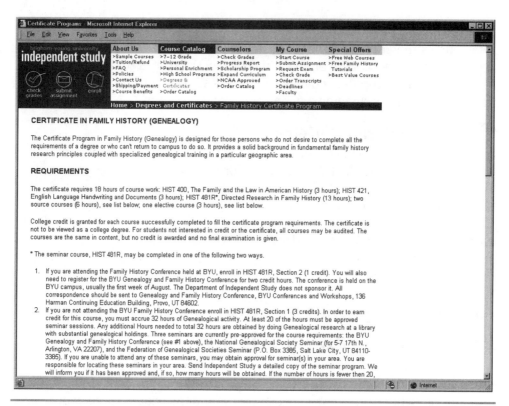

FIGURE 5-2. *BYU, an accredited school, offers college-level genealogy courses through its independent study program over the Web.*

(Canada) have designed a series of courses (Basic, Intermediate, Advanced, and Electives) leading to various Certificates in Genealogical Studies with specialization in various countries. These courses are web-based and aimed at both family historians and professional genealogists. Countries included are the U.S., Canada, England, Germany, Ireland, and Scotland. There are also certificates in Librarianship and General Methodology.

Details can be found at www.genealogicalstudies.com/.

Search College Sites for Other Courses

Search any major search engine for "genealogy courses independent study" or "genealogy courses distance learning" and you will come up with many smaller colleges and institutions that offer at least a course or two, if not a certificate program like BYU's or UT's.

Also, go to the site of the nearest community college, junior college, or other higher learning site and simply search for "genealogy." Often Library Science and Information Science majors will include a course or two in genealogy.

Offline

For some genealogy education opportunities, you have to go to the site. Trips to genealogy conventions, institutes, meetings and conferences can be very rewarding in terms of getting further along in your research as well as meeting other enthusiasts.

NGS' American Genealogy and Youth Resources

Besides the online courses previously mentioned, NGS offers you chances to learn about genealogy in other ways. You might also want to investigate the resources for helping young people learn about genealogy.

Sites Listing Offline Genealogy Events

- **About.com Genealogy Conferences**
  http://genealogy.about.com/cs/conferences/

- **Cyndi's List** http://www.cyndislist.com/events.htm

- **Eastman's Genealogy Newsletter**
  http://www.rootsforum.com/, each week has a list of conferences and meetings

- **Genealogy Forum** http://www.genealogyforum.rootsweb .com/gfaol/events/Conference.htm

- **Geniespeak** http://www.geniespeak.com/event.html

- **Genealogy Events Web Ring** http://www.rootsweb.com/ ~ autwgw/gencon/ring.htm

American Genealogy

For many years, NGS has offered a home-study *correspondence* course, *American Genealogy: A Basic Course.* The NGS recommends that you take the online Introduction course first and then move on to the home study course, which covers some of the same topics in more depth, and includes many more besides. Those who successfully complete the online Introduction course will receive a discount coupon that can be applied toward the home study course. Check the NGS website for the current fees.

The package includes lessons, resource materials, government publications useful to genealogists, help request forms, and the envelopes and postage needed to mail in your lessons.

The 16 lessons are "hands on" and require trips to libraries, courthouses, and other sites, as well as the ability to write well about your research. The NGS website, however, has online resources to help the student. Most people take 18 months to complete the course, although extensions are granted.

Youth Resources

Teachers can find lesson plans; suggested books; articles on genealogy as a tool in teaching social studies, writing, literature, and research skills; a list of websites; and other materials for teaching young people about genealogy on the NGS page at www.ngsgenealogy.org/youth.htm. You can also find information on the Rubicam Youth Award, a $500 prize for 8th through 12th graders for original genealogy work.

University of Washington Genealogy and Family History Certificate

A nine-month evening certificate program for teachers, librarians, amateur researchers, and others interested in researching their own families, this on-campus program is described at www.outreach .washington.edu/extinfo/certprog/gfh/gfh_main.asp. Participants develop a completed family history project as part of classes that meet one evening per week on the UW campus in Seattle.

Through lectures, discussions, readings, and field trips, students learn how to use the resources and methods necessary to develop a family history and to examine such topics as the migration of ethnic groups, population shifts, and the differences in urban and rural lifestyles. Students have access to the resources of the University of Washington libraries while enrolled.

Participants get nine Continuing Education Units (CEUs) and a certificate when they complete the program. Check the website for fees.

NGS Regional Conferences

Held two to three times a year, the National Genealogical Society conferences cover a wide range of topics over a one- or two-day period. Check out the latest schedule and costs at www.ngsgenealogy.org/conf.htm.

FGS Conferences

The Federation of Genealogical Societies (www.fgs.org) holds a national conference each year for genealogists of all levels of experience. The conferences spotlight management workshops for genealogy organizations, genealogical lectures by nationally recognized speakers and regional experts, and exhibitors with genealogical materials and supplies. Check the website for fees, which historically have been under $200.

National Institute on Genealogical Research

Information on this oldest of genealogy institutes can be found at www.rootsweb.com/~natgenin/. The National Institute on Genealogical Research started in 1950 and is sponsored by the American University, the American Society of Genealogists, the National Archives, and the Maryland Hall of Records. The National Archives provides strong support, including meeting space. The cost is usually around $350.

The Institute's program takes an in-depth look at federal records of genealogical value located primarily in the Washington, D.C. area. The program is for *experienced* researchers (genealogists, historians, librarians, archivists), not an *introductory course in genealogy*. For example, sessions for 2003 included Advanced Census Research Methodology, Federal Land Records, and Cartographic Records.

Institute on Genealogy and Historical Research

Held at Samford University (Birmingham, Alabama) every June, this five-day event is for intermediate to advanced genealogists. Small classes are held during the day. Each evening of the Institute features a dinner with a speaker, as well. Details and registration information can be found at www.samford.edu/schools/ighr/ighr.html. Check the website for fees, which historically have been under $400.

The Genealogical Institute of Mid-America, University of Illinois Springfield

GIMA is a four-day program of intensive study at the University of Illinois Springfield, with a web presence at www.rootdig.com/gima.html.

The Salt Lake Institute of Genealogy

Held at the Family History Library in Salt Lake City, Utah, by the Utah Genealogical Society, this is a week-long, hands-on event, usually held early in the year. Check the website for fees, which historically have been under $400. In 2003, attendees could choose from ten different courses of lectures, including topics on American, Canadian, and German research.

Regional and Local Workshops and Seminars

DearMYRTLE's schedule of classes is indicative of what you can find in local resources. DearMYRTLE's Genealogy for Lunch Bunch is held at Rachel's Gardens Bed and Breakfast in Bradenton, Florida every Monday. She teaches a four-week course on getting ready for a research trip to Washington, D.C., which includes what you can expect to find, how to organize your genealogy chores, and how to make the most of your time. She also teaches genealogy at the local vocational school.

"The classes vary from time to time. We have a snowbird season, so it fluctuates," DearMYRTLE says.

Many state historical societies hold seminars. An example is the Wisconsin State Genealogical Society, which has two events each year—

one in conjunction with the annual meeting in the spring, and one in conjunction with the fall meeting. Events are open to the public for a nominal registration fee. Each one features a nationally known expert, speaking on a facet of genealogical research of particular interest to Wisconsin researchers. The Spring Gene-A-Ramas are held at various locations around the state, whereas the fall seminars generally alternate between the Madison and Milwaukee areas. Details and registration forms can be found at www.rootsweb.com/ ~ wsgs/.

Success Story

Ann Lusk, attending a beginning genealogy course in her hometown of Huntsville, Alabama, learned about platting deeds. To plat a deed, you draw a picture of a piece of land from the description on the deed. Taking what she learned from the class, Ann worked with two Tennessee deeds, described in metes and bounds, a method that notes adjoining land. By platting two deeds for land owned by men with her husband's surname, cutting them out, and laying them on the table together, she saw the two pieces fit together "like hand and glove." This helped her show that the two men were father and son, and from that she could look for the original family plat. This information not only helped her DAR application, it also qualified her for the First Families of Tennessee (http://web.utk.edu/ ~ kizzer/ethisctr/ 1stfamtn.htm).

Finding a local class, seminar, workshop, or other event near you is the best way to start. Query a search engine for "genealogy" and the name of the town you live in or will be visiting. Also, check Cyndi's List page (www.cyndislist.com/events.htm), Dick Eastman's weekly newsletter, and DearMYRTLE's sites often for announcements.

Wrapping Up

- ♦ Taking beginners' courses can save you some time and effort in your research.

- ♦ Seminars, conferences, and courses are a good way to meet other genealogists and expand your skills.

- ♦ Local, regional, and national programs give you a wide choice of how to learn about genealogy.

Chapter 6

Search Engines

Throughout this book, I will try to point you to the best genealogy newsgroups and websites. Nevertheless, plenty of reasons exist to search the Internet for other sources. Things change incredibly fast on the Internet: Websites disappear or move to a new server, which changes a site's Uniform Resource Locator (URL). Also, new sources of genealogical information appear daily on the Internet, so you might miss an important new resource if you don't do your own searches once in a while. Finally, as a genealogist, you've experienced the thrill of discovering things for yourself—it can be quite a kick to find a website or newsgroup none of your friends know about. To do this, you need a way to find genealogical resources on the Internet on your own. That's where search sites come in.

Defining Terms

Search engine is an all-purpose label used to describe anything that will let you search for terms within a group of data. That data could be on a single site, such as DearMYRTLE.com, or on the entire Internet, or some subset in between the two. Just about anything that lets you search gets called a *search engine,* but some other terms are more accurate for specific sites.

A *spider* is a program that looks for information on the Internet, creates a database of what it finds, and lets you use a web browser to run a search engine on that database for specific information. As noted, this can mean millions of pages or only the pages on one site. A search site might have one or more search engines and can claim to search "the whole Web," but, in reality, it probably covers about 15 percent of the Web at any given time. This is because pages quickly appear and disappear on the Web. That's why you might want to use several different search sites when you are searching for specific information or for general types of sites. Or, you might want to try one of the many metasearch engines that try several search sites at one time.

A search site called a *directory* or a *catalog* uses a search engine to let you hunt through an edited list of Internet sites for specific information. The value of these sites is that in a directory or catalog, the newsgroups and websites are sorted, categorized, and sometimes rated.

Yahoo! (www.yahoo.com), shown in Figure 6-1, is one of the first catalogs or directories established online; it is also a good example of a *portal,* which offers other services such as chat, news, forums, and more. A portal is a little bit of everything: a search engine for the Web at large, a catalog of sites the owners recommend, and usually a group of other features, including stock prices, web-based e-mail, shopping, and so on.

A metasearch engine submits your query to several different search sites, portals, and catalogs at the same time. You might get more results, and you will usually be able to compare how each one responded to the query. These searches may take longer, however.

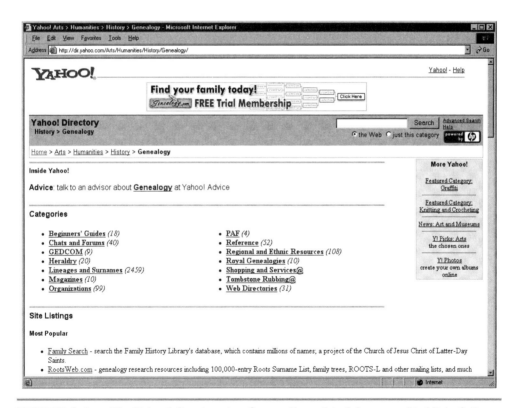

FIGURE 6-1.   *The Yahoo! directory is a frequently updated, human-edited list of sites, sorted into categories.*

Searching with Savoir Faire

First, some general search tips:

♦ *Use phrases instead of single words in your searches.* Type several words that are relevant to your search. Typing `Spencer genealogy Ohio` will narrow a search well.

♦ *Enclose phrases in quotes.* Searching with the phrase `Spencer family history` without quotation marks will match all pages that have any of those three words included somewhere on the page, in any order, and not necessarily adjacent. Searching with the phrase `"Spencer family history"` (with quotation marks) will return only those pages that have those three words together. The order of the words, however, may or may not be relevant in the search, depending on the specific search engine. For some search engines, "Abraham Spencer," even in quotes, will return items on Energy Secretary Spencer Abraham.

♦ *The more specific you are, the better.* Searching for `Irish genealogy databases` will give you fewer, but closer matches than searching for `Irish genealogy`.

♦ *Use plus and minus signs in your searches.* A word preceded by a plus sign (+) must appear on the page to be considered a match. A word preceded by a minus sign (−) must not appear on the page to be considered a match. No spaces can be between the plus and minus signs and the words they apply to. For example, entering

`+Spencer -royal genealogy`

would ask the search engine to find pages that definitely used the word "Spencer," but don't use the word "royal," with "genealogy" preferred, but optional. Most search engines would get some Spencer genealogy pages but leave out those that include Lady Diana, Princess of Wales. More about this type of search can be found in the following sidebar about Boolean searches.

♦ *Narrow your searches if you get too many matches.* Sometimes the page with your search results will have an input box to narrow or broaden the search. This might mean adding terms or deleting terms and then running the search again only on the results from the first search. You can also run searches within search results to help narrow choices. This is the easiest way.

Using Boolean Terms

Searching the Internet is no simple matter. With literally hundreds of thousands of sites, millions of documents, and more words than you can imagine, finding exactly the right needle in all that hay can be daunting. The key, of course, is crafting a precise query.

Boolean operators are handy tools for honing your searches. Named after George Boole, the nineteenth-century mathematician who dreamed up symbolic logic, *Boolean operators* represent the relationships among items using terms such as OR, AND, and NOT. When applied to information retrieval, they can expand or narrow a search to uncover as many citations, or *hits,* as you want.

The Boolean OR

When you search for two or more terms joined with an OR operator, you get back hits that contain any one of your terms. Therefore, the query `Powell OR genealogy` will retrieve documents holding "Powell" or "genealogy," but not necessarily both. Note that nearly all search pages default to OR—that is, they assume you want any page with any one or more of your terms in it.

You can see it makes good sense to use OR when you search for synonyms or closely related terms. For example, if you're looking for variations on a name, search for `SPENCER SPENCE SPENSER`. The average search engine will assume the OR operator and find any page with any one or more of those terms.

The Boolean AND

In the Boolean boogie, joining search terms with AND means all terms must be found in a document, but not necessarily together. The query `George AND Washington` will result in a list of documents that have both the names "George" and "Washington" somewhere within. Use AND when you have dissimilar terms and need to narrow a search. Usually to get AND in a search, you type a plus sign (+) or put the term AND between the words and enclose everything within parentheses, like so:

```
(Spencer AND genealogy)
```

Remember, a simple AND doesn't guarantee the words will be next to each other. Your search for George Washington could turn up documents about George Benson and Grover Washington.

The Boolean NOT

When you use NOT, search results must exclude certain terms. Many search engines don't have this functionality. Often, when you can use it, the syntax is to put a minus sign (hyphen) in front of the unwanted term.

The query `Powell NOT Colin` will return all citations containing the name "Powell," but none including "Colin," regardless of whether "Powell" is there. Use NOT when you want to exclude possible second meanings. "Banks" can be found on genealogy surname pages as well as on pages associated with finance or with rivers. Searching for `banks AND genealogy NOT river` increases the chances of finding documents relating to Banks (the people, not riversides). In some search engines, the minus sign often takes the place of NOT.

The fun part is combining Boolean operators to create a precise search. Let's say you want to find documents about the city of Dallas. If you simply search for `Dallas`, you could get irrelevant hits about Dallas County in Alabama (county seat, Selma), which might not be the Dallas you want. To avoid that, you would use AND, NOT, and OR in this fashion:

```
(Dallas AND Texas) NOT (Selma OR Alabama)
(Powell AND genealogy) NOT (Colin AND "SECRETARY OF STATE")
```

Note that parentheses group the search terms together.

Beyond AND/OR/NOT

In most web search engines, unless a phrase option is specifically offered, the capitalization or order of the terms isn't important: A Venetian blind is the same as a blind Venetian. However, some search engines enable you to fine-tune a search further. The WITH operator, for example, searches for terms much nearer each other. How "near" is defined depends on the engine. Some would look at "George WITH Washington" and deliver documents only containing the words "George Washington" next to each other. Others might consider words in the same sentence or paragraph to be near enough.

Check the search engine's help files to see if it uses wildcards or word stemming (for finding all variations of a word, such as ancestry, ancestral, ancestor, ancestors).

Using these techniques, you can search the Web much more efficiently, finding just the right document on George Washington Carver or a genealogy site on the right set of Powells. Learn the steps to the Boolean boogie and you'll soon be web dancing wherever you please!

Search Sites

Lots of search sites are out there, some of which are more useful to genealogists than others. The following is a list of genealogy-related catalogs, portals, and search engines, in alphabetical order.

Access Genealogy

At this site, www.accessgenealogy.com, you can read and search free of charge for many different types of records for genealogy research, including newspapers and periodicals, emigration and immigration forms, census reports, voting records, and archives from libraries, cemeteries, churches, and courts.

Biography Guide

Was any ancestor of yours a member of Congress? Search for biographies of members by last name, first name, position, and state at this site, bioguide.congress.gov/biosearch/biosearch.asp. If your ancestors are in the database, this fascinating site can add a new dimension to your family history.

Cyndi's List

The site www.cyndislist.com catalogs over 98,000 genealogy websites. You will find links to the genealogy sites and sites that simply would help a genealogist, worldwide. This is the first place many new online genealogists visit. The links are categorized and organized, and there's also a search box for finding the subjects you want quickly. As shown in Figure 6-2, this is a very popular site.

Cyndi Howells works on the list every day, updating, deleting, and adding sites. To keep up, you can frequently check the pages on the list that interest you. Each new or updated link will have a small "new" or "updated" graphic next to it for 30 days.

The main index is updated each time activity occurs on Cyndi's List. Check the date under each category heading to determine when the last update was made for that category. The date is also updated at the bottom of each category page.

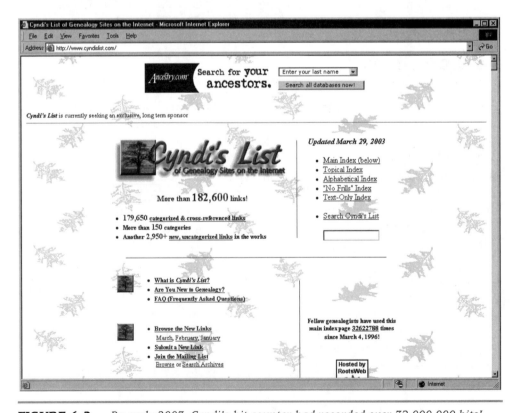

FIGURE 6-2. *By early 2003, Cyndi's hit counter had recorded over 32,000,000 hits!*

But the easiest way to keep on top of the changes is to subscribe to CyndisList Mailing List. This is a free, announcements-only, e-mail mailing list detailing the updates and news regarding the website. You will usually get an update once a day during the work week. To subscribe, send an e-mail message to CyndisList-request@rootsweb .comand. In the body of the message, type only the word **subscribe**.

Similarly, to unsubscribe, send an e-mail message to CyndisList-request@rootsweb.com. In the body, type only the word **unsubscribe**.

Be sure not to include your automatic signature when sending either of the previous commands to the RootsWeb mailing list server.

Genealogy Pages

A collected catalog of genealogy sites, the website www.genealogypages .com also offers you a free e-mail box and a browser-based chat site, so it qualifies as a portal.

You can browse the collection of links by category or search the entire collection. Because it's all about genealogy, you don't have to put that term in the search box. For example, a search for `South Carolina Powell` in the regular search box turned up nothing, even though in the Advanced Search I could choose between AND (the default) and OR. And even if it was recognized as a phrase, I couldn't get a match on all three. Searching on `South Carolina` got good results, however, as did searching on `Powell`.

GeneaSearch.com

This portal, www.geneasearch.com, is along the lines of Genealogy Pages. Several search options exist, but searching by surname is your best bet. GeneaSearch gives results similar to those of Genealogy Pages. They will both return submitted GEDCOMs from users that will be secondary sources for genealogy.

The site's services include free genealogy lookups, free genealogy sites, family surname newsletters, data, books from genealogy societies and individuals, surname queries, female ancestors, new site announcements, a beginner's genealogy guide, and free clip art. Other genealogy resources include tools, links, and lists of societies. Also, there are free genealogy databases and genealogy resources for each state.

GenealogyPortal.com

A joint venture of Steve Wood, who founded the original Genealogy Home Page, and Matthew Helm, of Genealogy Toolbox, www .genealogyportal.com is a site that uses one form for eight separate search engines to help you efficiently search the Web.

It is designed to assist genealogists in finding information that is not readily accessible through traditional genealogical link sites. All search engines contained in GenealogyPortal.com are free to all users.

You can use GenealogyPortal.com's eight separate search engines to assist you in researching your family history. Here are some specifics:

- ◆ Ancestors and families can be found in the Names and Personal Sites, Location-Specific, and Primary Records search engines.

- ◆ Census and vital records can be found in the Location-Specific and Primary Records search engines.

- ◆ Local histories/collections can be found in the Archives and Libraries, Location-Specific, and Historical Sites search engines.

- ◆ Research help can be found in the Research Guides search engine.

- ◆ Genealogical products/services can be found in the Research Supplies and Software and Utilities search engines.

The site also includes a short, edited catalog of sites under headings such as Archives and Libraries, Primary Records, and Guides to Research. You can browse the catalog by clicking the links to these categories from the front page of the site.

GenGateway

Another version of a catalog of websites organized into categories for genealogists is www.gengateway.com, by Steve Lacy. It indexes thousands of web pages and sources. Choose the category you want to search, such as surname or obituary, and you'll get well-sorted results.

To navigate the site, use one of the many useful gateways listed in the navigation bar to the left of the opening page. If you're new to the site, first try the Beginners Gateway or the Search Pages.

For example, the Beginner's Gateway link will give you links to general guides, such as "20 Ways to Avoid Genealogical Grief"

(www.naesmyth.com/20ways.htm). The Search Pages link is a
metasearch engine that uses several sites, such as Infoseek, Magellan,
Excite, and Yahoo!, with limiters. It also searches specialized sites,
such as Irish on the Net, for surnames.

GenServ

An all-volunteer effort, GenServ, at www.genserv.com, is a collection
of donated GEDCOMs with a sophisticated set of search commands.
(Remember, this is all secondary source material. When you seem to
have a match, you need to contact the submitter to determine what
primary source material he or she might have.) The database has over
25,000,000 individuals in more than 19,000 databases. All this family
history data is online and available by search and reports to subscribers.
You can search a limited amount of the data in a free trial (see Figure 6-3).

GenServ has been online since 1991 and on the Web since early
1994. To access the system, you have to at least submit your own

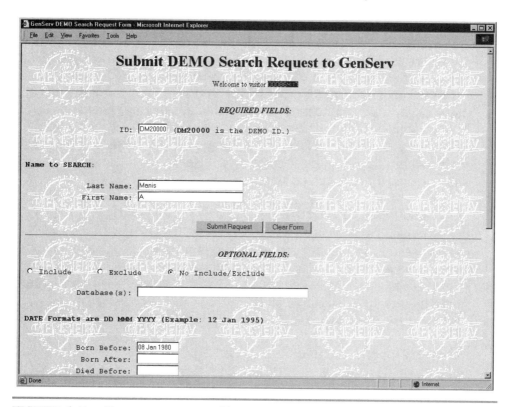

FIGURE 6-3.   *You can get a taste of how powerful GenServ is for free.*

GEDCOM. If you pay the optional yearly fees, you can perform many more searches per day than the free access allows.

The capability to do complex searches on the databases means a real learning curve exists. Furthermore, only the "surname count" search can be done from the Web; all the rest are done via e-mail messages. This has the advantage of letting you input your terms and then surf on to other sites. The results, meanwhile, come back by e-mail (and quickly, too!).

Uploading your data and learning how to query this set of databases is worth your time.

GenSource

The specialized genealogy directory site www.gensource.com provides the online genealogist with three databases to assist with research online.

The first database is called Search Common Threads, which will help you find other genealogists researching your family name. If you're at a "dead end" finding information on an ancestor, add an entry to Common Threads so other family members can find you.

Search the second database, I Found It!, to locate genealogy sites on the Internet. You can use the I Found It! search engine to locate pages on surnames, one-name studies, ship passenger lists, genealogical societies and associations, researchers, software, books, family mailing lists, online records of churches, census data, cemeteries, and more.

Search the third database, the IFI (I Found It!) Archives, for sites containing actual historical records. Many people have taken the time to transcribe records and place them on the Net for your use, all of which are indexed for research purposes.

GenealogySearch.com

Like GenSource, genealogysearch.com has GEDCOM databases for you to search, specific to its site. All the information is uploaded by volunteers and is secondary source material.

It also has a small, edited catalog of online genealogy sources, sorted into the categories Starting Points, Family Pages, Books, Software, Royalty, and Web Page Tools.

General Search Sites

Many web-wide search engines and portals can help you find genealogy resources. Using the search techniques previously mentioned, you'll probably have good results trying these general search engines. Some of them have catalogs of genealogy sites. For those that do, information on how to browse them is provided in the following list. On all of them, though, searches as described in the beginning of this chapter will work:

- **AOL NetFind (search.aol.com)**   Browse to Main | Society | Genealogy. The search engine is based on Google.

- **AskJeeves (www.ask.com)**   Click Browse By Subject | Society | Genealogy.

- **C|Net Search (www.search.com)**   Type "genealogy" and/or the surname and/or the location you need in the Search box.

- **Dogpile (www.dogpile.com)**   This is a metasearch engine. One search will query several other search engines. It also uses the + and – Boolean searches. Don't bother with the Dogpile "Web directory," because it's simply a listing of their paid advertisers. The search function, however, is fast and gives good results.

- **Excite (www.excite.com)**   Click the Family link in the Explore Excite box.

- **FastSearch (www.alltheweb.com)**   Type "genealogy" and/or the surname and/or the location you need in the Search box.

- **Go.com (www.go.com)**   Type "genealogy" and/or the surname and/or the location you need in the Search box. The search engine is based on Google.

- **Google (www.google.com)**   Simply type "genealogy" and/or the surname and/or the location you need in the search box. This is the leader in search engine technology at the moment, and many search engines are based on the Google programming. You can use it to search news (for obituaries, for example) and web sites. Another important feature is page translations. Click Language Tools from the main Google page. You have a choice of putting in a page you already found, or simply pasting in a block of text to be translated. Also, if a regular Google search turns up non-English pages, one of your choices will be "Translate this page." Great for when you get beyond the boat to the "old country"!

- **Hot Bot (www.hotbot.lycos.com)**   From the home page, click Society | Genealogy.

- **MetaCrawler (www.metacrawler.com)**   Browse to Lifestyles | Hobbies | Genealogy & Heraldry.

- **NBCi (www.nbci.com)**   Click the Search and Find tab, and then click the Genealogy link under the Living subheadline, or browse through to Society & Politics | Culture and Heritage, and then choose your country. You will also find a link to NBCi's Genealogy channel, with news and articles about genealogy.

- **Yahoo! (www.yahoo.com)**   Search the whole Yahoo! catalog by typing "genealogy" and/or the surname and/or the location in the search box, or browse to Arts | Humanities | History | Genealogy. Yahoo!'s new search engine is faster than before, and it gives you a choice of opening a link in a new window to make browsing through results easier. Also, you can now search news, pictures and U.S. maps as well as web pages.

Obituary Search Pages

Several pages enable you to search recent and older obituaries:

- **Legacy.com (www.legacy.com/NewspaperMap.asp)**   Has a page called ObitFinder that searches recent obituaries by name, keyword, and location.

- **Obituary Links (www.geocities.com/ ~ cribbswh/ obit)** Searches cemetery records, obituaries, and other pages from sites such as Ancestry.com, RootsWeb, and so on. This is a metasearch engine that focuses on death records.

- **4Obituaries (4obituaries.4anything.com)**   Has a list of links to modern obit pages.

Origins.net

This is a for-fee genealogy search site; you can try a sample search for free. Users pay a license fee for use of the Origin Search software at $5 for 24 hours or $15 for 14 days. Origins.net provides access to databases of genealogical data for online family history research in the United Kingdom, Canada, Australia, New Zealand, and the U.S.

Origin Search (www.originsearch.com) is a new service from Origins.net, which allows searching, via a single search request, of millions of web pages containing genealogy data. By entering a surname and any other relevant information, such as forename, year, place of birth, or residence, the search engine will link you directly to sites where that name and information appears.

The free Irish Origins service is based on the same software and functionality as the overall service. If you are considering using Origin Search, you can check thoroughly the functionality and quality of service you will receive before committing to pay for Origin Search.

The site has 11 categories of data available for searching, ranging from birth and death records to military and immigration records. Origin Search does not hold any primary data, such as the General Register Office for Scotland records that used to be held on Scots Origins. Origin Search is not an interface for databases but rather a specialized genealogical search engine that saves users time and ensures they find information that may not be found on general search engines such as Google, Excite, and so on.

Surname Web

Located online at www.surnameweb.org, Surname Web has a database of names submitted by users, as well as pages from other websites. Simply input the surname.

WorldConnect

WorldConnect (worldconnect.rootsweb.com) is a division of RootsWeb (Figure 6-4). RootsWeb's motto is "Connecting the world, one GEDCOM at a time." People are free to upload to and search in this collection of GEDCOM databases. All you need to do is fill out the form with name, place of birth and death, and dates of birth and death. You can choose an exact search if you're sure of your facts, or a range of 2 to 20 years for dates and Soundex searches for names and places. It's fast, but the results depend entirely on the uploaded GEDCOMs. If you have no hits, consider uploading your information for others. If you already uploaded your information, you can exclude your own database from future searches.

Like GenServ, WorldConnect is all volunteer, amateur information. You must contact the submitter of a database to find out the sources for the data. However, unlike GenServ, you can do the searches via the Web.

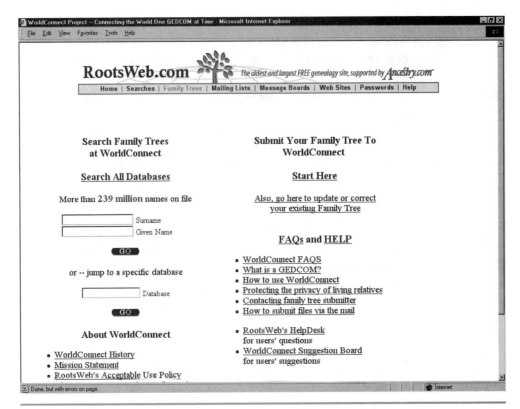

FIGURE 6-4. *You can search other genealogists' research at WorldConnect on RootsWeb.*

Yourfamily.com

Yourfamily.com is a database of genealogy pages by individuals, submitted by the users themselves. To use the search function, click the Family Homepages button. The resulting page gives you a search box to input the surname you need. The site presents you with a list of pages by genealogists, both amateur and professional, who are searching that surname.

White Page Directories

So far, you've looked at search engines and directories for finding a website. But, what if you need to find lost, living relatives? Or, what if you want to write to people with the same surnames you're researching?

In that case, you need people search engines, called *White Page directories.* Like the White Pages of your phone book, these directories specialize in finding people, not pages. In fact, all the search engine sites mentioned previously have White Page directories.

The AT&T site (www.att.com/directory), shown in Figure 6-5, has an excellent set of directories for people and businesses, with a reverse phone number lookup (put in the phone number, get the name).

Switchboard (www.switchboard.com) is one of many White Pages services on the Web. It's free, and it lists the e-mail addresses and telephone numbers of millions of people and businesses, taken from public records. It's also a website catalog. If you register as a user (it's free), you can ensure that your listing is not only accurate but has only the information you want it to reveal.

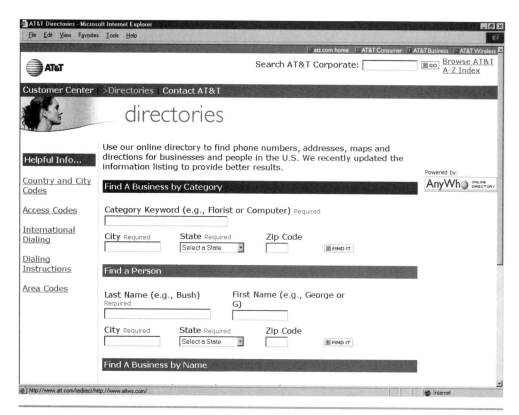

FIGURE 6-5. *AT&T has one of the best White Pages search sites.*

BigFoot (www.bigfoot.com) is another such effort to catalog people, with the same general rules: Input your information and you get searches that are more specific. BigFoot also has surface mail addresses in addition to e-mail and telephone information.

Wrapping Up

♦ Learn to use Boolean search terms to target your web searches.

♦ Use genealogy-specific sites to search for surnames and localities.

♦ Use general search sites and catalogs that gather news and links about genealogy.

♦ Use White Pages search sites to find living people.

Chapter 7

Chat: Hail Thy Fellow Genealogists on the Net!

Sometimes you might want to talk to a fellow genealogist to resolve problems you're encountering in your research. The online world can help you there, too, with chat.

Where's Amos?

by GenHostMike

It was the night of January 5th, 2003 when I wandered into Uncle Hiram's Chat Cabins at www.bhocutt.com. I thought it best to familiarize myself with my new "digs" before the following night's grand opening and my hosting debut.

Thinking I'd be alone to try this and that, I was surprised to find three chatters in a deep genealogical discussion. They told me that DearMYRTLE's newsletter had guided them to this corner of cyberspace. I could tell by their conversation that they were veterans in the field, but I pressed on and asked if there was anything I could do to help them with their research.

One chatter stepped forward and presented his brick wall. The ancestor's name was Amos, Amos HURLBUT. He had recently found him in the 1870 census in Iowa and was looking for his parents. The census told him that he was born in New York and was 36 years old. He already knew that Amos and wife Sarah POTTER were married in NY and that Sarah was from Franklin County, NY. He ended by telling me that Marvin HURLBUT was also found in the same part of Iowa as Amos and may be related. Eager to please, especially on my first "unofficial" day, I told him I would look to my resources and see what I could find.

I always feel it best to start with the facts, so I pulled up the 1870 census to see what the chatter saw. With ease I found Amos in the Iowa 1860 and 1870 census, and I saw the Marvin HURLBUT he was speaking about. But this didn't get me any closer to Amos's parents.

I thought, hmmm, if Sarah was from Franklin County, NY, maybe Amos was as well. So I decided to search the 1850 census with Soundex for HURLBUTs in that county, but all matches came up empty. Not an Amos to be found.

I turned to other facts in the case. Who was this Marvin fella? I decided to search for his name to see what I could find. To my surprise, Iowa Cemetery Records showed a Marvin HURLBUT born in 1826 in Onondaga County, NY. This seemed to match the age of the Marvin previously found on the census. My next thought: If Marvin was born in 1826, he just might be a head of household in 1850. A search produced a Marvin HERLBUT in Chautauqua County, NY matching the age and wife of the Marvin I've been seeking. Marvin seemed to be found, but where's Amos?

Assuming Marvin was related and that families moved in packs, I decided to give a look in 1850 for other HURLBUTs in Clymer, Chautauqua County, NY. And it was there in the index where I found Daniel HERLBUT. When I viewed the census for Daniel, I let out a yell, for there was a son named Amos at home at the age of 17. Perfect match.

I could have ended there, but my curiosity took over. I then found Daniel in the same town in the 1840 census. Then I found a Daniel in 1830 in Onondaga County (yes, the same county in which Marvin was born).

Although I have a strong feeling, I cannot prove that Amos and Marvin are related, or that Marvin is Daniel's son. But the information I found on Marvin led me to find Amos. It just goes to show you that any piece of information found can be vital to your research.

Can We Talk?

Online chat has been around for a long time. From the earliest days of The Source and CompuServe to the era of America Online (AOL) and the Web, *chat* has been a staple of online communication. Chat is useful whether you're collaborating on a genealogy project, sending digital reunion memos to your extended family, or discussing your hobby with a large crowd.

Chatting Up the Internet

Internet Relay Chat, better known as *IRC,* used to be the most popular form of chat. Although IRC can support one-to-one, one-to-many, and many-to-many messages, usually IRC is a lot of people on a "channel" typing messages back and forth in a many-to-many format. IRC uses a system of clients and servers that enables people all over the world to communicate in real time by typing on their computers. So, for example, folks in Australia, France, Hong Kong, Kenya, British Columbia, and Vermont can all sit at their computers at the same time, log in to the same server, connect to the same channel, and type messages interactively, each seeing what all the others are saying.

A group of people chatting on a channel at the same time are said to be in a *chat room*. You can create private, invitation-only chat rooms or join in on a public one.

If you just wander into any old chat room, you may be dismayed at the level and tone of the conversation. Everyday chat conversations tend to be either mundane or racy. You need to search the chat server for rooms devoted to the subjects of family history and/or genealogy.

Even when you do get into a genealogy chat, the conversations overlap. This makes it hard to keep track of who's saying what. Unmoderated, general chat rooms (sometimes called *drop-ins*) are like strolling by the corner coffee shop. You don't know whom you'll find there or whether anyone inside will be of help to you. Typically, a lot of what's going on will be totally irrelevant to your search.

A moderated or hosted chat, however, is more like attending a class or a genealogy club meeting. There's usually a specific topic being discussed, an expert or two available, and a system for asking and answering questions, so the conversations are at least a little easier to follow. A one-on-one chat between yourself and a buddy can be even more productive. If you can set up a specific time and channel to discuss a problem or a great find, you can get a lot done this way.

The most popular form of chat today is instant messaging or instant message, thanks in large part to America Online's Instant Messenger program, known to users as AIM. In this form of chat, a select, invited list of people (from two to a whole "room") exchange typed messages in real time. This feature has become so popular that instant messaging is used 200 million times a day, according to AOL PR people. Another example is ICQ (I-seek-you), a different instant messaging program that AOL recently bought out; it gets hundreds of new users a day. And newer programs exist, such as Microsoft Meeting, which can be used as an intranet/Internet collaboration tool.

The latest versions of all the instant messaging programs reviewed in this chapter also have sound and video capability. However, you will find these bandwidth-hogging applications are not used much in genealogy circles.

Web-based chat uses Java or ActiveX in your browser to present the conversations. This is slow, and I've found few rewarding web-based genealogy chats. However, searching for "web genealogy chat" in a search engine might turn up some links. In general, the best genealogy chats are on instant messaging systems, then IRC, then voice chat with Internet radio show hosts.

Chat Flavors

Different programs enable you to have one-on-one and multiperson conversations with people. Some require you to sign on to a chat server, where the program you use doesn't matter. Others only let you chat with people using the same program, who have allowed you to put them on their "buddy list." The former lets you connect with more people; the latter gives you more security. A few, as noted, will let you do both.

AOL Instant Messenger

You can find AOL Instant Messenger (known as *AIM*) at www.aim.com. It's free and it's a proprietary type of service, unlike IRC, which is open. AOL's Instant Messenger (AIM) program, which is separate from the instant message facility on the AOL service, but coordinates with it, is the most widely used instant messaging program. The Instant Messenger software gives Internet users the capability to send instant messages and create chat rooms with other AIM users, whether or not they use AOL (see Figure 7-1). Although easy to use, AIM doesn't have all the features of ICQ (covered later). The program is available as a Navigator or Eudora plug-in and comes in Windows 9*x*, NT, and CE versions, as well as a version for the Macintosh. There is also an all-Java version called *Quick Buddy* that runs in your browser, but it's very slow. The newest edition of AIM also supports voice chat, which is discussed later in the chapter.

MSN Messenger

This program comes already installed on many Windows machines, and it works very much like AIM. You register as a user for free, choosing a screen name and a password. If you already have a Passport account, you can use that login info.

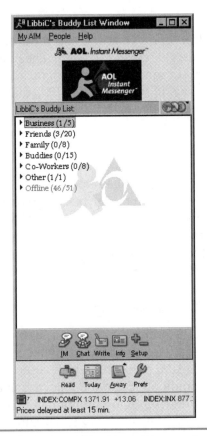

FIGURE 7-1. *AOL Instant Messenger can be used by people who do not subscribe to AOL.*

MSN Messenger has a link to chat rooms on MSN. In the chat rooms, you have to scroll through long lists of role playing and other topics to find one on genealogy. One good genealogy chat room is GenPals, which you can access from www.geocities.com/genpals2002/.

Success Story: GenPals Solves a Mystery

Charlene Hazzard CharAH1@aol.com (NY "G" families) and Mary Martha Von Ville McGrath marymarthavonville@ hotmail.com (Ohio "G" families) solved a mystery through GenPals.

"When new to the Internet, I found a message on Guenther/Ginther/ Gunter/Gunther (from Charlene Hazzard), and when I finally figured out how to write a message, got an answer from her. She had my line into what is now a different country in Europe and had it back two generations from there!" Mary Martha had a town name of HERSTOM in Germany. Charlene knew that this was the common nickname for Herbitzheim, which is now in France. Charlene had communicated directly with the Herbitzheim (aka Herstom) town historian until he died in 2000.

"I had only a nickname for the town of origin, and Charlene explained the real name of the town. By the way, her message was from 1999, and she is the only one who had info from Europe," said Mary Martha. *"What an answer to a 30-year-old prayer. Thank you, GOD!"*

Mary Martha and Charlene are the coordinators on GenPals for the descendants of this family who settled in NY and OHIO (many are still in both states) and want this information out to the world.

Their line: GUENTHER/GUNTHER/GUNTER/GUINTHER/GINTHER/GINTER

(The children went by many different versions of the name, which only added to the unlikelihood of finding a connection.)

Peter GUENTHER 11NOV1814-20NOV1890 + (Cordelia MORGAN 26JUN1812-1881), both born Herbitzheim/Herstom (Germany) France and died in GLENMONT, HOLMES OHIO)

Peter GUNTHER/GUNTER 1790-1882 + (about 90 yrs. old!) (Catherine ZIMMER 1793-1882 parents: John ZIMMER and (Marie) MULLER) (born Herbitzheim, GE d. Mohawk Hills, Lewis County, NEW YORK)

Jacques GUNTER 16JUN1723-20JUN1795

(+ Barbara ORDITZ 21JUN1750-9AUG1823) born and died in Herbitzheim (nicknamed Herstom) Germany in what is now Alsace, FRANCE 2003

Charlene's 1999 posting and Mary Martha's finding it in almost the year 2003 (and being brand new to the Internet) was truly a miracle in their book.

Yahoo! Messenger

Yahoo! Messenger works just like MSN and AIM. Go to www.yahoo.com, click Chat, click Genealogy, and pick a room for web-based chats, or you can download Yahoo! Messenger to set up your own private chat rooms.

ICQ

ICQ (available at www.icq.com) is a system similar to AIM that's free of charge. ICQ is a one-to-one or multiple person chat in the instant messaging model. When you're online, it registers your presence with the secure ICQ server, so other ICQ users can "see" you. You can keep a buddy list and be informed when your buddies log on. You can send messages and files, even talk by voice or send live video. All the while, the program runs in the background, taking up a minimal amount of memory and Net resources, so you can continue to surf the Web or run your genealogy program. You can start ICQ and then look for ongoing genealogy chats, as shown in Figure 7-2.

mIRC

You can buy mIRC at www.mirc.co.uk/get.html for $20. With it, you can talk to others on IRC channels whether they are using mIRC or some other IRC program. mIRC is an excellent—and popular—program with many features. You can set favorite IRC servers, change the colors of messages sent by different people, and more. A popular IRC program, mIRC is shareware, so you can try it for a while before you send the author the money for it.

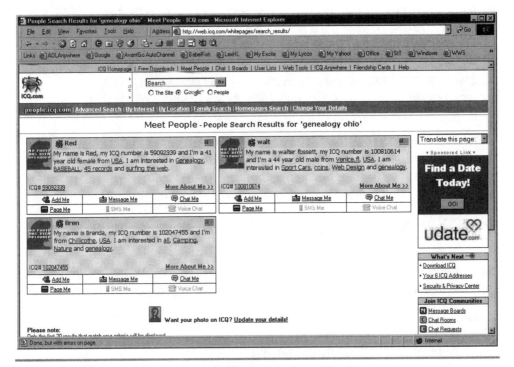

FIGURE 7-2. *ICQ has one-to-one and many-to-many functions.*

How They Work

How do chat services and programs work? You use the client program to log on to a chat server. Where to find servers is covered at the end of this chapter.

If it's an open, public chat server, such as Internet Relay Chat (IRC), you can use a program like mIRC. You log on and search for a channel that suits your interests. If there isn't one at the moment, you can create one (calling it #genealogy, perhaps) and wait for interested people to come chat with you. Once the chat gets going, it's a lot like citizens' band radio, but in print.

Other programs like AOL Instant Messenger are set up so that only people using the same program can contact you. With such a program, you can usually indicate your status (gone, accepting calls, connected but away from your desk, and so on) and keep a list of people you want to contact (often called a *buddy list* or *address book*), as well as those who are allowed to contact *you*. (Alas, you can't import a buddy list from your e-mail address book—you usually have to ask permission to add someone to your list!) To find people to add to your list, you can look them up by e-mail address, or e-mail them an invitation to use the same program you are using, and then exchange ID names.

When someone hails you, a sound or small message window (or both) will alert you. Chatting typically takes place in two panes of one window: one for your outgoing messages and one for incoming ones.

If you're worried about security or just want to be left alone, fret not. Most of these programs let you shield your presence from specific people or from the world at large, as suits your mood. You can also let yourself be "seen," but not heard, with an online "I'm-busy-now" indicator.

You can choose a *handle* or nickname for your login ID. This is the name by which people will know you on IRC (everyone in a channel must have a unique nickname). Remember, hundreds of thousands of people are on IRC, so it's possible someone might already be using the nickname you've chosen. If that's the case, simply choose another one. Some programs record your preferred nickname in the setup screen and let you choose an alternative if someone is using your first choice in a certain channel.

Also, be sure to make use of the chat program's help files. They'll help you get the most out of your chat time.

How to Chat

IRC and instant messaging programs work in different ways but have many of the same functions. Let me urge you again to read the help file of your program. Most of the time, the help file is a mini manual that will tell you how to best use the client.

Many modern IRC chat programs type your commands for you. You just choose what you want to do from a menu. Still, you should learn a few commands.

When you join an IRC chat room, the server will send you the Message of the Day (MOTD). Some IRC programs show you this in a side window, some in the main window. If the MOTD flies by too fast for you to see it, type the command **/MOTD** into the same place you would type a message. Note that anything preceded by a slash (/) is a command in an IRC chat room. The MOTD usually has a greeting, some statistics about how many people are on the server right now, and, sometimes, the rules for this particular server.

Most IRC clients will log you in to the default channel, usually called *Lobby,* while you search for the channel or room you want. You must choose a handle, or nickname, to log on. Once you find a good channel and log on, lurk for a moment, reading the messages. If this is a room you want to join, send a polite greeting such as "Hello, everyone!" You might find some rooms so friendly that the moment you log on, someone sends you a greeting. Politely acknowledge it.

Besides /JOIN and /MOTD, the most important IRC command for you to know is /IGNORE (or whatever the equivalent is for that server). When someone is offending, bothering, or flaming you, typing **/IGNORE < badguy's handle >** will keep that person's messages from appearing on your screen.

If the chat is moderated, you often have to send a line with a question mark, wait for the moderator to recognize you, and then send your question or comment.

Instant messaging programs, such as AOL Instant Messenger, enable you to block people from paging you or chatting with you.

Chat can be a useful Internet tool, especially when moderated and when a specific subject is chosen. But it can also be addictive, and if you're not careful you might find yourself doing more chatting than researching. Just remember, I warned you!

Where to Chat

Any evening you can find a good genealogy chat on AOL in the Golden Gate Genealogy Forum (keyword: ROOTS). The rooms can be accessed on AOL by going to keyword ROOTS and clicking "Chats," where you will find icons for the five main rooms. Additional rooms (for example, those for the Canadian provinces) can be found by going to the menu in the lower-left corner and scrolling down to the last item, Related Chat Rooms. The times given in the following table are Eastern Standard Time.

Topic	Day	Time (EST)	Room
African-Ancestry Chat	Tue	9–11 P.M.	Ancestral Digs
	Sat	9–10:30 P.M.	Golden Gates
	Wed	3–4:30 P.M.	Golden Gates
Alabama/Mississippi/Georgia Chat	Sun	8 P.M.	Root Cellar
American Civil War History Chat	Thurs	11 P.M.	Golden Gates
AOL/Computing Basics Chat	Tue	7–8 P.M.	Golden Gates
Beginners	Sun–Sat	8 P.M. to 12 A.M.	Beginners
Beyond Beginners	Thurs	7–8 P.M.	Golden Gates
British Isles Chat	Mon	10–11 P.M.	Golden Gates
Central Heartland Chat	Thurs	7–8 P.M.	Root Cellar (AR/MO/NE/KS/TX)
Connecticut	Sat	10 P.M.	Root Cellar
Dear Diary	Thurs	8–9 P.M.	Golden Gates
Evening Canada Chat	Wed	9 P.M.	Ancestral Digs
Florida Chat	Sun	7 P.M.	Root Cellar
France Chat	Tue	11 P.M. to Noon	Ancestral Digs
French Canadian	Thurs	9–10 P.M.	Golden Gates
French Language Chat	Tues	10 P.M.	Quebec Chat Room
General Genealogy	Sun–Sat	8 P.M. to 2 A.M.	Family Treehouse
GENTREK	Mon	8–10 P.M.	Golden Gates
Great Lakes U.S. Chat	Mon	10–11 P.M.	Ancestral Digs
Indiana/Illinois/Iowa Chat	Tue	9 P.M.	Root Cellar
Irish & Scot Chat	Fri	10 P.M. to Midnight	Ancestral Digs
Italian Chat	Wed	9–10 P.M.	Golden Gates
Jewish Chat	Thurs	10–11 P.M.	Golden Gates
Kentucky Chat	Wed	8 P.M.	Root Cellar
Late Nite Canada Chat	Tue	Midnight	Golden Gates

Topic	Day	Time (EST)	Room
Maine Chat	Sat	7 P.M.	Root Cellar
Maritimes Chat	Sun	8–9 P.M.	Ancestral Digs
	Sun	10–11 P.M.	Root Cellar
Michigan Chat	Mon	9 P.M.	Root Cellar
Mid-Atlantic U.S. Chat	Tue	9–10 A.M.	Root Cellar
	Thurs	4–5 P.M.	Ancestral Digs
	Tue	10 P.M. to Midnight	(NY/NJ/PA/MD/DE/ WV/DC)
			Golden Gates
Minnesota/Wisconsin	Sun	9 P.M.	Root Cellar
Mugs & Hugs Family Hour	Mon–Fri	9–10 A.M.	Ancestral Digs
Native American Chat	Sun	10 P.M. to Midnight	Golden Gates
	Fri	4–5 P.M.	Golden Gates
New England Chat	Wed	3–4 P.M.	Ancestral Digs
	Wed	10 P.M. to Midnight	(ME/NH/VT/MA/CT/RI)
			Ancestral Digs
Newfoundland Chat	Sun	9 P.M.	Newfoundland Chat Room
New Hampshire/Vermont Chat	Sat	8 P.M.	Root Cellar
New York Chat	Fri	9 P.M.	Root Cellar
NJ/NY Chat	Tue	10 P.M.	Root Cellar
North Carolina Chat	Mon	7 P.M.	Root Cellar
Ohio Chat	Wed	9–10 P.M.	Root Cellar
Ontario Chat	Mon	11 P.M.	Ontario Chat Room
Pennsylvania Chat	Thurs	9–10 A.M.	Root Cellar
	Fri	10–11 P.M.	Root Cellar
Polish Chat	Thurs	8–10 P.M.	Ancestral Digs
Portuguese Chat	Wed	11 P.M. to Midnight	Golden Gates
	Sun	8–9 P.M.	Golden Gates
Quebec Chat	Fri	9 P.M.	Quebec Chat Room
Scandinavian Chat	Fri	10 P.M. to Midnight	Golden Gates
South Carolina Chat	Mon	8 P.M.	Root Cellar
Southern U.S. Chat	Fri	3–4 P.M.	Ancestral Digs
	Sat	9 P.M.	(VA/NC/SC/GA/ FL/AL/TN/KY/MS)
			Ancestral Digs
Tennessee Chat	Tue	8 P.M.	Root Cellar
Virginia & West Virginia Chat	Wed	7 P.M.	Root Cellar
War Between the States Chat	Fri	9 P.M.	Golden Gates

Another good resource for regular chats is Bill Holcutt's site, www.bhocutt.com/cgi-bin/gtchat/chat.pl. These web-based chat rooms, or "cabins," have had topics such as General Genealogy, Beginner's Genealogy, Church Records, and Jefferson Moak, Archivist from the NARA Mid-Atlantic Region. You have to create a username and a password to log on, but that only takes a couple of minutes.

Okay, let's say you have mIRC, or some other text-based program that uses public, open chat servers. Several genealogy sites have both scheduled and impromptu chats. RootsWeb (point your chat client to irc.rootsweb.com, port 6667, alternative 7000) is just about the best place for genealogy chats.

The chat server is hosted in conjunction with the International Internet Genealogical Society (IIGS) at www.iigs.org. If you point your IRC chat client to irc.IIGS.org, it'll send you on to irc.rootsweb.com in a couple of seconds. There's usually an impromptu open chat going on among the people who manage genealogy websites. However, among the most wonderful resources on the whole Net are the moderated, as opposed to the impromptu, RootsWeb/IIGS chats. The scheduled ones are listed at www.iigs.org/cgi/ircthemes/ircthemes. The topics range from very general, such as Diana Hansen's question-and-answer sessions to discuss all aspects of genealogy research and methodology, to very specific, such as Estill County, Kentucky genealogy.

Besides the wonderful experts and helpful people, the niftiest thing about this IRC server is the translation bot—a program on the server that enables you to log on to a chat channel and have the conversations translated into another language. DearMYRTLE told me of a recent chat where people speaking German, Spanish, and Norwegian were all able to ask her questions (which were translated into English for her) and receive her answers (translated back to their respective languages).

Another good source of scheduled chats is the About.com set of pages—specifically, About.Genealogy. The page genealogy.about.com/hobbies/genealogy/mpchat.htm has a list of the scheduled genealogy chats.

In particular, look for the channels on the servers listed here:

Server	Channels
irc.chat.org:6667	#FTMCC (Family Tree Maker Chat), #genealogy
irc.IIGS.org:6667 or irc.IIGS.org:7000	#Australia, #Benelux, #Canadian-Gen, #cert, #Cogenweb, #CZER-Group, #DEUgen, #genealogie.fr, #Ger-Rus, #htmlhelp, #IIGS-Ontario, #IIGS-Ukgen, #IIGS-UK-IRE, #IIGS-UnivHelp, #Ireland-gen, #KY-Estill, #NewEngland, #SE-USA, #SHANNON

Server	Channels
irc.dal.net:7000	#Canadian GEN #Fianna (Irish Genealogy), #genealogy-events, #genealogy-help, #Genealogy_IRC, #Gen_Family_Tree, #Gentrace, #lunie-links (Lunenburg Co., NS, Canada)
irc.another.net:6667	#genealogy
irc.afternet.org	#GenealogyForum, #Genealogy-n-UK
irc.rootsweb.com	#DearMYRTLE, #IIGS-UnivHelp, #htmlhelp
irc.newnet.net:6667	#family_history, #genealogy, #genealogy101
irc.rootsweb.com:6667 or irc.rootsweb.com:7000	#MSGenWeb
irc.scscorp.net:6667	#genealogy
irc.superchat.org:6660	#Genealogy
irc.webmaster.com	#TMG (The Master Genealogist software discussion)

Wrapping Up

♦ Moderated chats are like online classes, with exchange of information or a question-and-answer format.

♦ Unmoderated chats can be more annoying than productive.

♦ Instant messaging is the most common form of chat.

♦ All chat forms can be addictive—handle with care!

Chapter 8

Genealogy Mail Lists, Newsletters, and Newsgroups

Communicating with other genealogists is one of the best things about genealogy online. Mail lists, newsletters, and newsgroups can all help you join in the fun.

It should be noted that Usenet is not as popular as it used to be because of the unsolicited bulk e-mail (spam) situation. The unforgivably aggressive marketing techniques of the unsolicited bulk e-mailers have just about ruined what was once a thriving communications medium. Still, several genealogy newsgroups have active participants.

Note

If you subscribe to Usenet, disguise your e-mail address. Sign up for a free mailbox at Yahoo! or another portal to use for posting, or write out your address as your_name at yourisp dot com.

Electronic mail lists are electronic discussion groups based on e-mail messages. All subscribers can send e-mail to the list and receive e-mail from the list. Messages sent to the mail list get forwarded to everyone who subscribes to it. Replies to messages from the list get sent to the list, where they are forwarded to all participants. And so it goes.

Mail lists can be completely automated, with a program taking care of subscribing people to the list, forwarding messages, and removing people from the list. Or, people can get into the loop, handling any and all of the mail list functions that programs can do. Such "moderated" mail lists can take two forms: They might have restricted memberships where you need to be approved to subscribe, or a moderator (or moderators) might let anyone join but would review each incoming message before it gets distributed, preventing inappropriate material from getting on to the list. Some newsgroups are moderated in that messages that are off-topic or spam may be deleted quickly after posting.

Many mail lists and newsgroups focus specifically on genealogy. In addition, many more lists and newsgroups, although not specifically for genealogists, cover topics of interest to genealogists, such as ethnic groups and historic events.

General Tips

With a decent mail program (see Chapter 2), participating in mail lists is easy. You simply have to figure out how to subscribe, manage, and unsubscribe to a list. Often, the instructions are included in the mail list's home site.

Mail List Subscribing

Say you want to subscribe to a Kent, England genealogy mail list and you know you need to send e-mail to eng-kent-request@british-genealogy.com with the message "subscribe" to join the list. Here's how you do it:

1. Click the Compose Mail icon in your mail program.

2. In the To: box, type **eng-kent-request@british-genealogy.com**.

3. In the Message box, type **subscribe**. Don't add anything else. If your mail program is set to append a signature file automatically, disable it for this message.

4. Click the Send button.

This is the general procedure. For some lists, you might also have to add your full real name. For other lists, you might have to add the actual name of the list after the word "subscribe." In all cases, don't put any signature at the bottom, or else put "end" on the line after the "subscribe" line, as shown in Figure 8-1.

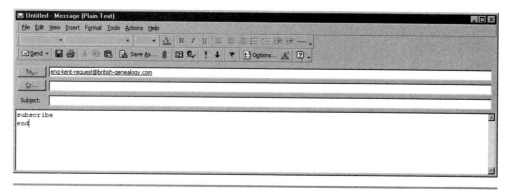

FIGURE 8-1.   *If you're in doubt whether an automatic signature might slip into a message to a listserv program, put "end" after the subscribe command line.*

You will receive a welcome message, which you should save to a text or document file. It will tell you how to manage your subscription to get off the list, suspend it temporarily, and prevent your own messages to the list from coming to you from the server.

Note that in some mail list programs, you can send a command— who or reveal—to find out who is subscribed to a certain list. If you do not want to be listed in the who command, you often have to send a command to the list server noting that. The welcome message will tell you how, but it's usually the command CONCEAL.

Success Story

The most meaningful success I have had was because of posting to boards. I found an aunt I never knew I had. Got to go meet her. She lives about 40 miles from me. I was adopted, so finding a biological relative was great. It was from an old posting, so keep posting everywhere. You never know when you will see results!

—GFS TUPPER
Host of Maine Genealogy Chat, Beginners Chat,
and Beyond Beginners Chat on AOL

Usenet Newsgroup Subscribing

Subscribing to Usenet newsgroups is slightly different. Subscribing in this case is simply telling your program that you wish to retrieve and read certain newsgroups. No Usenet command reveals who is subscribed; if you only lurk and never post, the others on the newsgroup will not know you exist.

You do not have to correspond with any program or person except your newsreader. Both Outlook Express and Netscape's mail reader come with the ability to subscribe to a newsgroup. Look under Tools | Accounts in OE and under Mail | Preference in Netscape. Other shareware newsreaders, such as News Rover, Agent, and TIFNY are worth looking into for their automation and filtering features.

Also, you can read Usenet messages on some web portals, if you register as a member. In Google, for example, go to groups.google.com, click soc., then click soc.genealogy for web access to 20 newsgroups about genealogy (see Figure 8-2).

On AOL, CompuServe, and other proprietary ISPs, go to the Usenet area and set up your preferences. To hide your e-mail address from

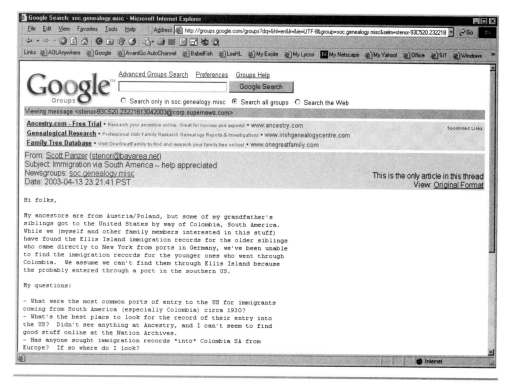

FIGURE 8-2. *You can read Usenet newsgroups on portals such as Google.*

harvesters, look for an option to enter your e-mail as something such as sam345@aol.comnospam.

Proper Addressing

Most mail lists have two e-mail addresses. You use one address to subscribe or change how you use the mail list and the other to post messages to the other people on the mail list. Some other mail lists might have a third address to use for certain administrative chores, such as reporting some violation of the list's rules to the moderator. Later in this chapter you'll find plenty of mail lists to subscribe to.

Addressing to Usenet newsgroups, again, is simpler, because it is done within your newsgroup readers. Remember to disguise your e-mail address, or use a false one, to protect yourself from unsolicited bulk e-mail.

Frequently Asked Questions (FAQ) Files

Many newsgroups post files of information called FAQs. About once a month, these get posted to their own newsgroup and to the newsgroup soc.answers. Look for a message called the Meta Genealogy FAQ, posted about the 22nd of each month to most of the soc.genealogy newsgroups. This message will show you how to get the FAQ files for the individual genealogy newsgroups.

Binary Files on Usenet

Some newsgroups carry binary files (recognizable because they usually have binaries in their names). This isn't seen so much on Usenet anymore because the Web is far superior for trading sounds, pictures, and programs. Still, sometimes people do encode a binary file, which has nontext characters, into ASCII codes that can transfer on Usenet.

Some newsreaders automatically take care of this for you. On AOL, you have to jump through a few hoops, however.

When you first join AOL, your account is set to the default to block all binary files in Usenet because most of the binaries sent over Usenet are pornographic. To turn this default behavior off, go to Keyword Parental Controls and select the screen name. Click the More Controls

Where to Find the FAQs

You don't have to wait for a certain date to roll around to read FAQs on your favorite topics. Try these sites, which have the latest versions:

- **Internet FAQ Archives**   http://www.faqs.org/
- **JewishGen FAQ**   http://www.jewishgen.org/infofiles/faq.html
- **The Genealogy Meta-FAQ**   http://www.woodgate.org/FAQs/meta-faq.html

drop-down button and choose Newsgroups. Uncheck the box Block Newsgroup File Download. You may, however, want to block the "adult" newsgroups in the same window.

Encoded binary files are often broken up across several different messages. Gathering the pieces, putting them together, and converting them to their original form used to be a real hassle. America Online's FileGrabber feature makes the process simple now. You have to set this feature for each newsgroup individually by checking the box in the Preferences window.

AOL's newsreader alerts you when you're viewing encoded data, and it gives you three choices: Download the file (the AOL software will automatically decode it for you), download the article that contains the code or piece of it (you will then have to decode the pieces yourself), and cancel. (Remember, CompuServe is running basically the same software as AOL now, so all this works there, too.)

Again, I caution you: Don't download and decode binaries on Usenet unless you know and trust the sender.

Mail List Example: ROOTS-L

Imagine a worldwide, never-ending conversation about genealogy, where novices and experts exchange help, information, ideas, and gossip. Now imagine this conversation is conducted by electronic mail (e-mail), so you needn't worry about missing anything. You've just imagined ROOTS-L, the grandparent of genealogy mail lists on the Internet.

ROOTS-L has spawned entire generations of newer genealogy mail lists—some large, some small—but this is the original. The mail list page at lists.rootsweb.com hosts over 26,0000 mail lists about genealogy and history (see Figure 8-3). ROOTS-L is the oldest, and still the largest.

To subscribe, you need to do two things:

1. Make sure your e-mail inbox is large enough to hold the volume of messages you'll receive. If you have limited space, use digest mode, if available, and check your mail box more than once a day.

2. Send an e-mail message to roots-l-request@rootsweb.org, with the message "Subscribe." You don't need to include anything else in the message—no signature block, no name or address.

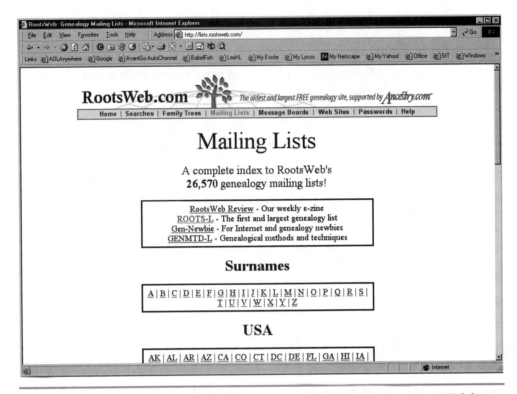

FIGURE 8-3. *From surnames to localities to genealogical computing, RootsWeb has mail lists on all aspects of genealogy.*

Some ROOTS-L Rules

ROOTS-L clearly states its rules in its welcome message. It would be wise to apply these rules to every mail list you join, whether or not they're explicitly stated:

◆ Memorize this rule: Messages to people go to roots-l@rootsweb.org. Commands to programs go to roots-l-request@rootsweb.org. I use this trick: I save the "request" address in my e-mail's address book under the name ROOTS-L REQUEST and the posting address under ROOTS-L POST. When I'm ready to send a message to one or the other, I choose it from the address list, just as I would a person's address.

◆ The list isn't a place to bring up wars of the past, or to discuss religion or politics.

♦ Advertising or selling a product is not, in general, acceptable. You can, however, post a new-product announcement.

♦ Make sure you spell the word "genealogy" correctly in all your messages.

♦ Don't post messages longer than about 150 lines unless you're sure they'll be of very general interest.

♦ Don't include a "surname signature" in your messages. These are lists of surnames that appear at the end of every message some people send. The surnames play havoc with the list's archive searches, so don't use them.

♦ Don't post copyrighted material, such as newspaper articles, or e-mail messages sent to you by other people.

♦ Quote *only* enough of previous messages to be clear about what the discussion is about. Never quote previous messages in their entirety because this bogs down the list.

Success Story: The Web Helps a Mobility-Challenged Genealogist

Being mobility challenged and on a very limited income, I have to depend mostly on the Internet at this time for my genealogy work, and I've had some success.

I had a query on an Irsch surname board for my great-grandfather and the fact he had married a Pitts in Noxubee, Mississippi in 1860. I just happened to decide to go to the Pitts surname board and posted the same query for a Lucretia Emmaline Pitts, who had married a Frank Irsch.

I received a tentative confirmation from someone whose great-grandfather had a sister who had married an Irsch about that time. A few back-and-forths later we thought we might have a connection; I asked if she had ever heard the names Aunt Em and Uncle Henry Hill. I had heard my grandmother speak of them, but didn't know if they were blood relatives.

We both knew we had established the connection. "Aunt Em" was the sister of her great-great-great-grandfather, Lafayette Newton Pitts, and another sister, Lucretia, had married Frank Irsch. Their father's name was James W. Pitts and their mother's name was Mary. We still haven't discovered her maiden name.

She had a picture of some of the Irsch family that Lizzie Eaton/Bennett had identified for them as her brother and family and Grandma Pitts. She wasn't sure if the older woman was her Grandma Pitts, but she didn't think so. Lizzie Eaton/Bennett was my *grandmother, and if she identified the older woman as Grandma Pitts, it would have been her grandmother, Mary ?-? Pitts. I remember my mother telling me of Aunt Annie Irsch and Grandma Pitts sending Christmas gifts when she was little.*

Now we proudly know we have a picture of our shared great-great-great-grandmother. We are working on other shared lines, but I would call this a wonderful tale of success from the Internet!

—Louise McDonald

Communicating with People and Programs

I mentioned this rule earlier in the chapter, but people tend to get confused about it, so here are more details. If you're already sure you know where to send messages to people subscribed to ROOTS-L, as opposed to sending commands to the software at ROOTS-L, you can skip the rest of this section.

It can be hard to remember the distinction between the list server that runs a mail list and the list itself. This problem is common to most mail lists. The *list server* gets all the commands: subscribe, unsubscribe, send message digests, and so forth. The *list* gets messages you want to send to other people. For ROOTS-L, messages addressed to roots-l@ rootsweb.org go to the mail list. Messages addressed to roots-l@rootsweb .org get posted on the list for all to see.

So, if you want to request help finding information about your Aunt Tilly, send your message to roots-l@rootsweb.org. If you want to request a copy of the Roots Surname List (described in the next section), send your message to roots-l-request@rootsweb.org.

Putting ROOTS-L to Work

Now that you've subscribed to ROOTS-L and you know all the rules, it's time to learn how to put the list server to work. You can control your subscription from your e-mail program. But, you must remember this: You can only control your subscription from the same e-mail account with which you subscribed in the first place. The commands you send will be processed automatically by the list processor—if you remember to send them to roots-l-request@rootsweb.org. If you send your commands to roots-l@rootsweb.org, you'll only succeed in irritating the people running the list.

When you first subscribe to ROOTS-L, you're subscribed in *digest* mode. This means, once or twice a day, you'll receive a large message from ROOTS-L containing a list of all the messages that have been posted to the list since the last digest message. For each topic, there's a topic number, a subject, and the name of the person who posted it.

Digests from ROOTS-L tend to be larger than many e-mail programs—including AOL—can view. Instead of showing the whole message, you might get a display of only the first part of the message, or even a blank message with an icon noting an attachment. A copy of the entire message is converted into a text file and stored as an attachment that, on AOL, you have to download (most e-mail programs, such as Eudora, will download the attachment automatically unless you have set the default not to). From there, it's up to you to open the file with a word processor or text editor and read the messages.

You can get around this by telling the list server to give you each message separately by switching to *mail* mode or *index* mode. Instructions on how to switch modes are included in the files rootsl.welcome2 and rootsl.welcome3. To get them, send an e-mail to roots-l-request@ rootsweb.org, put the word "archive" (without the quotation marks) in the subject line, and, as the message, include the following commands:

```
get roots-l.welcome2
get roots-l.welcome3
```

Note that the letter *l* (ell) appears after the dash, not the number 1. Don't include your name, tagline, signature, or anything else besides the commands.

If you just like to browse the messages, go to http://listsearches .rootsweb.com/cgi-bin/listsearch.pl?list = ROOTS to the Archives; then click the date you want to see. The Daily Indexes are where a separate page for each digest is posted in HTML form, with associated message numbers. The searchable archive is where you can select one year, search for a string of letters, such as SPENCER or POWELL, and get the corresponding messages (see Figure 8-4).

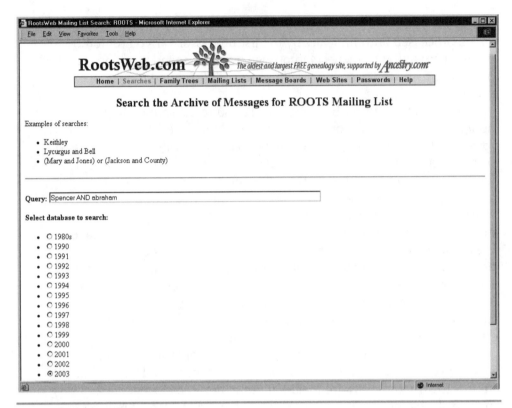

FIGURE 8-4.   *You can search all the archives of the ROOTS-L mail list for keywords.*

Losing Contact with a Mail List

It's possible you'll stop receiving messages from a mail list, even though you didn't unsubscribe. If this happens, it may be because:

♦   Your Internet service provider (ISP) could be having trouble with their e-mail service. Any service can have intermittent service problems. Sometimes, a whole section of the Internet might be out of order for a few minutes or even for hours. In fact, AOL has had such problems in the past, as have many other online services. If all your e-mail stops coming in—not just mail from a mail list— this could be the cause.

♦ Your mail list may be sharing an IP address with a known spammer, through no fault of the list owner. Contact your ISP to tell them to let your mail list through as legitimate mail.

♦ You're using a different e-mail address than the one you used to subscribe to the mail list. Most e-mail server programs will only send to the return address of the subscribe message.

If all else fails, subscribe to the mail list again. That should get the messages flowing for you.

Newsgroups of Interest to Online Genealogists

Once upon a time, only one online genealogy Usenet newsgroup for genealogists was available: soc.roots. As more genealogy researchers came onboard, more messages were posted. Trying to deal with an overwhelming array of genealogical topics—ranging from beginners' questions to historical epochs—soon became unwieldy. Thankfully, after much discussion and soul-searching, we now have an embarrassment of riches in genealogical newsgroups.

However, the ebb and flow of genealogy newsgroups is as constant as it is bewildering. To find genealogy newsgroups, sign on to your ISP and search the list for the word "genealogy." For example, in Outlook Express, I would click the news server, click the Newsgroups button in the toolbar, and then type **Genealogy** in the Display Newsgroups Which Contain box (see Figure 8-5).

Here are some newsgroups you might find particularly interesting:

♦ **alt.adoption**   A newsgroup that discusses adoption issues, including the search for birth parents.

♦ **alt.genealogy**   A genealogy group that discusses more general topics. Copied to the ALT-GENEALOGY mail list.

♦ **alt.culture.cajun**   A newsgroup devoted to discussions of Cajun history, genealogy, culture, and events.

♦ **fido.eur.genealogy**   For those researching European genealogy. FidoNet is a message network for dial-up bulletin board systems; some FidoNet discussion groups are copied to Usenet, as this one is.

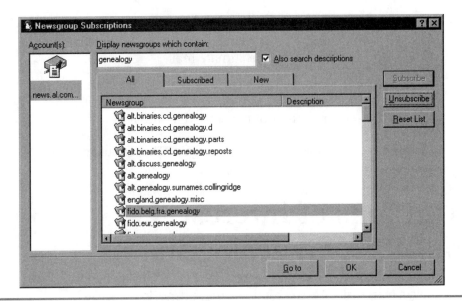

FIGURE 8-5.   *Search for newsgroups that contain GENEALOGY in your newsreader.*

- **fido.ger.genealogy**   The same as fido.eur.genealogy, but intended for German gencalogy research (with most messages posted in German).

- **fr.rec.genealogie**   Copied to the GEN-FF-L mail list for the discussion of Francophone genealogy, the genealogy of French-speaking people (with messages posted in French).

- **soc.genealogy**   These original RootsWeb newsgroups have been inactive for most of the first half of 2001. They may be revived later, but at press time they have little or, in some cases, no traffic.

- **soc.genealogy.African**   When active, this newsgroup is about African genealogy, but at press time the last post was in March 2001.

- **soc.genealogy.computing**   An exception to the previous ones, this newsgroup remains popular. It has information about various genealogical programs and their corresponding bugs (including how-to instructions). Topics mostly concern software (with some hardware discussions). Copied to the SOFTWARE.GENCMP-L mail list.

- **soc.genealogy.french** Genealogy of French-speaking peoples (with most messages posted in French). Copied to the GEN-FR-L mail list.

- **soc.genealogy.german** Discussions of family history for those with Germanic backgrounds (messages are mainly in German). Copied to the GEN-DE-L mail list.

- **soc.genealogy.hispanic** Genealogical discussions as related to Hispanics (some centering around Central and South American family lines), with many messages in Spanish.

- **soc.genealogy.jewish** A moderated discussion of Judaic genealogy. Copied to the JEWISHGEN mail list.

- **soc.genealogy.marketplace** Here, you can buy, sell, and trade books, as well as read about programs, seminars, and so forth related to genealogy.

- **soc.genealogy.medieval** Copied to the GEN-MEDIEVAL mail list for genealogy and family history discussions among people researching individuals living during medieval times— loosely defined as the period from the breakup of the Western Roman Empire until the time public records relating to the general population began to be kept (roughly from A.D. 500 to A.D. 1600).

- **soc.genealogy.methods** A general discussion of genealogy and methods of genealogical research. Copied to the GENMTD-L mail list, but it has been inactive of late.

- **soc.genealogy.misc** This is what became of soc.roots. It's essentially a general discussion of genealogy, and it copies to the GENMSC-L mail list. This is a catchall for topics that don't fit into other soc.genealogy.* categories.

- **soc.genealogy.Nordic** Offers genealogical products and services pertaining to Northern Europe.

- **soc.genealogy.Slavic** Slavic genealogy, with some messages in Slavic languages.

♦ **soc.genealogy.surnames.***   Several different newsgroups for surname queries. Besides the root newsgroup soc.genealogy .surnames, there are subgroups for German, British, Canadian, U.S., and miscellaneous.

♦ **soc.genealogy.uk + Ireland and soc.genealogy.uk**   Copied to the GENUKI-L mail list for the discussion of genealogy and family history. Also used for discussions among people researching ancestors, family members, or others who have a genealogical connection to people in any part of the British Isles (England, Wales, Ireland, Scotland, the Channel Isles, and the Isle of Man).

♦ **soc.genealogy.west-indies**   Covers Caribbean genealogy, and most, but not all, of the messages are in English.

In addition to this list are several groups in the soc.history hierarchies that discuss issues genealogists typically face, such as the authentication of records and sources, and so on. These include soc.history.medieval, soc.history.war.us.civil-war, and soc.history.war.us-revolution, among others.

Read-Only Mail Lists

Another category of lists is the "read-only" or "announcement-only" list. This type of list is compiled—sometimes by a staff, sometimes by an individual—with news and announcements on genealogy. You don't post to them; instead, you simply receive them like a newsletter or a magazine. Some worth your attention are detailed in this section.

Ancestry Daily News

Ancestry Daily News is a daily news service from the Ancestry site with free family history tips, news, and updates. Subscribe at www.ancestry .com and click Free Newsletters.

DearMYRTLE

DearMYRTLE's daily column can be delivered to your mailbox if you don't remember to visit her site. Simply go to www.dearmyrtle.com and click Subscribe in the navigation bar to the left. Click the List (every column individually, as it's posted) or Digest (consolidated columns, once or twice a week) button. A message will be generated in your e-mail program. Be sure to take out any automatic signatures before you send.

Eastman's Genealogy Newsletter

Dick Eastman is one of the most respected online genealogists, and his weekly newsletter, *Eastman's Genealogy Newsletter,* provides "a weekly summary of events and topics of interest to online genealogists." It's always worth reading! You can subscribe at www.rootsforum.com/newsletter.

Everton's Family History Newsline

This newsletter has breaking news on the genealogy industry, including mergers, acquisitions, and product releases. You can subscribe at www.everton.com.

Genealogy Newsletter

The *Genealogy Newsletter* (GenealogyNewsletter.com) is sponsored by the Genealogy Gateway to the Web (GenGateway.com). This publication provides free genealogy-related informational materials to family researchers and casual family seekers. The mission is to publish information that is useful, interesting, and current. Subscribe at www.genealogynewsletter.com/archive/menu.htm and just fill in the form.

Missing Links and RootsWeb Review

Missing Links contains articles on all aspects of genealogical research worldwide, research success stories, book reviews, "Somebody's Links" notices (genealogical treasures, such as bibles, diaries, old letters, and photos), announcements of genealogical conferences, seminars, workshops, family reunions, and humor. *RootsWeb Review* provides news about RootsWeb, its new databases, mail lists, home pages, and websites. Both are weekly. Subscribe by sending a blank e-mail to rootsweb-review-subscribe@rootsweb.com.

What's New on Cyndi's List

This is a daily update of new sites added to Cyndi's List. To subscribe, send an e-mail message to CyndisList-request@rootsweb.com. In the body, include only one word: subscribe. To unsubscribe, send an e-mail message to CyndisList-request@rootsweb.com and, in the body, include only one word: unsubscribe. Be sure to turn *off* your automatic signature file when sending either of the previous commands to the RootsWeb mail list server.

Other Mail List Sites

Use your favorite search engine to look for "genealogy newsletter" and you will be amazed! You'll find newsletters based on surnames, locations, and software programs. Here are some other sites where you can subscribe to mail lists:

- **Coollist (http://directory.coollist.com/society/ genealogy)** Coollist is a site where you can join or create a mail list by simply filling out a form. The list can be viewed by anyone or by only members who signed up through the website, as the list owner chooses.

- **eScribe (http://www.escribe.com/genealogy)** This site has a few lists—some general, some surname specific, and some about history of a certain region. eScribe provides a free, web-based set of tools for list management, including a completely searchable web-based archive of messages, bulletin boards, polls, classifieds, chat rooms, and so forth. eScribe offers personalized service and support.

- **JewishGen (http://www.jewishgen.org)** The Jewish Genealogy site hosts two or three dozen groups based on geography, projects of the site, and other interests. Go to the home page and scroll down to Discussion Groups; then click the link for Special Interest Groups (SIGS) for a current listing.

♦ **Branching Out (http://communities.prodigy.net/genealogy/)**   This monthly newsletter has news on special events, news of interest to all Prodigy members concerning software upgrades and new features, genealogy tips from expert Myra Vanderpool Gormley, and other special features as time and space allow.

♦ **USRoots/Rootsquest (http://www.rootsquest.com)**   This site has surname-based mail lists. You can e-mail the site owners to start your own mail list. Of course, before you start one, check ROOTS-L, FamilySearch, and other sites to be certain you aren't replicating an existing list.

♦ **Yahoo! (http://groups.yahoo.com)**   Yahoo! has thousands of discussion groups based on surnames, geography, and ethnicity. Some are public, which means anyone can post to them, and some require you to sign up before you can post to them. Go to the groups.yahoo .com page and search for "genealogy" and/or the surnames you need. Yahoo! and eGroups merged a couple of years back; any references you see to an eGroup now refers to groups.yahoo.com.

Finding More Mail Lists

Even though it may seem like we've covered more mail lists than you can shake a stick at, many more exist. To find more mail lists, first check out the RootsWeb website for their ever-growing list. If you point your web browser to www.rootsweb.org/ ~ maillist, you'll have access to the hundreds of mail lists hosted by RootsWeb.

Also, John Fuller and Christine Gaunt maintain a categorized directory of genealogy mail lists at www.rootsweb.com/ ~ jfuller/ gen_mail.html (see Figure 8-6).

Cyndi's List (www.CyndisList.com/magazine.htm) is a good site to visit to keep up on the latest in mail lists and newsletters.

Finally, you can search a database of publicly accessible mail lists at the Publicly Accessible Mail List site, http://paml.alastra.com/. You can search this database by keyword or browse the index of hundreds of mail lists.

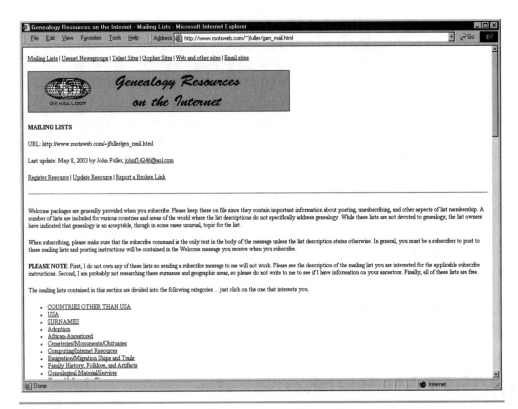

FIGURE 8-6. *Mail lists are catalogued at John Fuller and Christine Gaunt's page.*

Wrapping Up

♦ E-mail discussion lists bring other genealogists right to your electronic mail box. Usenet requires a newsreader, but it can be more anonymous.

♦ When you subscribe to a mail list, always save the reply message, which usually has the "unsubscribe" instructions as well as the rules of the list.

♦ Usenet is less useful than it used to be, but active genealogy newsgroups still exist.

◆ When you subscribe to a Usenet newsgroup, look for the FAQ to be posted or go to the FAQ archive to retrieve it.

◆ Hide or disguise your return e-mail address in any Usenet posting to protect yourself from unsolicited bulk e-mail.

◆ Most mail lists are interactive and have one address for subscribing and another for posting messages.

◆ Some e-mail lists are "read-only." That is, you subscribe to them, but you don't submit to them.

Part III

Specific Online Resources

Chapter 9

Vital Records

Vital records are the milestones of life: birth, marriage, and death. Other important records are naturalization, census records, and land ownership. More and more, you can find at least clues to these records online; in some cases you can get to digitized versions of the records themselves.

Among the best of the online sites maintained by the United States federal government are the Library of Congress (LOC) and the National Archives and Records Administration (NARA). Both the LOC and the NARA sites have been recently revamped, with links to genealogy guides, tips, and resources gathered together for easy access. Still, you'll find these sites useful to help you decide what to ask for by mail or if you should visit in person. You'll eventually want to visit an NARA branch or the LOC in person because, although many resources are online, not every book or document is available that way.

Other important federal records online are the Bureau of Land Management records of original land grants and patents, immigration records, and naturalization records. Some states and counties also have certain vital records and censuses, sometimes online, and sometimes just the contact information for ordering a copy.

This chapter gives you a short overview of what's there and how to access the resources of these sites.

Library of Congress

The mission of the Library of Congress (www.loc.gov) is to "make its resources available and useful to the Congress and the American people and to sustain and preserve a universal collection of knowledge and creativity for future generations." To that end, the LOC, since its founding in 1800, has amassed more than 100 million items and become one of the world's leading cultural institutions. The LOC website, shown in Figure 9-1, makes a small portion of the LOC's contents available to the world through the Internet.

Four sections of the website are of particular use to genealogists:

♦ **The Local History and Genealogy Reading Room page (www.loc.gov/rr/genealogy/)**   This page has information on how to prepare for a visit to the site.

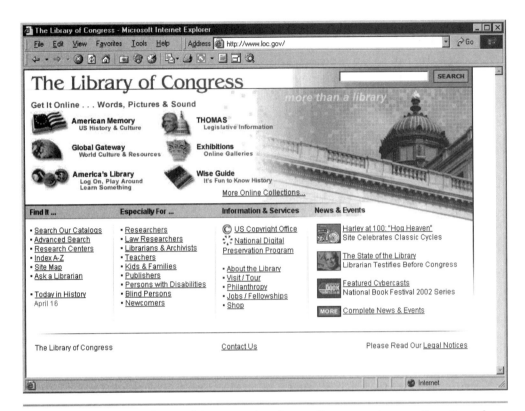

FIGURE 9-1. *The Library of Congress site gives online access to a small portion of the holdings.*

♦ **The American Memory section**   This section contains documents, photographs, movies, and sound recordings that tell some of America's story. A direct link is http://memory.loc.gov/.

♦ **The Research Tools section**   This section of the site offers many online databases and connections to resources at other sites. The direct link is www.loc.gov/rr/.

♦ **The American Treasures section**   This section of the site is of interest more for the wonderful historical artifacts found there than for any specific genealogy information. The direct link is www.loc.gov/exhibits/treasures/.

American Memory

Click the American Memory link to begin your exploration of the LOC site. The subtitle for this page is "Historical Collections for the National Digital Library." This project is a public-private partnership designed to create a digital library of reproductions of primary source material to support research into the history and culture of the United States of America. Because this is an ongoing project, you can expect the resources here will continue to grow for the foreseeable future.

If you're researching African-American roots, you'll want to look at the African-American Odyssey page at memory.loc.gov/ammem/ aaohtml/aohome.html. This exhibition examines the African-American quest for full citizenship and contains primary source material, as well as links to other African-American materials at the LOC.

Going back to the American Memory home page, you can click Collection Finder to explore other primary source material. The collections are grouped by subject, then time, then place, then library division. You can also browse by format, if you want a sound or picture. Each collection has its own distinct character and subject matter, as well as narrative information to describe the content of the collection. Whereas searching all the collections at once could leave items of interest to you "buried" in a long list, visiting a collection's home page and reading the descriptive information about the collection can give you more direction in finding what you want.

Click the Social Sciences link from the Collection Finder page, and you'll find listings from folklore in Florida to the San Francisco earthquake of 1906 to first-person narratives of the American South.

The drawbacks to the Collection Finder are that it's a catalog you browse—not an index you search—and it doesn't always list every single item in a collection but, instead, gives an overview of the topic. For instance, if only a few items in a collection pertain to the broad topic of "agriculture," the collection might not appear under that topic. Clicking a category is like saying, "I want to see a collection mainly about a certain subject." The complete list of subjects is at memory.loc.gov/ ammem/collections/collsubjindex1.html. Say you know an ancestor owned a hotel in the early twentieth century. In that case, the collection "Hotels 1870–1930" might help you research that ancestor.

Searching the American Memory

You can search for phrases or keywords across all collections and look at essays, images, and primary source material, but do realize you'll get a lot of hits. Searching for the word "genealogy" across all collections gave me 168 hits, which included a genealogy of Pocahontas, letters written to Abraham Lincoln about genealogy (see Figure 9-2), and Memoirs of a Southern Woman Within the Lines (Civil War).

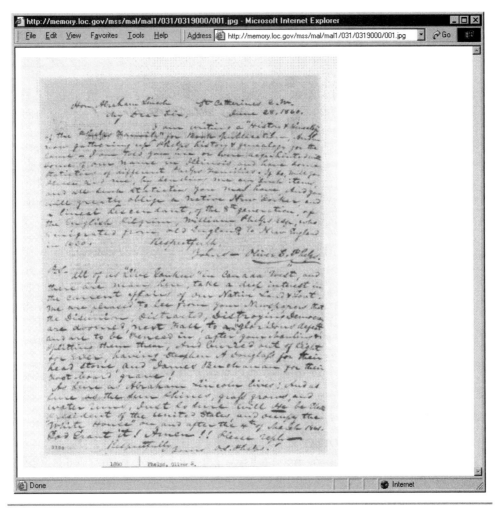

FIGURE 9-2.   *This letter to Abraham Lincoln starts, "My Dear Sir, I am writing a 'History and Genealogy of the Phelps Family'...."*

Some of the items you can find in the American Memory include:

♦ Almost 200 books describing the personal experiences of individuals in and on the way to California during and after the Gold Rush

♦ Hundreds of objects dealing with the Women's Suffrage movement

♦ Significant and interesting documents from Americans obscure to famous, as collected in the first 100 years of the Library of Congress Manuscript Division

♦ American Life Histories: Manuscripts from the Federal Writer's Project, 1936–1940

A third area of the American Memory section of the LOC for you to explore is the Maps section. On the Subject page mentioned previously, click Geography. Then you can search collections containing hundreds of digitized maps from 1639–1988. You can find city maps, conservation maps, exploration maps, immigration and settlement maps, military maps, and transportation maps, to name a few. And the amazing thing is this wealth of maps is only a tiny part of the LOC's full 4.5-million-item Geography and Map Division holdings.

Using the Library of Congress

Click Using the Library of Congress on the home page, and you can click your way through an excellent tutorial on the ins and outs of researching the library in person. Specifically, pay attention to the Local History and Genealogy page in this section, lcweb.loc.gov/rr/genealogy. This tells you about tours, how to prepare for a visit to the LOC, and links to other Internet genealogy resources.

Remember, not everything is available online. If you need to make a trip to the LOC, reading this section first can save you some time and frustration.

The Library Today

This link from the home page tells you about new exhibits, collections, and events at the LOC and its website. Visit it at least once a week because anything new posted to the website will be announced here.

Research Tools

The Research Tools page at lcweb.loc.gov/rr/tools.html takes you to a large set of useful links of interest for researchers, both on the LOC site and on other World Wide Web sites. These include desk references you can use on the Web, the LOC card catalog of all materials (including those not online), and special databases.

The Vietnam Era Prisoner of War/Missing in Action and Task Force Russia Databases at lcweb2.loc.gov/pow/powhome.html are examples. This URL takes you to a page that gives you access to a massive database of over 137,000 records pertaining to United States military personnel listed as unaccounted for as of December 1991. At the bottom of this page is a link to Task Force Russia at lcweb2.loc.gov/frd/tfrquery.html, a set of documents dealing with Americans who are believed to have been held in the former Soviet Union.

Exhibitions

Under the Exhibitions heading on the LOC Home Page, check out Featured Attractions. You'll find reproductions of dozens of the most treasured objects in the Library's collection. Each one of the objects featured—from the *Whole Booke of Psalmes Faithfully Translated into English Metre, 1640,* to an image of the *New York Herald's* story on the sinking of the Titanic, to a baseball program from a game between the Kansas City Monarchs and the Indianapolis Clowns in 1954—has some special historical significance. You might not find any long-lost ancestors when browsing this collection, but such artifacts can fill in the details of the times of our ancestors' lives.

Ask a Librarian

New features of the site include Ask a Librarian and Chat with a Librarian. Click Ask a Librarian from the home page, and you'll first get a help page with answers to frequently asked questions about collections and formats. The Local History and Genealogy link gives tips on what the service can and cannot do.

Here's what you can get:

♦ Basic research assistance related to genealogy, U.S. local history, and heraldry

♦ Answers to queries requiring resources unique to the Library of Congress

♦ Response within five business days

However, you cannot get extensive research in genealogy or heraldry. If you cannot find the answers to your questions on the general links, you can e-mail your question to a librarian. Furthermore, certain topics, such as American Memory, have specific times of day when a librarian is available for a live, web-based chat.

National Archives and Records Administration

Since the last edition of this book, the NARA site has been completely revamped, from the URL, which is now www.archives.gov/index.html, to the guides and tips for genealogists. Printer-friendly versions of the web pages, news, and events notices, a drop-down box with direct access to web pages (see Figure 9-3), a site index, and an FAQ page are just some of the improvements. The result is a site that gives you much-needed improvements in navigation, uniformity, and appearance. Furthermore, there is now accessibility to users with disabilities.

Now, floundering around the NARA site trying to find the genealogy stuff is a thing of the past! The site's pages now work in intuitive and consistent ways, making it easier for you to find what you are looking for and know where you are within the website. There are specific pages for researching African-American and Native American genealogy (see Chapter 14), for FAQs, and for helpful pages that are not part of NARA but may help your search, governmental and otherwise.

With an eye-catching image of the National Archives Rotunda, the opening page has easy access to the website's major topic areas, which allow browsing and searching through information about federal government records, services provided by the National Archives, and online presentations of exhibits. The drop-down box at the top has the most-used pages of the site, including genealogy.

FIGURE 9-3.   *The redesigned NARA site is much easier to navigate for genealogists.*

The Genealogy Page

This is a general outline of the finding aids, guides, and research tools to help you for preparing yourself before you visit one of the NARA facilities, for requesting records from NARA, or for using the Web to look for information. It links you to various documents and sites for specific genealogy tasks.

Notice the list Genealogy News and Events on the genealogy page (see Figure 9-4), which is where NARA workshops are announced. As noted in Chapter 5, attending workshops such as these can help you with techniques and resources you might otherwise take years to uncover.

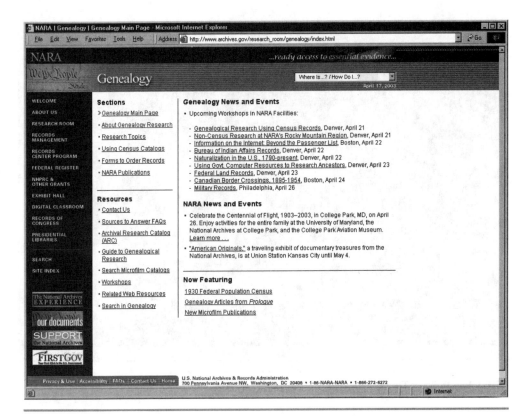

FIGURE 9-4. *The Genealogy page on the NARA site includes a list of workshops.*

You still want to start at the Research Room link in the navigation bar to the left of the opening page and go to Genealogy from there, or you can go straight to www.archives.gov/research_room/genealogy. Here you'll find information for beginners, such as the page "About Genealogy Research" and a list of research topics in genealogy with links to NARA resources that deal with them. Worth a read: The message from John W. Carlin, Archivist of the United States, about the perennial urban legend that the NARA is going to start limiting access to the records genealogists need.

More advanced genealogists will want to read about the census catalogs, the online catalogs, Soundex indexing, and the latest additions to the collection. All genealogists should read the FAQ file, the latest list of genealogy workshops, and the information on the latest version of the NARA Archival Information Locator (NAIL).

After touring this general help, you're ready to tackle the specific resources on the NARA site.

NARA Web Databases

You can search various subsets of the NARA holdings from their web databases, starting at search.nara.gov. Click Search in the navigation bar at the top of every page in the NARA site to get there.

On the Search page, you can input any term and search the entire NARA website. You can also search individual databases, which find items that could be on other websites, on the NARA website, or might be at some regional NARA site.

To search the main site, simply put in a term or two in the box at the top. Entering **Powell genealogy**, for example, gets over 2,000 hits—obviously an embarrassment of riches! Note, however, you can search the results to narrow them down, you can exclude the Presidential Libraries, and so on. So, instead, you might want to choose Advanced Search.

On the Advanced Search page, you can uncheck the boxes by the sites to search:

◆ Main: Full text of all web pages

◆ Presidential Libraries: Full text of all web pages on Presidential Library websites

◆ ARDOR, a prototype collection of selected federal agency records' schedules and manuals

You can also define search words in Boolean terms: must (AND), must not (NOT), and should (OR). You can limit the date of the results and how many hits to display on a page.

Using genealogy as a "should" term and Powell as a "must" term, searching only www.archives.gov, still gets over 2,000 hits. But making both terms "must" cuts the results down to 123. You can see how the advanced search can be a powerful tool.

AAD

The Access to Archival Databases (AAD) page is outlined in the Spring 2003 issue of *Prologue,* the NARA quarterly publication. AAD gives you a way to search a selection of nearly 50 million historic electronic records created by more than 20 federal agencies on a wide range of topics. It also gives you the ability to search for records with the specific information that you seek, important contextual information to help you understand the records better (including code lists), explanatory notes from NARA archivists, and for some series or files in AAD, related documents.

> ## Note
>
> *Go to the Prologue Magazine link in the drop-down box at the top of every page, or directly at www.archives.gov/publications/prologue/index.html.*

You can reach the AAD from the drop-down box at the top of every page in the NARA site, or you can go directly to www.archives.gov/aad/index.html.

On your first visit to the page, use the AAD Pathfinder (from the link on the left or at www.archives.gov/aad/getting_started.html), a graphical representation of the overall AAD research process, to see how to use the system. You can see where you are in the process at any time by clicking the "Where Am I?" link. You'll also find a narrative overview and a sample search to help you understand how to use AAD.

Finding what you need is a three-step process. You will first need to determine the series and file unit that may contain the information you want, because AAD will permit you to search only one data file at a time.

To begin, you have to determine which series you want to search. AAD provides several avenues to assist you. NARA's archivists have categorized all the series in AAD into the following areas.

♦ All Series

♦ People

♦ Indexes to Other Records

♦ Subject

♦ Geographic Areas

♦ Organization

♦ Time Spans

♦ Creator

Select an area, and it will display either further subtopics or a list of series.

Click any series title, and the next page will show information about the series, such as why it was created and how it was used. This should help you decide if the records in the series are relevant to your research. Each series has one or more file units associated with it.

Clicking the file unit will provide further information about it. The file units will have one or more data files associated with them.

Next, you can search a data file. AAD will allow you to search only one data file at a time. Once you have selected a data file, you will need to determine the columns (or data fields) and the values you want to use to build your search.

Finally, you display the results. After you submit your search, AAD will display all the records that match your request. You can select the ones for which you want to see the full record, or you can print out the results of your search or download them.

On the Record Detail page, AAD provides the meaning for many of the columns where only coded values exist in the original data file.

ARC

The Archival Research Catalog (ARC) is the online catalog of 20 percent of NARA's nationwide holdings in the Washington, D.C. area, Regional Archives, and Presidential Libraries.

> ### Note
> *You access ARC by selecting it from the drop-down box at the top of the page, or directly at www.archives.gov/research_room/ arc/index.html.*

ARC has replaced its prototype, the NARA Archival Information Locator (NAIL). You can still perform keyword, digitized image, and location searches. ARC's advanced functionalities also allow you to search by organization, person, and topic. The NARA staff is working to expand the catalog, and eventually it will reflect all the holdings.

Part of what is so wonderful about this updated catalog is the quick access to specific collections, such as the Guion-Miller Roll Index, the Index to the Final Rolls (Dawes)—two censuses of Native American populations from the 1800s and early 1900s—the World War II Army and Army Air Force Casualty List, and the World War II Navy, Marine, and Coast Guard Casualty List.

ALIC

The Archives Library Information Center (ALIC) is designed to provide NARA staff and researchers nationwide with convenient access to content beyond the physical holdings of the two traditional libraries. ALIC provides access to information on American history and government, archival administration, information management, and government documents to NARA staff, archives- and records-management professionals, and the general public.

Note

Access ALIC from the drop-down box at the top of every page, or directly at www.archives.gov/research_room/alic/index.html.

The Archive Library Information Center pages have links to collected resources on specific topics. The genealogy one, at www.archives.gov/research_room/alic/reference_desk/genealogy_links.html, has links to various government and private websites as well as articles of interest (see Figure 9-5). You can see in the figure that a host of topics, from Archives and Records to Women, are covered in this manner.

ERA

The Electronic Records Archives (ERA) will theoretically be helpful to genealogists a hundred years from now. The goal is to preserve the electronic records of the government, such as memos, e-mails, presidential speeches, and so on. As such, it has very recent records, and it's still a pilot program.

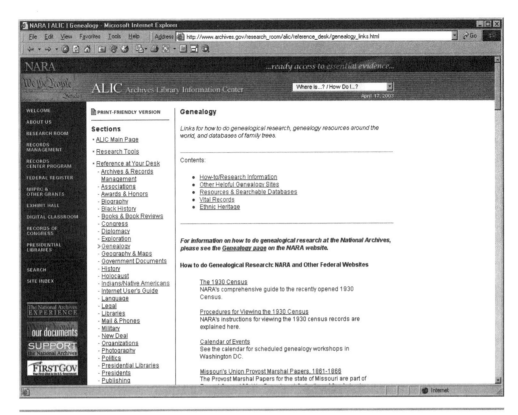

FIGURE 9-5.   *ALIC has pages that gather information and links together by topic.
Great for beginners!*

Note

*Get to the ERA from the drop-down box at the top of every NARA
page, or directly at www.archives.gov/electronic_records_ archives/
index.html.*

Microfilm Publications Search

From the NARA Genealogy page, you can click Search Microfilm Catalogs.
The catalogs list the various microfilms you can purchase, rent, or view

onsite from NARA; the 3,400 microfilms can be searched by keyword, microfilm ID, record group number, and/or NARA location.

Most of NARA's microfilm lists and descriptive pamphlets are not online. By searching for microfilm publications in the Microfilm Publications Catalog, however, you will be able to find out if a roll list or descriptive pamphlet is available. You will need to contact one of the NARA locations listed in the Viewing Location field(s) of the microfilm publication description to find out how to get a copy of the descriptive pamphlet or roll list.

Federal Register Publications

The *Federal Register* is a legal newspaper published every business day by the National Archives and Records Administration (NARA). It contains federal agency regulations; proposed rules and notices; and executive orders, proclamations, and other presidential documents. NARA's Office of the Federal Register prepares the *Federal Register* for publication in partnership with the Government Printing Office (GPO), which distributes it in paper form, on microfiche, and on the World Wide Web.

NARA Library Catalog

If you click the link for the NARA Library Catalog from the search page, you get another page that directs you to www.archives.gov/ research_room/alic/research_tools/online_public_access_catalog.html. Some of the research tools are available only to the archivists at NARA, which means you must go to a NARA facility and ask the staff to do the search for you to get the actual record or document you're looking for.

Other parts of the NARA Library Catalog, however, are available from the Web. As explained in Chapter 12, looking at a card catalog before you go can save you a lot of time and frustration during your visit. If what you need is available by loan or can be copied for a fee, it might save you a trip altogether.

You simply fill out a form with the desired terms. The page comes back just the same as before, except the number of hits is shown in red at the top. You then have to click the button that reads Display Search Results. From the resulting page, you can sort by subject or author as well as see complete records for the items you select.

As with any card catalog, you get the call number, details on the size of the work, and links to related items on the same subject.

Prologue

The quarterly NARA magazine *Prologue* has a web page you can link to from the NARA home page or go to directly at www.nara.gov/publications/prologue/prologue.html. Special issues, such as the recent "Federal Records in African-American Research," may be posted almost in their entirety, but usually a regular issue has one or two features on the website, plus the regular column, *Genealogy Notes*. A list of previous columns can be found at www.nara.gov/publications/prologue/artlist .html#genea. This site is worth bookmarking.

Some Experience Helpful

Much of what is available at the LOC and NARA sites would be most helpful for intermediate-to-advanced genealogists: The best way to use these sites is to know what you're looking for before you start, such as a specific military record or a particular Work Projects Administration (WPA) oral history from the 1930s. The beginner will find the schedules of workshops on the NARA and the how-to articles on the LOC helpful, as well.

Bureau of Immigration and Naturalization

Under the "About Us" section of the Bureau of Immigration and Naturalization (BIN) home page, you'll find the History, Genealogy, and Education page at www.immigration.gov/graphics/aboutus/history/index.htm. Here, you can find a lot of good tips, guides, and information (see Figure 9-6).

Information you can retrieve online includes articles on immigration history, some naturalization records, and information on the Chinese Records. Some of these links from the BIN take you to the NARA, but the BIN site has explanations of these resources.

Immigration Records

The site has pages explaining ports of entry, their records, and links to each state with a port, as well as a list of U.S. cities with ports of entry from Canada. The Immigration Arrival Records page has links to

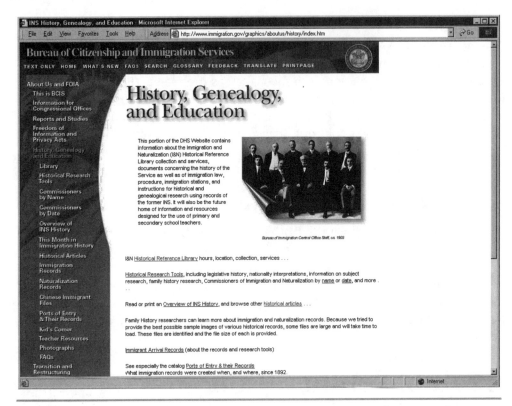

FIGURE 9-6. *The Bureau of Immigration and Naturalization site has a page for guiding genealogists to records.*

information of these and other topics, such as ships' passenger lists (Ellis Island and other entry points) and an overview of the history of the BIN.

Of special interest will be the historical articles, including "Changing Immigrant Names," which shows some of the variations that can occur, "Women and Naturalization," and the series "This Month in Immigration History."

Naturalization Records

Many of the links from here will take you back to the NARA, but the site points out that Immigration and Naturalization Service (INS) naturalization certificate files, known as *C-Files,* include all U.S. naturalizations from all states and territories, and from all courts (federal, state, and local). The INS maintains an index to the C-Files and can retrieve individual records based on name, date of birth, and place of birth. C-Files from 1906 to 1956 have been microfilmed and are available via a Freedom of Information/Privacy Act request to the INS headquarters in Washington, D.C.

For naturalization records after 1956, Freedom of Information requests should be sent to the appropriate INS district office.

Chinese Records

Responsibility for enforcement of U.S. Chinese Exclusion law transferred to the Immigration and Naturalization Service in 1903, and continued until repeal of the Chinese Exclusion Act in 1943. The old Chinese Service transferred into the INS along with its records, which the INS maintained as a separate set until 1908. Those files on Chinese matters kept separate from general immigration files at Washington, D.C., until 1908, are referred to as *Segregated Chinese Files* and are today found at the National Archives in Washington, D.C. The INS continued to file records of Chinese in separate file series at major ports of entry and district offices, and those files are today found at Regional Archives across the country.

Several articles on these records are on the site; links to them are in the table at the bottom of the page at www.immigration.gov/graphics/aboutus/history/chinese.htm.

Library

The INS has a Historical Reference Library in Washington, D.C. The I&N Historical Reference Library collection focuses primarily on the history of the Immigration and Naturalization Service and its predecessor agencies, then on the history of immigration to the United States and the history of the federal government in general. Their text collection has an automated catalog, in addition to books, periodicals, and other published sources, as well as agency publications and unpublished reports, studies, papers, and other documents dating from the turn of the twentieth century to the present. The catalog is not online at this time. The library also has a collection of uncatalogued photographs, videotapes, and other media.

Another Source

In 2001, the Statue of Liberty-Ellis Island Foundation published an online database of records from Ellis Island during the peak immigration years (1892–1924). This database of 22 million names—representing 60 percent of all United States immigration records—has opened the floodgates for a huge increase in the number of amateur genealogists. Jupiter Media Metrix listed the Ellis Island site in its latest "Top Newcomers" list. See Chapter 11 for an explanation of how to use this site.

Government Land Records

I just "glowed" when I found this resource, the Government Land Office (GLO) site. You can search for, and view online, original land grants and patents between 1820 and 1928.

Note

Land patents document the transfer of land ownership from the federal government to individuals. These land patent records include the information recorded when ownership was transferred.

Land Patent Searches

Go to www.glorecords.blm.gov and click Search Land Patents in the navigation bar. Input the state and name, and you'll get a list of matching records. For individual records, you can see a summary, the legal land description, and the document image (see Figure 9-7). You can also order a certified copy. In addition, you will find a link to a glossary page with details on what the search fields mean.

This site does not cover the 13 colonies, their territories, and a few other states, although the site does have resource links for most states. This is because in the very early years of the United States, the Congress of the Confederation declared it would sell or grant the unclaimed lands in "the West" (that is, what is now Alabama, Michigan, parts of

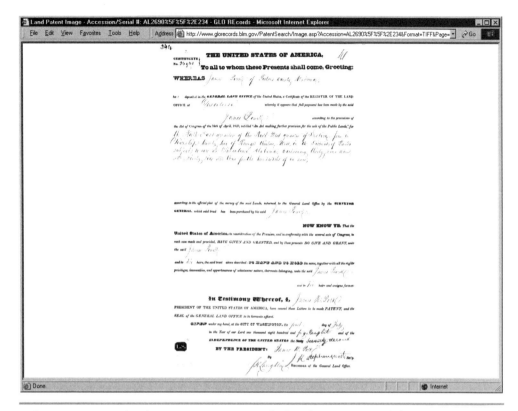

FIGURE 9-7. *A land patent to James Powell of Pickens County, Alabama, 1820.*

Minnesota, Mississippi, Illinois, Indiana, Ohio, and Wisconsin). The United States could then sell this unclaimed land to raise money for the Treasury. In turn, the United States gave up its claims to any land within the boundaries of the original colonies.

Not all states are available now, but they are working hard to include them. There is a page with links to state pages that can help in deeds, grants, and patents concerning land at www.glorecords.blm.gov/visitors/StateResearch.asp.

Maps

A PDF file at www.or.blm.gov/lo/Maps-Index.pdf will show you how to order maps of various documents and maps concerning the Bureau of

Land Management and its holdings. The Montana division has maps of Montana as well as North and South Dakota at www.mt.blm.gov/faq/ maps/index.html.

Note _____

Remember a PDF file needs Acrobat Reader to be displayed. You can get Acrobat at www.adobe.com/products/acrobat/.

Getting Certified Copies

With the online shopping cart, you may request certified copies of land patents electronically or through the mail. Hard copy will be on a letter-sized sheet of paper (8.5 × 11 inches) of your preference (plain bond or parchment paper).

Census Records

U.S. census records are available in a variety of forms, both online and offline. For other countries, check out Census Links, http://censuslinks .com/, which has transcriptions of censuses such as "Roll of Emigrants That Have Been Sent to the Colony of Liberia, Western Africa, by the American Colonization Society and Its Auxiliaries, to September, 1843" and "Ecclesiastical Census of Revilla (Mexico)—1780."

Another good source is the Archives of Canada. The first census in Canada was in 1666 by Intendant Jean Talon, who listed 3,215 inhabitants. Talon is considered the "father" of modern census taking in Canada. Regular censuses did not begin until 1841, however. Several Canadian censuses are searchable online at www.archives.ca.

Use your favorite search engine to find "census" and the country you are looking in to find other census resources. For example, Brazil's census information has an English page at www1.ibge.gov.br/english/ default.php.

Success Story: Stepping Back Through the Censuses

The Internet is one of the few spaces in genealogy that is friendly to people not running Windows, so instead of using CD-ROMs, I subscribe to Images Online at Ancestry.com for easy access to the handwritten census pages. Reading originals instead of relying on transcribers and indexers was part of my success in finding my great-great-grandparents. Tracking my family back through ten-year steps is what worked for me.

I had inherited a genealogical chart of my male Downs/Downes line in Connecticut, showing the names of the wives but nothing else about them. So I knew only that my great-grandmother was supposed to be a Charlotte Smith. First, the 1900 census showed my grandfather living with a Charlotte Thompson, described as "Mother" and shown as being born in 1849. The step back to 1890 had to be skipped, of course, because of the destruction of those records. Then the 1880 census showed my grandfather at the age of five living in Oxford, Connecticut with a Jane M. Burnett, who called him her grandson. This allowed me to leapfrog over the puzzle of my great-grandmother Charlotte and jump directly into the puzzle of my great-great-grandmother Jane.

Note

A fire in 1921 destroyed many of the original records of the 1890 census in Washington, D.C. An account of this incident is on the NARA site at www.archives.gov/publications/prologue/ spring_1996_1890_census_1.html.

I reasoned that for Charlotte to have been a Smith, it was necessary for this Jane M. Burnett also to have been a Smith when Charlotte was born, so I went to the 1850 census in search of Jane M. Smith. The 1850 schedules list everybody by name, but the index lists mostly heads of household—meaning that almost all wives and children are invisible until you read the original pages. After spending two months following the wrong Jane M. Smith with no baby Charlotte, I abandoned the index and started wading through every name in Oxford and then in the surrounding towns. In 1860 Naugatuck, I found a Jane M. Smith whose age fit that of Jane M. Burnett, but still no Charlotte.

Tracking that family back into the 1850 census, I couldn't find them in Naugatuck or in Oxford, but I did find them next door in Middlebury. And there, finally, was one-year-old Charlotte along with Jane and—for the first time with certainty—my great-great-grandfather David S. Smith. Since then, the census has helped me to solve many parts of the puzzle.

The next steps—back to 1840 and beyond—will be much more difficult, because those earlier schedules do not list names of family members except for the head of household. But I am very happy with my success so far.

—Alan Downes

The Census Bureau

The Census Bureau generally provides only summary and statistical information for the first 72 years after a census is taken. The data on individuals is kept private until then. That means the 1930 census is the most recent available for public use.

The only services the Census Bureau provides related to genealogy are the Age Search Service and the counts of names from the 1990 census.

The Census Bureau does not have old census forms available. Copies of decennial census forms from 1790 through 1930 are available on microfilm, for research at the U.S. National Archives and Records Administration in Washington, D.C., at Archives Regional Centers, and at select federal depository libraries throughout the United States. In addition, these records are available at various other libraries and research facilities throughout the United States.

The other important information at the Census Bureau site is their FAQ at www.census.gov/genealogy/www/faqgene.txt.

CDs and Microfilms

Several vendors provide CD-ROMs and microfilm of census records—sometimes images of the actual census form, and sometimes transcriptions. Here's a list of some of them:

- ◆ AllCensus.com
- ◆ Ancestry.com

- CensusDiggins.com

- Everton.com

- FamilySearch (LDS)

- Genealogy Today

- HeritageQuest

- SK Publishing

Your local library, LDS Family History Center, or genealogy club may also have copies of these microfilms and/or CD-ROMs with census images.

Online Searches

Ancestry.com and Genealogy.com have subscription-based services to let you search indexes of U.S. federal censuses and view the original pages. These are usually worth the money for at least a year's subscription, once you know what you are looking for.

The UK 1901 census is available for searching online at www.census .pro.gov.uk/. This site had a disastrous beginning: When it first went online, it had over a million hits in the first hours, the server crashed, and it was months before it was back up. Like Ancestry.com and Genealogy.com, you can search the index for free, but looking at the actual record costs a fee. Unlike Ancestry.com and Genealogy.com, you can pay per record, not subscribe for a length of time to look at the records. Viewing transcribed data costs 50p for an individual and then 50p for a list of all other people in that person's household. Viewing a digital image of the census page costs 75p.

Transcriptions

As mentioned earlier, www.censuslinks.com is one way to find census transcriptions from around the world. Christines' Genealogy Website (ccharity.com) also has an active volunteer transcription project, emphasizing African-American censuses. Also check Cyndi's List at www.cyndislist.com/census.htm. But the best place to find online

Some Census Sites

The Froyle Archive (www.froyle.demon.co.uk) is the official website of the village of Froyle in Hampshire, UK, with all census returns, baptisms, marriages, and burials.

The Ayrshire Free Census Project (www.speakeasy.org/ ~jgribble/ayr.html) aims to transcribe all nineteenth-century Ayrshire census records and upload them to a free-to-view online database. This is part of FreeCEN: UK Census Online Project.

Massac County, Illinois History and Genealogy (www.rootsweb .com/~ilmassa2/) is an ongoing project to transcribe records of births, cemetery records and tombstones, census pages, death records, land grants, marriages, obituaries, biographies, and wills.

1920 Yavapai County, Arizona Census Index online (http://sharlot .org/archives/census/index.html) is a local project. The Sharlot Hall Museum in Prescott, Arizona has posted transcriptions of the 1870, 1880, 1900, and 1920 Yavapai County census indexes. Genealogists can search the 1870, 1880, and 1900 census indexes for names and partial names and get page numbers.

African-American Census Schedules (www.afrigeneas.com/ aacensus) is a volunteer project to transcribe pre-1870 census schedules.

transcriptions of censuses around the world is at the USGenWeb project, at www.rootsweb.com/~usgenweb/cen_img.htm (see Figure 9-8).

Click Census Surname Search from the USGenWeb home page and then use the form to search all the census records or to narrow your search by state or year.

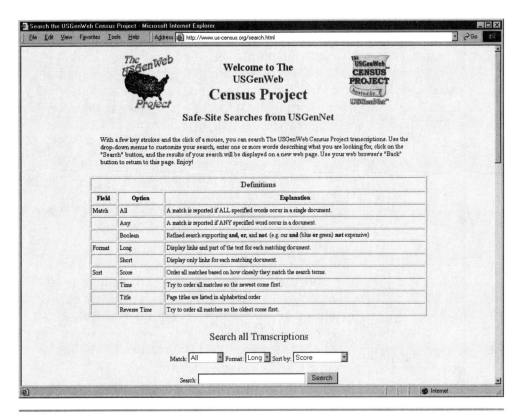

FIGURE 9-8.   *At the USGenWeb census site, you can search by surname.*

Be Part of the Project!

An important aspect of online genealogy is giving back to the resources on the Web. A great way to do this is to participate in the Census Project.

The USGenWeb Census Project was created to coordinate a U.S. federal census transcription effort. The mission is to recruit and guide volunteer transcribers in achieving the goal of providing free access to online research data for everyone. Each transcription will bear the transcriber's copyright and will be housed in the Census FTP Archives, maintained free of charge for all researchers to use. It's an ambitious project, and the 1930 census reel numbers and enumeration district descriptions have been added to the project.

To join the project as a transcriber, first check the Transcription Assignments section to see if the state, county, and year of your interest is available for assignment. The USGenWeb Census Project also provides "transcribing help" FAQs. Every transcriber must find a proofreader. You can volunteer to proofread a transcription by going to the Proofreader Exchange, filling out the form, and noting in the comments the censuses in which you are interested.

You must obtain access to copies of the census that you have chosen, either by renting or purchasing a microfilm or CD-ROM or by finding copies locally. A few census resources have been donated for transcription, but the project itself does not provide the original census material to be transcribed.

It will take a lot of folks to complete this project; try to be one of them!

State and Local Sources

Besides the U.S. federal census, some state and local governments will have taken censuses for tax purposes. Such states include Illinois, Iowa, Kansas, Massachusetts, Michigan, Minnesota, New Jersey, New York, and Wisconsin, to name a few.

You can often trace the migration of families in America when state census records are used with other records, such as the federal census after 1850; family bibles; death certificates; church, marriage, military, probate, and land records; and other American genealogical sources.

A major reference source is *State Census Records,* by Ann S. Lainhart (Genealogical Publishing Company, 1992); also check FamilySearch, or the catalog of a library, under your state of interest and then under the headings "Census – Indexes" and "Census" (see Chapters 10 and 12).

Search the Internet to see if state and local censuses have been indexed. See especially the AIS Census Indexes at Ancestry.com (searching Ancestry's indexes is free; seeing the original record is for paid subscribers only).

State Archives and Libraries

Many state archives and libraries have vital records and census information. For example, www.nysl.nysed.gov/genealogy/vitrec.htm is a guide to getting genealogical records from the state of New York. The Alabama Archives has a list of available census information from the state's early years, at www.archives.state.al.us/referenc/census .html. Search for the state you need, along with "census" or "archives," to find such sources.

Local Sources

Sometimes you can't find a birth, marriage, or death record in the "official" sources. In these cases, you can look in county and city court records, newspapers, cemetery and funeral home records, and local libraries. These sources can give you clues to parentage, marriages, and burials, which can help you discover where the records may be located—or that the records were destroyed in some way.

Wrapping Up

- ◆ The Library of Congress (LOC) and the National Archives and Records Administration (NARA) have online guides to genealogy, as well as some full-text and scanned-image resources.

- ◆ Both the LOC and NARA have several search functions to help you find records and materials.

- ◆ The Government Land Office (GLO) has original land records, viewable online, as well as certified copies.

- ◆ The Bureau of Immigration and Naturalization (BIN) has a web page of history and helps for the genealogist.

- Many volunteer projects are transcribing census records; you can also buy access to images and census records on CD-ROM.

- Using the online versions of these resources can help you before you visit a physical location—and visiting the physical location might be necessary.

Chapter 10

The Church of Jesus Christ of Latter-day Saints

The genealogy research work of the members of The Church of Jesus Christ of Latter-day Saints is unsurpassed in scope and size. Every genealogist needs to know how to use this wonderful resource.

FamilySearch Internet

The FamilySearch Internet Genealogy Service (www.FamilySearch.org) is a World Wide Web service sponsored by The Church of Jesus Christ of Latter-day Saints to help people find and share family history information. Launched in May 1999, it is the largest genealogical database ever to go on the Internet, where you can search for more than 400 million names of people who have died. These names are mostly from the United States, Canada, and the British Isles and have taken decades to compile. In addition, years have been spent developing, engineering, and improving core internal systems to provide this resource. Using the site (the opening page is shown in Figure 10-1) is free, although you can order some products, such as databases on CD-ROM and research guides.

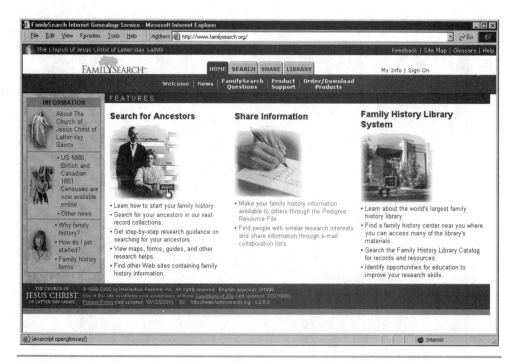

FIGURE 10-1.   *The FamilySearch site is one of the most important online genealogy resources.*

Here's a list of the main resources on the site:

- Ancestral File (explained later in the chapter)

- The 1880 United States, 1881 British Isles, and the 1881 Canadian censuses

- The International Genealogical Index, or IGI (explained later in the chapter)

- The Pedigree Resource File, or PRF, which is the collection of genealogical information uploaded to FamilySearch since its launch in 1999

- The U.S. Social Security Death Index

- The Vital Records Index for Mexico and Scandinavia

- The Search Family History websites

The FamilySearch site protects privacy in two ways: The data on the site is already publicly available at other locations, and living people are not identified.

Records contained in the Family History Library and in the FamilySearch databases have been collected from a wide variety of sources. Individuals, families, and genealogical societies donate records to the Family History Library; the library also purchases other records, such as the U.S. Social Security Death Index, census records, and published family or county histories. Most of the microfilm collection has been produced by the Family History Department's own international effort to microfilm original sources. An index to many of these records is available online through the Family History Library Catalog. In cooperation with legal custodians of records worldwide, Family History Department employees are currently supervising microfilming projects in 47 countries.

Note

Both www.familysearch.org and www.familysearch.com work as URLs for the site.

Often what you get is a reference to a document on microfilm that you can rent or buy. The Church of Jesus Christ of Latter-day Saints put the 1880 U.S. and 1881 Canadian censuses online recently. New visitor traffic surged immediately to more than 500 percent and remained six to ten times above normal the following week. You can also search the Vital Records Index for Mexico and Scandinavia.

FamilySearch Internet is designed to be a first step in searching for family history information. When you're searching LDS proprietary sources, the first screen doesn't give you the information itself. The search results simply tell you if the information you need is available, with links to the website, Family History Library Catalog citation, International Genealogical Index (IGI), Ancestral File (AF) reference, or citation in one of the CD-ROMs the LDS has for sale.

This is more helpful than it sounds, however. Just finding a match in the Family History Library Catalog can save you hours of research. Some FHCs are so busy, patrons are only allowed one hour a week at the computer! Searching the catalog before you go can make your trip much more productive. Finding a reference in the CD-ROMs might tell you whether it's worth the price for you to order it. Finding a reference in the IGI or AF can tell you if someone else has already found the primary record or source you're looking for, and sometimes how to contact the person who found it. In short, this can save you a lot of time and travel. Only rarely, though, can you use this resource to get to primary (original record) sources.

Most of the records in FamilySearch Internet are abstracts. If you find a reference to a record you want in the LDS sources, you usually can get a complete copy of it from a Family History Center (FHC). FHCs are located throughout the world and have many of the records found in FamilySearch Internet. You learn more about FHCs later in the chapter.

Another big advantage to this site is that it has more international data than most online sources. Although the greatest part of the data is from English-speaking countries, you can find some information from every continent. Asian sources are the most limited, whereas North American and European sources are the most abundant.

Some Background

Mormons consider it a religious duty to research their family history. The Church teaches that families are eternal, and for more than a century and a half, members have been encouraged to identify their deceased ancestors. A detailed explanation can be found at the LDS home site, www.lds.org. One of the LDS Church's objectives is to build its copyrighted databases, known as the AF and the IGI, and to continually improve their accuracy and the software used to search them. The IGI is a record of the Temple work.

The AF offers pedigrees the IGI doesn't. The PRF is all secondary material submitted by volunteers.

The results are archived at the church's headquarters in Salt Lake City, Utah and distributed in microfilm, microfiche, and CD-ROM to their many Family History Centers throughout the world. The data is in several forms, but the most important to the online genealogist are the AF and the IGI. The Family History Department maintains a climate-controlled, underground storage facility to safeguard master copies of all its microfilm records. The storage facility, built literally into a mountainside, is located about 25 miles from downtown Salt Lake City.

IGI

The International Genealogical Index (IGI) lists the dates and places of births, christenings, and marriages for more than 285 million deceased people. The index includes people who lived at any time after the early 1500s up through the early 1900s. These names have been researched and extracted from thousands of original records. Most of these records are compiled from public domain sources. The IGI database makes otherwise difficult-to-access information readily available to the public. You will find many duplicate records in IGI; in most cases, the duplication is caused by multiple people submitting the same name with slight variations in the data. When working on family history research, individuals are encouraged to contact other family members who are working on the same family lines so that duplication of information may be eliminated.

The IGI you view at the local Family History Center and the Internet version have the same data, but the Internet and Family History Center versions display that data differently:

- The Internet displays all events and relationships.

- The CD-ROM version displays only one event per entry.

The Internet version is updated more frequently and contains more information. However, you still have to order the documents by film number, just as you do with the CD-ROM version.

The IGI contains two basic kinds of entries: submissions by individual LDS members of data on their ancestors (which may or may not be accurate), and submissions from the extraction program, which is a systematic and well-controlled volunteer program of the church. Members all over the world extract birth or christening dates, as well as marriage dates and locations from microfilms of original parish and civil records.

The source of the data from information provided for each entry is on the CD-ROM version of the IGI. But, always remember, the IGI is only an index. You should go to the source document to verify the information.

AF

The Ancestral File contains a compilation of genealogies of families from around the world and records that have been contributed by thousands of people, including users of the Church's Family History Library and Family History Centers. The information—mostly data about people who have died—is linked into pedigrees to show both ancestors and descendants of individuals. The file contains more than 35 million names.

PRF

The Pedigree Resource File is a searchable database of submissions from new FamilySearch Internet users. The Pedigree Resource File grows at the rate of 1.2 million names per month. Forty percent of the database is from outside North America and the British Isles.

The Pedigree Resource File contains compiled pedigrees submitted by users via the FamilySearch Internet Genealogy Service or gathered from printed family histories and other sources, including government archives. The Pedigree Resource File is becoming a reservoir of names to help individuals identify and link their ancestors.

The Pedigree Resource File is similar to the Ancestral File, and they're growing rapidly. The Pedigree Resource File is a new lineage-linked pedigree file containing genealogical data. Like the well-known AF, it contains pedigrees and family group sheet data in electronic form. Unlike the Ancestral File, it contains notes and source documentation, which varies in thoroughness, and it only contains the data as of that moment. Data isn't updated from CD-ROM to CD-ROM unless the submitter resubmits it for inclusion on another CD-ROM. It is almost all secondary material.

Using These Resources

The IGI, the AF, and the PRF are unrelated because data entered in one file doesn't necessarily show up in the other file. Each has a value of its own, and all files are worth searching. The advantage of the AF is that you can get pedigrees from it. The advantage of the IGI is that it provides more detailed information. The PRF has the work of other genealogists, which makes it one or two times removed from the original sources, but it's useful nonetheless.

Most non-LDS genealogists see the IGI as the more valuable of the two. Although errors turn up in both, the IGI is closer to the original records (data is normally entered into the IGI first), and it has excellent bits and pieces of information, especially its references to where the information originated. Therefore, many non-LDS genealogists always go to the IGI first, but the Ancestral File, with the new 5.5 GEDCOM format, enables you to find out what documentation supports the entry. Considering you can get the submitter's name and address, as well as pedigree or descendant charts, the Ancestral File is also a valuable resource.

Although errors do exist, the percentage seems low. Plenty of genealogy books printed in the past 100 years have more errors than these databases.

Treat the PRF, AF, and IGI the same way you treat a printed book about a surname—with informed caution. Use it as an excellent source of clues, but always crosscheck it with primary records. Although the computer increases the amount of data you can scan, making your work much easier, it doesn't necessarily improve accuracy. Human beings are still the source of the data.

Success Story: FamilySearch Proves a Family Legend

I had the names of my great-grandfather, his two brothers, and both parents—along with the name of the little town they were born and raised in Wales. For three years, I searched for evidence of the parents who were presumably named Hugh Jones and Mary Ellen Williams. The information was furnished by their grandson.

In the quest to acquire as much evidence as possible on every person in my line, I ran a query on the LDS site (www.familysearch.org). Some of this information is transcription, and some is by submission of family group sheets (without source citations). I was fortunate to find what could potentially be my great-grandfather's christening record as a transcribed set of bishop's records for the parish. Correct place, correct year, wrong parent names—or so I thought. I was able to run a query using the parents' names only so that I could find all birth records in that county where these two names appeared as mother and father. Sure enough, each of the other two boys and a bonus daughter appeared. The parents were Moses Jones and Elizabeth Jones.

Subsequent research further supports the information. In fact, both died before the grandson informant was even born! Perhaps he mistook an "adopted" set of grandparents as his own... who knows? Three years of trying blown away by a total of five minutes worth of Internet research. I use the Internet for a large portion of my research.

—*Heather Jones DeGeorge*

The LDS apparently wants to make the AF and IGI available to more people. Originally, you had to visit the Family History Library in Salt Lake City, Utah to use these databases. Today, that library has CD-ROMs on a LAN that's connected to the Joseph Smith Memorial Building next door and about 200 access terminals scattered about the buildings.

About 15 years ago, the church set up local Family History Centers (FHCs) around the world. In 1988, they started selling the databases on microfiche. In 1991, the Church released them on CD-ROM to their local centers, and later to societies and libraries. The New England Historic Genealogical Society has a copy at their library in Boston, as does the California State Sutro Library in San Francisco.

The pattern here is more and more access via more and more means. The Mormons are cautious, though, and they take small steps, one at a time. The Church hasn't worked out all the legalities of online access, and it's concerned about presenting a useful, viable program and database for its members and the rest of the world. The main concern of the Church is not to turn out a bad product.

A Run-Through

The opening page of FamilySearch Internet was shown in Figure 10-1. To the left is a navigation bar with links to information on the Mormon church and genealogy in general. On the top is a navigation bar to the most-often used features of the site. It's worth your while to click "Why Family History?" and "How Do I Get Started?" (see Figure 10-2) on this page. These take you to basic how-to files.

On every page, you will see four tabs on the navigation bar: Home, Search, Share, and Library.

Home Tab

Under the Home tab, you find links to the resources: Search for Ancestors, Share Information, and Family History Library System under the word "Welcome" in the navigation bar. All of these are explained later in this chapter.

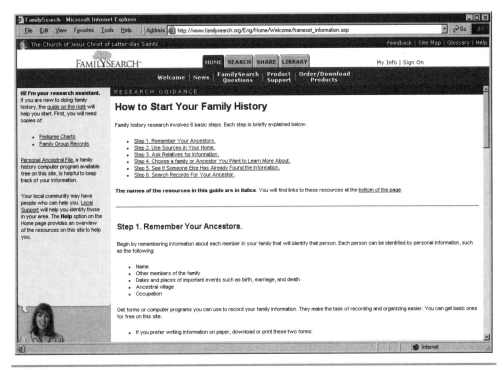

FIGURE 10-2.   *"How Do I Get Started?" is a good beginner's guide to genealogy on the FamilySearch site.*

The News link is where you go to find out about new features, updates, and news releases on the sites.

Family Search Questions is the link to the FAQ files for the site. There you'll find answers to common questions about everything from GEDCOMs to the Church. The About the Church link presents some basic beliefs about The Church of Jesus Christ of Latter-day Saints and allows people to request more information if they desire.

Product Support helps you with frequently asked questions about each product, as well as provides questions organized by topics, common solutions, information about how to contact people locally who may be able to help you, and instructions on how to use the built-in online support that comes with the many CD-ROMs and other software you can buy from the LDS Church.

Order/Download Products is the link to the online store, which offers books, forms, CD-ROMs, and other items. You can also download the free PAF program using this option. All you have to do is register. The new PAF version has a Palm computer option.

Search Tab

Click Search for Ancestors, and you get the screen shown in Figure 10-3. You can type information about an ancestor and find out whether any of the cataloged Internet sites, resource files, and donated information available through the service may contain additional information about the ancestor. You can search through all resources or choose just one from the Ancestral File; the 1880 United States, 1881 British Isles, or the 1881 Canadian census; the IGI; the PRF; the U.S. Social Security Death Index; the Index to Vital Records from Mexico and Scandinavia; and the catalog of genealogical websites.

You can get to the same page by clicking the Search for Ancestors link from the Home/Welcome page. The link above the input form—Tips on How to Search for Your Ancestors—is worth exploring. This tells you in plain language what can work and what won't work on the search page (you can't search for just a given name, for example), and how to narrow your search.

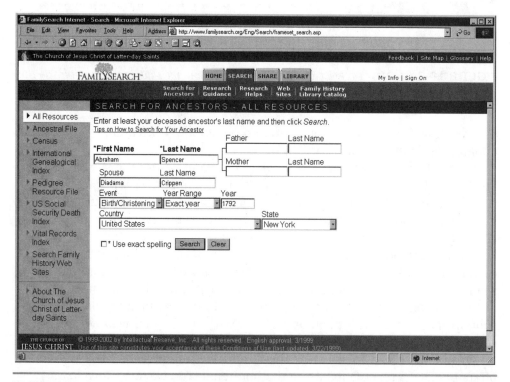

FIGURE 10-3. *Enter your search terms in the boxes on the Search screen. Default searches all databases.*

Using a pedigree chart form on this screen, you can input only a last name, or both first and last names, and even the names of a spouse and parents if you know them. Of course, the more information you put in, the fewer matches you get. The less specific you are, the more matches you get.

I searched for my family's most elusive ancestor, Abraham Spencer. We know he was born in New York in 1792, so I limited my search to that year and to the United States. The results are shown in Figure 10-4.

The record gives the known data, with links to download the information, view a pedigree of the individual, and the family group sheet.

The Research Guidance link goes to LDS publications. They are all online in PDF and HTML format; there are also links to order hard copies. Research Outlines on genealogy techniques and resources are alphabetized by location.

Research Outlines can help you decide what records to look for next. They list the best records to use, recommend the order in which to search them, provide step-by-step instructions for finding information in

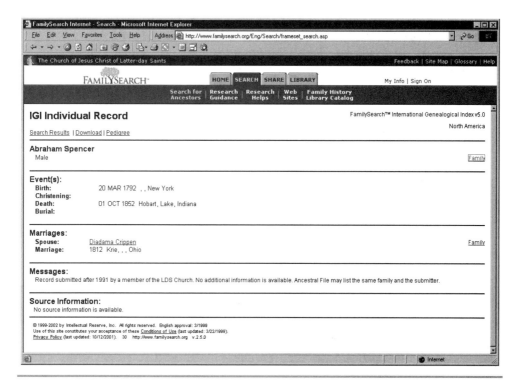

FIGURE 10-4.   *An IGI record for an individual shows the known data.*

the records, and tell you where the copies of the records may be located. Select a place where your ancestor was born, christened, married, or died. If you aren't sure of the country, click Determining the Country Where Your Ancestor Lived for some ways to nail it down. Only places for which research guides have been created are listed on the page. As more are added, they'll appear. So, for example, you can find guidance for Baden, Germany, but not for Zaire.

Research Helps is another way to access the Research Outlines, as well as many other publications, such as almanacs, gazetteers, and blank charts for organizing your research. These include forms, maps, historical backgrounds, information on how to find such documents from other sources, name variations, and so forth. You can sort the list of links by place, title, subject, or document type. You can sort by document type and choose helps that are forms, government publications, LDS research guides (excellent resources, and they're all available online!), maps, and word lists.

Web Sites links you to the catalog of genealogy sites that have been submitted and reviewed by genealogists. Like Yahoo!, this catalog is organized by category. The site has guidance on the quality and usefulness of other genealogy websites. Hundreds of volunteers review every genealogy-related website linked to the service and classify the sites according to an established cataloging system. The resulting index allows users to make advanced searches by category, place, surname, subject, country or locale, family relationship, and so forth.

Finally, Family History Library Catalog takes you to the FHL card catalog, which is discussed in the "Library" section.

Share Tab

Under the Share tab, shown in Figure 10-5, you find two links: Share My Genealogy and Collaboration E-Mail Lists.

Share My Genealogy allows you to submit personal genealogies in a GEDCOM format to the Church for preservation in the Granite Mountain Records Vault and to be published on CD-ROM in the PRF. Your information stays separate from the others in the PRF. (However, this same information may be submitted to other systems in the future, such as the Ancestral File.) You have to agree to this use before you upload. When you submit your data, it will all be available for searching through the PRF. When a person uses Search for Ancestors, the service searches the entire index. If it finds information that might be relevant,

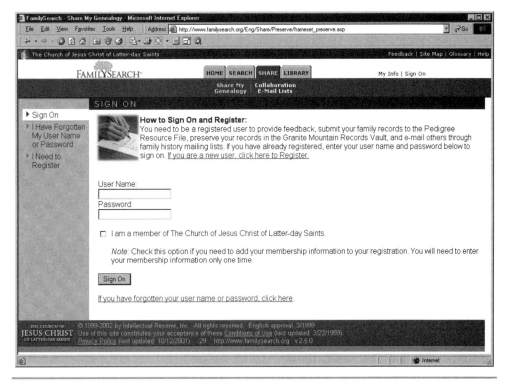

FIGURE 10-5. *The Share tab leads to discussion groups and GEDCOM upload.*

the user gets a reference to which resource (AF, PRF, IGI, and so on) had matches.

To participate, you have to fill out the free registration form.

The Collaboration E-Mail Lists link takes you to the sign-up for mail lists. When I registered as a user and accepted the terms of service, I searched the mail lists, such as those shown in Figure 10-6.

One click on Join and I was a member of one of the lists. Lists exist for specific persons as well as for general surnames.

Library

The Library tab of the navigation bar leads to information on the Family History Library in Salt Lake City, a search form to find a Family History Center near you, an online version of the card catalog to the Family

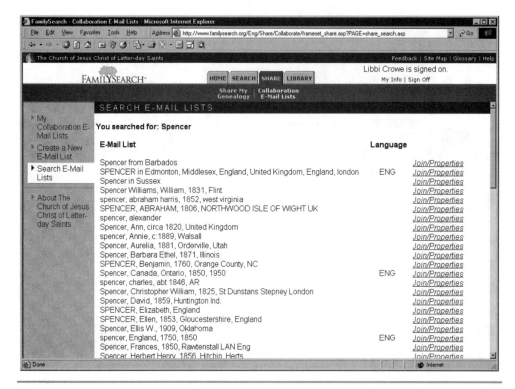

FIGURE 10-6. *Search the mail lists for the names or places that interest you, or start your own.*

History Library, and a list of courses and classes on the library and genealogy.

With a custom-built search engine, the Family History Library Catalog describes the library's more than 3 million microfilm, microfiche, and books, letting you pinpoint available resources. Many of the cataloged items can be ordered for use at any one of the more than 3,400 Family History Centers worldwide. This new search engine has been designed to search specifically for defined relationships, not just names.

Family History Library, the first selection on the Library tab's navigation bar, gives you details of how to find the Salt Lake City facility and some statistics on it.

Family History Centers is a link to a form to search for the FHC nearest you. As explained in the "A Visit to an FHC" section, FHCs are in LDS parishes and are considered branches of the Family History Library, providing access to most of the microfilms and microfiches in the FHL to help you in your research. The general public is welcome to come to the centers and use Family History Center resources.

Family History Library Catalog is a form for searching the holdings of the FHL in Salt Lake City. Click the Help link and you'll find hints on searching each available field: Surname, Place, Film/Fiche, Call Number, and Author. For example, the help files tell you that a surname search mainly finds family histories. The more of a surname that you type as a search term, the smaller the list of results will be.

The results list will have the title and author of each hit; click the title and you get the complete library record for that work, including its call number. You can use that to have the work, microfilm, or microfiche sent to your local FHC for a short time so that you can copy it or make notes.

> ## Note
>
> *The link to the left—Use Research Guidance to Find Catalog Records—takes you back to the Search tab page, which lists all the publications.*

Education in the navigation bar of this section will take you to a list of classes on genealogy offered at the FHL in Salt Lake City. There are also lists of publications from the library on subjects such as forms and letter-writing guides. You'll find a list of conferences and classes offered by other organizations, such as the National Genealogical Society, and a list of university and home-study courses. See Chapter 5 for more discussion on how valuable these can be.

Other Cool Stuff

You can use the site for records preservation: Families can already post their histories to their own or other websites, but some sites are transitory, lacking a commitment to long-term preservation. The FamilySearch website offers long-term storage. You can also use the site's message boards for online collaboration.

Even though you give LDS certain rights to your information, uploading it to FamilySearch Internet doesn't limit your right to publish, sell, or give the information you submit to others.

In Add a Site, you can register your existing genealogy site with FamilySearch Internet. The editors of the site then review your information and decide if it will be included in the database of web pages to be searched from the opening page of the site.

Freedman's Bank Records

You can buy on CD-ROM some records collected by the LDS Church; one such resource is the Freedman's Bank Records CD-ROM (see the following illustration). Released in February 2001 by the Church of Jesus Christ of Latter-day Saints, this database contains biographical information on the roughly 500,000 African-Americans who deposited money into Freedman's Bank following the Civil War. It is estimated that 8 to 10 million African-Americans living today have ancestors whose records are contained in the Freedman's database. This CD-ROM has records that cover 1864 to 1871 and document the names and family relationships of those who used the bank.

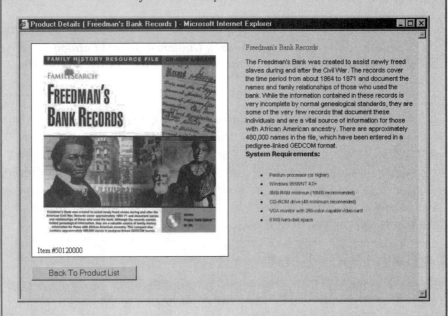

The information contained in these records is rather fragmentary by normal genealogical standards, but they are some of the very few records that document these individuals and are a vital source of information for those with African-American ancestry. There are approximately 480,000 names in the file, which have been entered in a pedigree-linked GEDCOM format. This means that they are indexed for searching; before this CD-ROM the records were available but unindexed, making them very hard to use. It took 11 years to complete the indexing and formatting for the CD-ROM.

> The Freedman's Bank Records CD-ROM is available at a cost of $6.50. It can be ordered over the Internet at www.familysearch.org or by calling Church Distribution Centers at 1-800-537-5971 and asking for item #50120.

A Visit to an FHC

Terry Morgan (terryann2@aol.com), Genealogy Forum Staff Member on America Online, is also a volunteer at the two FHCs in Huntsville, Alabama. These setups are typical, Terry says, and she gave me a personal tour of the one closest to our homes.

"The best way to find one near you is to look in the White Pages of the phone book for the nearest Church of Jesus Christ of Latter-day Saints," Terry says. "Call them and find out where the nearest FHC is, and the hours. Honestly, because the hours vary so much from place to place, the best time to call is Sunday morning around 10:00. Everyone's at church then!"

If you call any other time, she says, give the staffers lots of rings to answer the phones, which might be on the other side of the church from the FHC. Or you could write to the LDS main library at the address in the note and ask for the latest list of FHCs. An excellent list of FHCs is maintained by Cyndi Howells at www.cyndislist.com/lds.htm, and a list of the larger FHCs at the LDS home site can be found at www.familysearch.org/Eng/Library/FHC/frameset_fhc.asp.

Note

The contact information for the main Family History Library is
35 North West Temple Street
Salt Lake City, UT 84150-3400
Phone: (801) 240-2331 or (800) 453-3860 x22331
FAX: (801) 240-5551
E-mail: fhl@ldschurch.org

All FHCs are branches of the main LDS Family History Library in Salt Lake City. The typical FHC has a few rooms at the local Mormon church, with anywhere from one to ten computers, a similar number of microfilm and microfiche readers, and a collection of atlases, manuals, and how-to genealogy books.

The FHC I was visiting had two IBM-compatibles that shared a printer in a room with a small library of about 25 reference books. In a room close by were two film readers and two fiche readers. Users are asked to sign in and out, and a cork bulletin board holds the latest genealogical technique brochures from the Salt Lake City Family History Library.

In some FHCs, Terry told me, the computers are networked, so patrons can use the CD-ROMs in a shared environment. The FHCs are going on the Internet and can access FamilySearch.org. Meanwhile, FamilySearch Internet and IGI are available at most FHCs, and usually only one person at a time can use them.

"Some centers offer training on the programs, some insist they train you before you start using the computers, and some only help if you ask," Terry says. "We offer help if you ask. We've not had much trouble installing ours here. The only tricks were the software has to have expanded memory, and you can have some TSRs (terminate-and-stay-resident programs, which sometimes cause conflicts) running, but few enough to have low memory and expanded memory as well."

The FHC computers usually are on a Windows platform. In the typical FHC setup, you must reserve a computer, and you're given a certain block of time to use it. Printouts of what you find usually cost a nickel a page. Some centers allow you to bring your own disk to record the information, but others insist that you buy certified virus-free disks from the FHC at a nominal fee.

Before you make a trip to the FHC near you, check out FamilySearch Internet and determine which resources you need. You can save lots of time!

Wrapping Up

- ♦ The LDS Church is the largest online resource for genealogy.

- ♦ The site also includes mail lists and a catalog of genealogy sites.

- ♦ Family History Centers are where you can view microfiches and microfilms of actual records as well as order copies of records.

Chapter 11

Ellis Island Online: The American Family Immigration History Center

Are you one of the 40 percent of Americans who can trace an ancestor to the immigration center at Ellis Island? If so, you definitely want to check out Ellis Island Online at www.ellisislandrecords .org. This site is the best thing to happen to online genealogy since the launch of FamilySearch. The interface is a little cluttered but still easy to navigate. The response to search input is fast, and the results are understandable.

The Family History Center is available on this website, as well as on a first-come, first-served basis, or by appointment, at the Ellis Island Immigration Museum. It features an electronic database of immigrants, passengers, and crew members who entered the United States through the Port of New York between 1892 and 1924, the peak years of Ellis Island's processing. The data, taken directly from microfilms of the ships' passenger manifests provided by the National Archives and Records Administration, has never before been available electronically. It was extracted and transcribed through the phenomenal efforts of 12,000 volunteers from The Church of Jesus Christ of Latter-day Saints, spending 5.6 million hours on the project. With over 22 million records, the countries with the highest representation in the database are Italy, Austria, Hungary, Russia, Finland, England, Ireland, Scotland, Germany, and Poland.

The opening page of the Ellis Island Online site is shown in Figure 11-1.

Note

Be sure to use the www.ellisisland.org URL. The site www .ellisisland.com has information on the park at Ellis Island concerning tours, hours of operation, and so on.

The Grand Opening

On April 17, 2001, the Statue of Liberty–Ellis Island Foundation (the Foundation), the National Park Service (NPS), Ellis Island immigrants and their families, dignitaries, and other guests gathered at the Ellis Island Immigration Museum to celebrate the opening of the American Family Immigration History Center. The website went online at 6 A.M. EDT that day.

The grand opening included appearances by Tom Brokaw, Charles Grodin, and Joel Grey; a search for Irving Berlin's immigration records

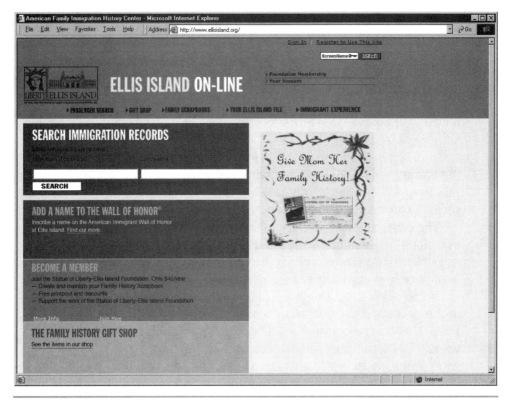

FIGURE 11-1. *Immigration records from 1892 to 1924 are available at EllisIsland.org.*

involving his daughters and great-grandson; an overview of the Family History Center's Family Scrapbook activity; and a presentation by Foundation Founding Chairman Lee A. Iacocca.

It was also the first annual Ellis Island Family History Day, an event that's cosponsored by the Foundation, the National Genealogical Society, and America's governors. That date in 1907 saw the largest number of immigrants ever processed on one day at Ellis Island—11,747 people, more than twice the usual number. This record-breaker will be honored every year.

The American Family Immigration History Center (not to be confused with a regular LDS Family History Center) provides easy access to information such as an immigrant's given name and surname, ethnicity, last town and country of residence, date of arrival, age, gender, marital status, ship of travel, port of departure, and line number on the manifest. The database is free of charge on the Internet or can be accessed at the Center for an entrance fee of $5, which includes a printout of an immigrant's arrival data. A scanned reproduction of the original ship's manifest, as well as a photo of the ship of passage, in the near future, will be available either on CD-ROM or on archival paper for an additional fee.

The Center, designed by Edwin Schlossberg Incorporated, also offers the Family History Scrapbook, which is discussed later in this chapter. As with previous Ellis Island projects, funding has come from the private sector, with no government funds employed.

The original ships' manifests show the passenger names, ages, and associated passengers, which is useful for clues to relationships. The ship information, often with a picture, gives the history and background of each ship that brought the immigrants.

If you register as a regular user, which is free, you can keep copies of the passenger records, manifests, and ship images in "Your Ellis Island File." This can be opened on the computers at Ellis Island or on this website. You can purchase copies of these documents at the online gift shop (more about this follows) or at the Interpretive Shop on Ellis Island.

If you join as a Foundation member at $45 per year, you can

◆ Annotate passenger records in the Ellis Island Archives

◆ Create and maintain your Family History Scrapbook

◆ Order one free copy of your initial Scrapbook (print or CD-ROM)

◆ Receive a 10-percent discount at the online gift shop or at the Center

◆ Support the ongoing work of the Foundation at Ellis Island

◆ Possibly get a tax deduction (check with your accountant)

A Guided Tour

The site has two parts: free services and services available only to Foundation members.

Even without the free registration, you can have access to "The Immigrant Experience," two sets of articles on the population of the United States. "Family Histories" gives real-life examples of people whose ancestors passed through Ellis Island. "The Peopling of America" is a series of articles showing the timeline of people coming to the United States from all over the world, beginning with those who crossed the Bering Straits 20,000 years ago.

To gain access to the free searches, you must register. This involves choosing a logon name and password and giving your name and address.

Searches

As a registered (free) user, you can use the Passenger Search. Simply put in a first and last name from the opening screen and then click Search Archives. If you want to perform a more targeted search, click Passenger Search at the top of the page and then click New Search. On that search page, you can input a first name and a last name and then choose Male or Female (or don't use gender at all).

The results will be presented to you in a table, as shown in Figure 11-2. If the results list is too long, you can refine the search with the choices in the bar at the left of the screen, filtering for year of arrival, ethnicity,

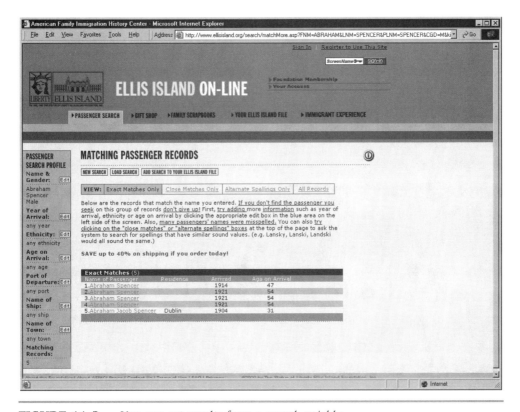

FIGURE 11-2. *You can get results from a search quickly.*

age on arrival, port of departure, and/or name of ship. For example, without the exact match, "Abraham" would also return "Ibrahim," "Abraam," and other near matches.

Choosing one of the names gives you a screen like the one shown in Figure 11-3. The details of the person as they appear on the manifest are listed. You can look at the transcription of the ship's manifest to see who is recorded near the person and click the Ship link to view details about the vessel. Registered members can save their searches and results in an online file for later reference and use.

Community Archives

Only members of the Foundation can create annotations to the records, but all registered users of the website can view them. Annotations supplement information in the record, telling more about the passenger's background and life in the United States. This information hasn't been

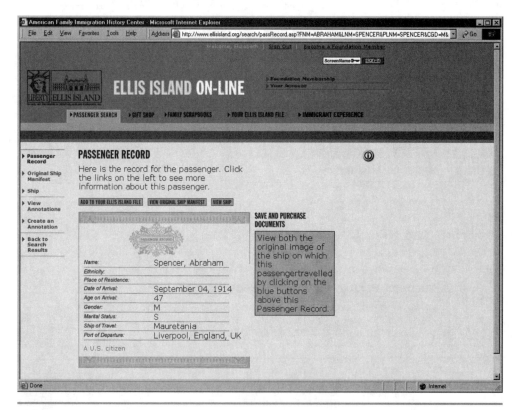

FIGURE 11-3.   *Details on each passenger include age and port of departure.*

verified as accurate and complete—it's simply what the annotating member believes to be the facts.

Click View Annotations on the passenger record (if no View Annotations button exists, the record hasn't yet been annotated). If you're registered with the site, you'll see a list of annotations. If you haven't yet registered, a screen will appear, enabling you to do so.

Ellis Island Family History Scrapbooks

If you've paid for a membership to The Statue of Liberty–Ellis Island Foundation, you can contribute Family History Scrapbooks on the website or at the American Family Immigration History Center itself on Ellis Island.

Family Scrapbooks combine member-submitted pictures, images from the Ellis Island archives, written stories and memories, and sound recordings. Members can choose to keep the Scrapbook private or add it to the publicly available Ellis Island Family History Archive. If you visit the Center, you can use a scanner, a camera, and recording equipment to work on Scrapbooks.

When you begin your Scrapbook, you have 16 pages to work on, including a title page and an author page. Ten of those pages have space for your images and four have space for an image from the Ellis Island Foundation archives. The site's documentation suggests you decide on a particular story or theme for your Scrapbook. Begin with a passenger search in the archives to find passenger records, ship images, and ship manifests to save in Your Ellis Island File and add to your Scrapbook, for example.

If you're a paying member, you can click Family Scrapbooks on the main menu and then click Start New Scrapbook (if this is the first time) or Create New Scrapbook (if previous Scrapbooks exist). You get to choose a style and create a title page and an author page. Once you complete those steps, you'll see the Scrapbook's table of contents. From there, you compose the Scrapbook pages. A page under composition is shown in Figure 11-4.

The Scrapbook pages can accept both pictures and audio recordings. The easiest way to do this is to gather everything you want to upload into one directory, to make them easier to find. On a Scrapbook page, under Add an Image, click Your Computer. In the Upload Image window, you can browse the local computer for the file or simply enter the filename. The files are uploaded one at a time, and they can be 180KB or smaller. If a file is larger than 210 × 210 pixels,

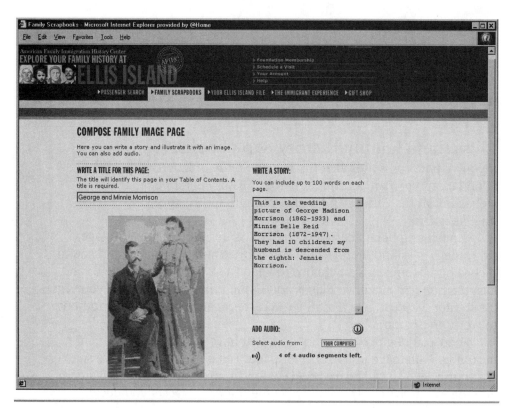

FIGURE 11-4.   *You can upload pictures and record stories of your ancestors.*

it will be resized, proportionally. If a file is smaller, it won't be resized. When Use Selected Image is clicked, the image will appear on the page and the window will close.

Members can also add files from the Ellis Island Library by clicking Our Library on a Scrapbook page under Add an Image. Your Ellis Island File may also contain passenger records, ship images, and ship manifests you saved during a passenger search. Click the left and right arrows to review the images in Our Library or Your Ellis Island File and then click Use This Image to add an image to the page. A finished page is shown in Figure 11-5.

On a Scrapbook page, under Add Audio, click Your Computer and choose an audio file. You can upload up to 1.8MB per file. Then enter a title for the audio file. When you click Use Selected File, the title assigned to the file appears on the page and the window will close. To remove an audio file, under Remove Audio?, click Delete This Audio File.

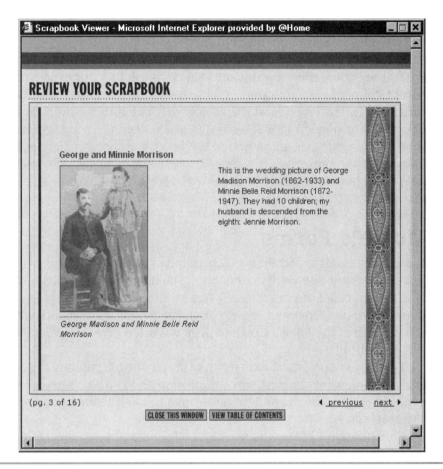

FIGURE 11-5. *Finished pages in the scrapbook have the elements you've chosen.*

At the online gift shop, paid Foundation members can order one free copy of their Scrapbooks, choosing either a high-quality print or a CD-ROM copy. Additional copies are available for purchase. At the table of contents, click Purchase Scrapbook.

Visiting in Person

You can also take care of these chores onsite at the museum, but you have to make an appointment within 90 days of your arrival. Click Schedule A Visit in the navigation bar at the top of any page on the site. You can simply choose to perform a passenger search ($5 entry fee to the museum) or to work on a Scrapbook (as with the online version, you must be an annual member of the Foundation to work on a Scrapbook).

You select the things you want to accomplish on your visit, list the number of people in your party (and whether any will need wheelchair assistance) up to seven, and then select the date and check-in time. Your appointment time will be assigned at check-in. You'll get a confirmation number at the end of the process to present at check-in. Print a copy to present at the desk. The screen also gives you links to articles on how to research and gather information for either a search session or a Scrapbook session.

Morse's Forms

The search as described on the Ellis Island site is better than it was the first summer the site went online, but it still has many steps. Dr. Stephen Morse, with collaborators Michael Tobias, Erik Steinmetz, and Dr. Yves Goulnik, created One-Step Search Tools for the Ellis Island site, which you can use at the Jewish Gen site page www.jewishgen.org/databases/eidb/intro.html.

This project consists of four separate search forms, but they necessarily overlap somewhat, causing some confusion about which one to use for a certain search. The major differences involve town searches and sounds-like searches.

An extensive FAQ on the site can be found at www.jewishgen.org/databases/eidb/faq.htm, with tips and explanations. You should read the FAQ before you try a search. I'll provide a quick overview here.

The Ellis Island search form lets you enter just the leading characters of the last name. It also allows you to search on ethnicity, ports, and ships. However, the search on the EI site requires you to first have an exact spelling match, whereas the Morse form does not. For example, suppose you are searching for a Polish immigrant named "Hoffman." To make sure you also get hits for "Hofman" (with a single *f*), you can do the search by entering only the first three letters—*Hof*. Then from the Ellis Island search page you would click edit-ethnicity.

White Form

The first form, called the *white form,* on the site searches all passengers, has a very restricted town search, and has a somewhat restricted sounds-like (or Soundex) search. It is shown in Figure 11-6.

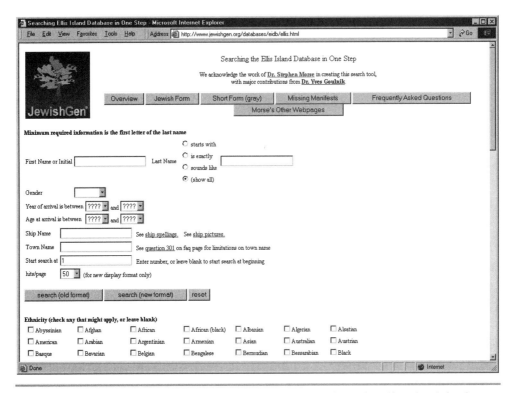

FIGURE 11-6. *The Morse white form is a general search on the Ellis Island database.*

On this form you should realize that the Ellis Island database will require an exact spelling match. You can find those spellings in the links at the bottom of the form, which sorts the over 700 port names by country.

You can also enter a town name at the bottom under Advanced Search Features. In this case you can enter just the starting letters of the town name. But the advanced search has a serious flaw: It doesn't do a real town search but instead downloads all matches regardless of town and filters for your match on your computer. Other problems are that it doesn't work perfectly with Internet Explorer, it requires tweaking to work with a Mac, and you have to manually edit a file to get it to work with Netscape 6/7. This experimental version is not ready for prime time.

The white form allows you to perform sounds-like searches on the last name only. But it does not use Soundex. Instead, it generates a list of all names that are known to be in the database and that sound like the name you are interested in. Then it searches for all passengers having those names. While this looks only for names known to be in the database, it also misses some similar-sounding names.

The town search and name search are mutually exclusive on the white form. You can do one or the other, but not both at the same time. There is no such limitation on the gray or blue forms.

Blue Form

The blue form searches the Ellis Island database for Jewish passengers only (see Figure 11-7). To get around the limitations of the Ellis Island search engine, Morse and his collaborators set up an alternate search engine that provides a true search-by-town capability and a true Soundex search capability; then they restricted the blue form's search engine to passengers having ethnicity of "Hebrew." What you get are pointers directly into the Ellis Island database for the passengers you find.

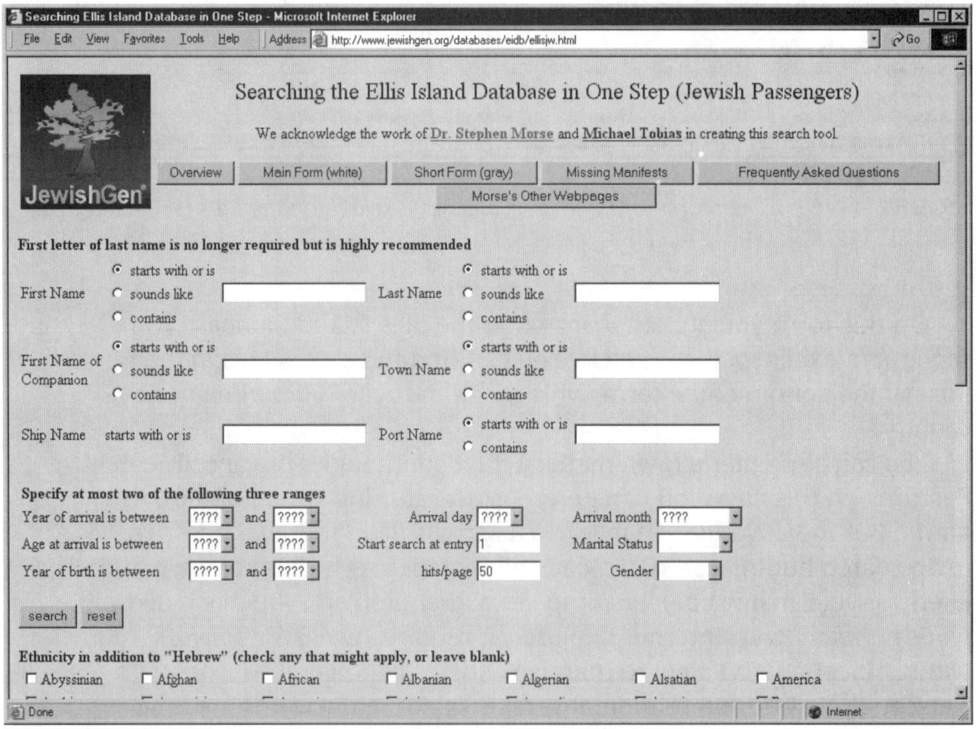

FIGURE 11-7.   *The blue form searches only Jewish passengers, although you can add a nationality to the search to further narrow the results.*

The blue form supports other fields, such as marital status, exact date of arrival, and year of birth. You can also search by just part of the ship's name. Therefore, the blue form is now a more powerful search tool than the white form, providing that the passenger being searched for has an ethnicity of Hebrew.

Gray Form

With the gray form you can find all the people who came from your ancestor's little village, if they came through Ellis Island. You input the name and the village as well as two dates (see Figure 11-8). The gray form uses the alternate search engine described for the blue form, only it looks at different fields. The Ellis Island search lets you search by ship, port, ethnicity, and gender, which the gray form does not. Therefore, you might find it beneficial to switch back and forth between the two when looking for passengers.

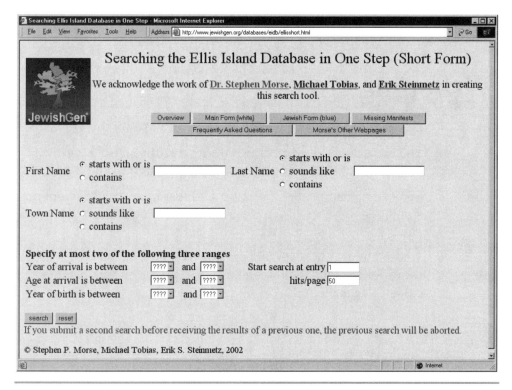

FIGURE 11-8. *The gray form is for searching for people from a specific town.*

Missing Manifests

The last form on the project searches for images that are torn or otherwise damaged, and therefore not indexed in the Ellis Island search form, though they do exist.

When you search for a passenger, get a passenger record, click View Original Manifest, and "NO IMAGE AVAILABLE" appears in a big black box, you have come across one of these manifests. Either the image did not get uploaded into the online Ellis Island database due to some error, or the image was uploaded but the link in the database is missing. If the image exists, but it did not get indexed, this form can find it.

Sometimes when you click View Original Manifest, you might get to an image of a manifest but for the wrong ship. This form can help with that as well.

This form can also help if you know the exact date of arrival and possibly the ship as well, but did not get a hit in the Ellis Island search page. In that case you can use the missing manifests page to view all the ships that arrived on that date and go through them line by line looking for the name you want, as shown in Figure 11-9.

Wrapping Up

♦ Ellis Island Online is a wonderful new resource on the Web.

♦ You can search for immigrants from 1892 through 1924—the peak years of Ellis Island's processing—by name, date, and ship.

♦ You can upload pictures, sounds, and text to an online scrapbook if you're a member of the Statue of Liberty Foundation ($45) or if you visit the museum itself in New York.

♦ Steven Morse and several others have created alternative search forms for the Ellis Island database that are faster and in some cases more useful.

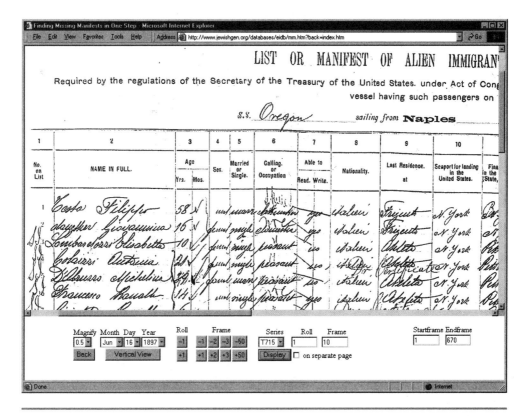

FIGURE 11-9. *You can examine specific manifests with the Missing Manifests form.*

Chapter 12

Online Library Card Catalogs

Despite all the wonderful things appearing online, many of your genealogical expeditions will still be in libraries. However, the online world can help you here, too.

One of the wonderful things about the online world is the plethora of libraries now using online card catalogs (OCCs). This greatly speeds up your search while you're at the library. Not only can you perform an instant search of all of a library's holdings (and, sometimes, even place a hold on the material), but also, with many terminals scattered throughout the building, you needn't look up your subject, author, or title on one floor and then repeatedly run to another floor to find the referenced material. If your local library hasn't computerized its card catalog yet, it probably will soon.

Going to the Library in Your Jammies

Oh, the joys of looking in the card catalog before you actually visit the library! You know immediately whether that library owns the title. With a few more keystrokes, you can find out whether the title is on the shelf, on reserve, on loan to someone, or lost without a trace. You can find out whether the book is available by interlibrary loan or found in a nearby branch library.

You can connect to online card catalogs in two main ways. The most convenient way is through the World Wide Web with a browser interface. Here, the card catalog appears like any of the web-based databases you encountered in this book.

With older online library card catalogs, however, the connection could be by telnet. If this is the case, you use a separate program to send commands to, and receive information from, the database. I'll explain this later in the chapter.

Note

Telnet is a telecommunications protocol that enables your computer to act as a remote terminal so that you can access a distant computer and function online using an interface that appears to be part of the your desktop system.

A third way to connect to an online card catalog is with a hybrid web-telnet connection. In this case, the library (or libraries) maintains a website with all the relevant information on how to use the card catalog. Then, when it's time to look at the card catalog database, your browser starts a telnet program to work with the database.

Connecting to OCCs by Web Browser

The easiest and most visually appealing way to connect to online card catalogs is via the Web. The mechanics of how this works is irrelevant. What's important is that a web-based interface lets you use the card catalog without having to install and load a telnet program.

A wonderful example is the University of Texas at Austin's UTNetCAT at http://dpweb1.dp.utexas.edu/lib/utnetcat. You can use the forms that appear at this website to search by author, title, subject, or any combination thereof. The results of the search are links to the card catalog. Click one and you get a full display of that item's record, as shown in Figure 12-1.

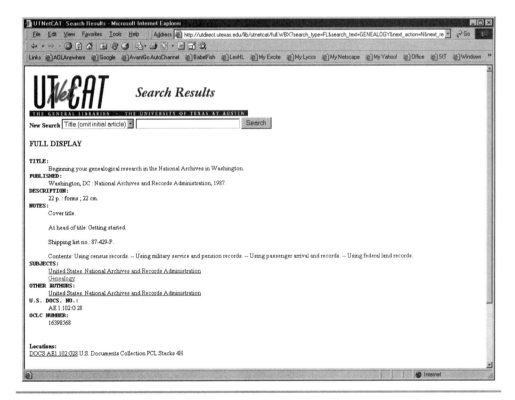

FIGURE 12-1.   *Information on a book on genealogy in the University of Texas at Austin library.*

Another slightly more complicated example is the Sirsi system. One example of this system can be found at www.uah.edu/library, the site for the University of Alabama in Huntsville's library. To log in, go directly to the card catalog's search page at library.uah.edu and click the I'm a Guest button.

Note

Sirsi is a company that specializes in software and databases for libraries and library websites. Their site is www.sirsi.com.

The search screen is shown in Figure 12-2. Once in the system, you can look for items in any field that contain certain words or phrases. Even better, by using Boolean options (AND, OR), you can specify that

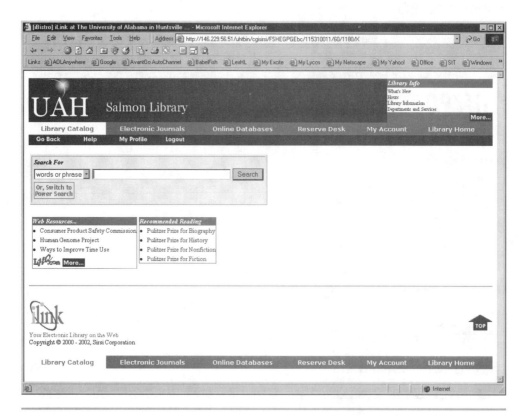

FIGURE 12-2. *Many libraries use a card catalog program from Sirsi on their websites.*

words, author names, title words, or subject terms must have a particular relationship to each other. If you want something written by a specific person, searching by author makes sense. If you know most of the words in the title, a title search can tell you whether the library has the item and where it's located. If you don't know an author or title, you can search by subject.

You can have better luck with your searches if you narrow them as much as possible. You can choose to search on Author and Title, Subject, and Word or Phrase, or any combination of these. You can also search recent issues of magazines using the Periodical Title option.

To show you how this works, I chose a search with "Alabama genealogy" in the general word or phrase field. Figure 12-3 shows the results of that search, which turned up four cards matching the search criteria. Each card has a short synopsis that appears on the results page.

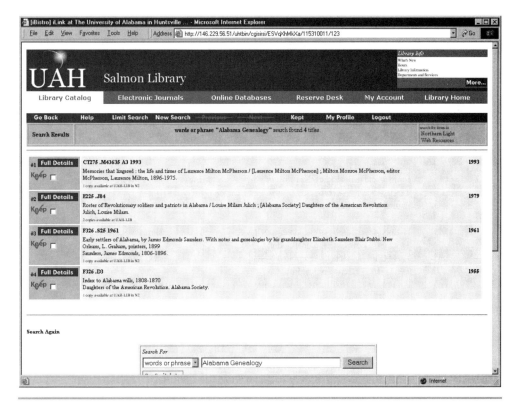

FIGURE 12-3. *Search results in a Sirsi system include short synopses.*

By clicking the View button next to a synopsis, you can get additional details about the book, such as the publication date, author, and cross-links to other relevant cards in the catalog. Then, if you like, you can print the results or have a copy of them e-mailed to you.

The Library of Virginia is home to a similarly powerful online card catalog, located at http://eagle.vsla.edu/catalog. This site has scanned images of Civil War records, family bible records, letters, and other material, all indexed and searchable by name.

I ran a test with "genealogy and Powell" as the search terms. The results can be seen in Figure 12-4. If I want to refine my search further, I could also use Boolean terms such as AND, NOT, and so on.

Overall, the Library of Virginia's card catalog is easy to understand and read—and, I might add, a pleasure to work with.

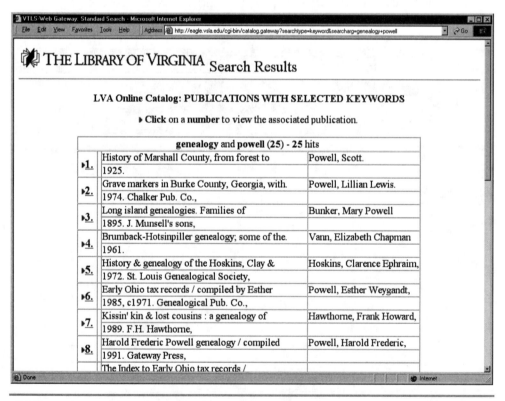

FIGURE 12-4. *The Library of Virginia's search results show title, author, and publication date.*

Don't Miss These Library Sites

♦ **The Allen County Public Library** (http://www.acpl.lib.in.us/) has one of the best genealogical collections in the country.

♦ **The Daughters of the American Revolution Library** (http://dar.library.net/) has over 160,000 books on American genealogy, and it's open to the public.

♦ **The New England Historical and Genealogical Society Lending Library** (http://www.newenglandancestors.org/rs3/ libraries/circulation/Default.asp) is available to members only. Consider joining if you have any New England ancestors!

♦ **The New York Public Library** genealogy section is called The Milstein Division. This department collects materials documenting American history on the national, state, and local levels, as well as genealogy, heraldry, personal and family names, and flags. The page at http://www.nypl.org/ research/chss/lhg/genea.html has good general information. The card catalog of the library at large is at http://www .nypl.org/catalogs/index.html.

♦ **The Newberry Library in Chicago** (http://www.newberry.org/ nl/genealogy/genealogyhome.html) has over 17,000 genealogies. Search the catalog to see if you need to make a visit!

Connecting to Card Catalogs by Telnet

Some card catalogs, although online, haven't been put in web format yet. This means you have to get at them another way. Enter telnet—a system that lets you connect to another computer as if your PC were a terminal on that computer. Although telnet is an older Internet service, it's still widely used for online card catalogs.

Windows comes with a basic telnet program that's activated by Microsoft Internet Explorer and Netscape Navigator whenever you try to connect to a telnet address. Just enter the address—for example, **telnet://seolib.state.lib.oh.us/**—on the browser's Address line, and a telnet window pops up, ready to go. (That address, by the way, is for the Southeastern Ohio Regional Library telnet catalog; the login is "library.")

A typical card catalog you can reach using telnet and the Internet is the South Carolina State Library card catalog (telnet://leo.scsl.state.sc.us). When you type the address in the Address box, the web browser automatically starts the telnet program, establishing a connection to the library. Afterward, enter the password (LION) listed in the first window (type it in where the cursor appears) and press ENTER. You see the library's welcome message, as shown in Figure 12-5.

I started by typing **1** to get into the LION card catalog, and then I searched by subject using the term "genealogy." As a result, the catalog returned a list of cards containing my search word. I also received several references to other sections of the card catalog. If you've ever used the electronic card catalog at your local library, such an interface should look familiar to you. By following the onscreen instructions, you

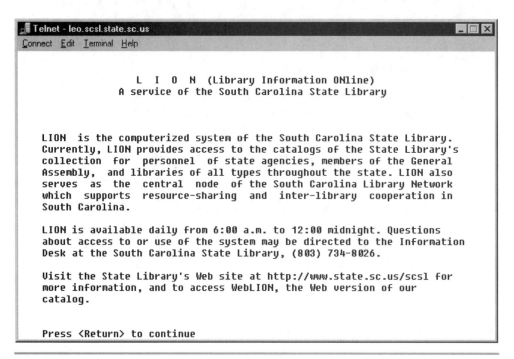

FIGURE 12-5. *The South Carolina State Library's card catalog has a telnet interface.*

can find out what titles are available and where they're located—in short, you can find all the information you would get if you were physically in the library, looking at the card catalog.

Where to Find More Online Card Catalogs

Once you explore the online card catalogs shown in this chapter, you'll probably want to find some more. Of course, first you'll want to use a search engine (see Chapter 6) and search for the term "library" and the town, province, or county you are interested in. Also, search for the name of a state and "public library" because many states have a network of their libraries. For example, the Ohio Public Library Information Network, shown in Figure 12-6, has a site with links to many public libraries in the state. The site is at www.oplin.lib.oh.us.

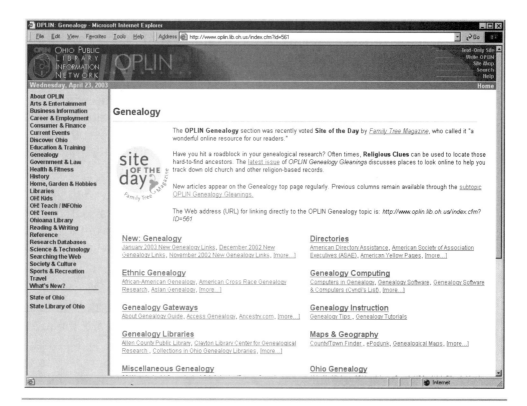

FIGURE 12-6. *OPLIN is just one example of a statewide network of libraries.*

Another place to look for both web and telnet OCCs is the Genealogy Resources page at the University of Minnesota. Browse down to the Libraries and Archives section at www.tc.umn.edu/~pmg/libraries. html. Other places to look for online library card catalogs include the following:

- **Library WWW Servers (http://sunsite.berkeley.edu/ Libweb/)** This site lets you search by keyword, state, and country for online library sites.

- **Gateway to Library Catalogs (http://lcweb.loc.gov/z3950/ gateway.html)** A page by the Library of Congress. This is a simple alphabetical list of sites.

- **Libdex (http://www.libdex.com)** A worldwide directory of library homepages, web-based OPACs, Friends of the Library pages, and library e-commerce affiliate links.

- **National Union Catalog of Manuscript Collections (NUCMC)** This site can point you not only to library card catalogs but also to archives and repositories with websites. You can find it at http://lcweb.loc.gov/coll/nucmc/index.html.

- **Repositories of Primary Sources (http://www.uidaho.edu/ special-collections/Other.repositories.html)** This site, by Terry Abraham of the University of Idaho, lists over 3,100 sites worldwide, arranged by region. It includes many of the major genealogical libraries with primary source documents.

- **The Library of Michigan** This site has a database with the locations of over 3,700 Michigan cemeteries and lists sources at the library where a researcher can find the names of those buried in each cemetery. The database can be found at http://michigancemeteries.libraryofmichigan.org or www.michigan.gov/hal.

- **USGenWeb (www.usgenweb.com)** When you visit this site, look under the state and then the county you're researching to see if the library catalog is linked.

♦ **Yale University Library (www.library.yale.edu/ pubstation/ libcats.html)**   This site has a page that includes connections to Yale library online catalogs, information about card catalogs, and connections to library catalogs from around the world.

♦ **The WWW Library Directory (http://www.webpan.com/ msauers/libdir/index.html)**   This is a list of library websites sorted by geography, not topic. However, it's very useful.

♦ **The Research Libraries Information Network (RLIN)**   This is a not-for-profit membership corporation of over 160 universities, national libraries, archives, historical societies, and other institutions that gathers and distributes the RLIN to make many resources available around the world. Libraries join the RLIN, and many libraries use a telnet connection to transfer RLIN records to their local systems for processing. You may find local libraries with an RLIN interface, allowing you to search the holdings of many different libraries.

Wrapping Up

♦ You can search the card catalogs of many libraries across the world from the Internet.

♦ Some libraries have begun scanning in images and actual text of their genealogical holdings.

♦ You can search for such libraries at several sites across the Internet.

Chapter 13

International Genealogy Resources

Sooner or later, you'll get "back to the boat"—that is, you'll find your original immigrant in a certain line. The first immigrant in your family might have arrived just a generation ago, or centuries ago. Either way, that doesn't have to mean your genealogy is "done."

When you find that first immigrant, finding the boat can be just as important. An excellent step-by-step guide to searching for immigrants is at Immigration & Ships Passenger Lists Research Guide (http://home.att.net/ ~ arnielang/shipgide.html). Check out Cyndi's List for links to ships' passenger lists projects at www.cyndislist.com/ships.htm. Also, search the Ellis Island site (see Chapter 11) and investigate the Immigrant Ships Transcribers' Guild at istg.rootsweb.com.

Of course, the next step is to start researching in "the old country," outside the United States. Can you do this online? Well, that depends on the country. Some countries do, indeed, have online records for you to search, especially those countries where English is spoken. But some countries only have sites with the most general information, and you'll be lucky to find the address of the civil records offices. You'll probably wind up doing a combination of online and in-person research and, possibly, some research by mail, too.

Beyond the Boat

In many of the places covered in previous chapters, you can find links to sites for genealogy beyond the United States. For online links, I recommend starting at Cyndi's List at www.cyndislist.com and RootsWeb at www.rootsweb.org. Other good places to look are:

♦ **National Archives**   A country's National Archives might have a web page describing genealogy how-tos for that country. For example, I recently searched for "Poland National Archives" in Google. Quickly, I found the English version of the Archives' website, www.archiwa.gov.pl/index.eng.html. That site has a page of links to other archives in Poland, from museums to church records. This sort of information can be very helpful.

♦ **Genealogical Societies**   Search in any major search site (Yahoo!, Google, Excite, and so on) for the country of origin for your immigrant and "genealogy." Often at the top of the list will be a genealogical society devoted to that particular nationality.

You need to learn how to research in those countries. Each place has its own method of recording vital statistics, history, and other information.

Before you start looking for records, you need to know what those records are called and who keeps them.

LDS Research Guides

The Church of Jesus Christ of Latter-day Saints has developed pamphlets on researching immigrants and ancestors around the world. The Research Guides are indispensable for these tasks. You can order them for a nominal fee from any Family History Center. Look in the Yellow Pages or in the White Pages for "The Church of Jesus Christ of Latter-day Saints" for a Family History Center near you.

The first one to read is the guide "Tracing Immigrant Origins," a 49-page outline of tips, procedures, and strategies (see Figure 13-1). You can find this publication online at FamilySearch (see Table 13-1, later in this chapter).

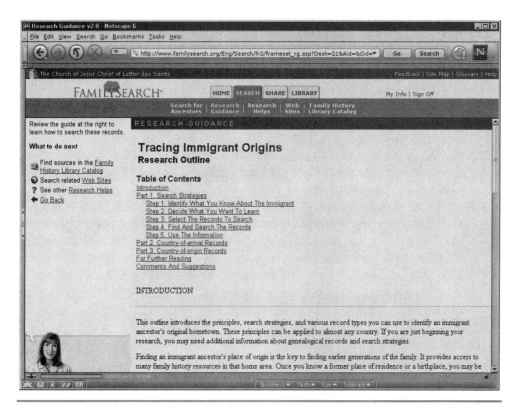

FIGURE 13-1. *You can find and print Tracing Immigrant Origins or you can get a printed copy at a local Family History Center for a small fee.*

Other Research Guides give you step-by-step pointers on the best way to pursue historical records in a particular state, province, or country. The letter-writing guides tell you what you need to know before you write the letter, where to write, how to address the envelope, how to enclose return postage, and a sample letter in the appropriate language.

Arm yourself with the research outlines and, if available, a letter-writing guide for the appropriate country, before you begin. Also, look at the LDS "word lists" for various languages; this can help you recognize the words for "birth," "marriage," "death," and so on in the records, even if you can't read the language.

WorldGenWeb

The WorldGenWeb Project was created in 1996 by Dale Schneider to help folks researching in countries around the world. The goal is to have every country in the world represented by an online website and hosted by researchers who either live in that country or are familiar with that country's resources. The site is at www.worldgenweb.org (see Figure 13-2).

When the WorldGenWeb Project opened on the Internet in October 1996, volunteers were recruited to host country websites. By coordinating with the USGenWeb Project, soon the major countries in the world had websites online. Throughout the next year, WorldGenWeb continued to grow. On September 13, 1997, the WorldGenWeb Project decided to move to RootsWeb. The support of the RootsWeb staff helped WorldGenWeb to expand to its present size.

Divided into 11 regions (Africa, Asia, British Isles, Central Europe, Caribbean, Eastern Europe, Mediterranean, Middle East, North America, Pacific, and South America), WorldGenWeb gives links to local sites with local resource addresses of county/country public records offices, cemetery locations, maps, library addresses, archive addresses, association addresses (including Family History Centers or other genealogical or historical societies), and some history and culture of the region. Other resources may include query pages or message boards, mail lists, historical data (including census records), cemetery records, biographies, bibliographies, and family/surname registration websites.

Between RootsWeb and WorldGenWeb, you should be able to find something about the country you need to search.

FIGURE 13-2. *WorldGenWeb can help you find genealogy sites in your country of interest.*

Other Good Starting Places

In addition to the places mentioned so far, there are many good starting places for an international search. Some are very general for all sorts of international research, and some are for specific locations. Here are some to get you started.

International Internet Genealogical Society

This all-volunteer effort aims to collect international genealogical material to one site, promote ethics in international genealogy, and promote cooperation among genealogists all over the world.

The main features of the site include the following:

◆ A list of volunteers involved at the Global Village Representatives page

◆ The many IRC chats held on a regular basis (including DearMYRTLE's weekly Monday gatherings)

◆ A library of links to resources all over the world

◆ Free online courses on how to conduct international genealogy

Translation Pages

Sites that can provide a translation of a web page into English include the following:

◆ **Alta Vista Babel Fish**
http://babelfish.altavista.digital.com/translate.dyn

◆ **GO Translator**   http://translator.go.com

◆ **Google Language Tools**
http://www.google.com/language_tools?hl = en

Asian Genealogical Sites

As noted in Chapter 9, the Bureau of Citizenship and Immigration Services has information on Chinese immigrants at their Chinese Immigrant Files page (www.immigration.gov/graphics/aboutus/history/chinese.htm). This collection of United States government records on immigrants is full of good information.

The Singapore Genealogy Forum at http://genforum.genealogy.com/singapore/ allows Singaporeans of all races to look for their relatives and ancestors.

AsianGenNet at www.rootsweb.org/ ~ asiagw is part of WorldGenWeb and has some sites, but needs hosts for many more.

Chinese Surnames (www.yutopian.com/names) is a fascinating page with the most common Chinese surnames and their history.

European Genealogical Sites

There are many sites where you can research your European roots. I recommend you start with the following.

Benelux   At Digital Resources Netherlands and Belgium (http://geneaknowhow.net/digi/resources.html) you can find resources from the Netherlands and Belgium, including over 350 Internet links to online resources (including more than 150 passenger lists), nearly 900 online resources on Dutch and Belgian bulletin board systems, and hundreds of digital resources.

Eastern Europe   Yahoo! has a category for Czech genealogy discussion and research at http://dir.yahoo.com/Regional/Countries/ Czech_Republic/Arts_and_Humanities/Humanities/History/Genealogy/ dir.yahoo.com/Regional/Countries/Czech_Republic/Arts_and_Humanities/ Humanities/History.

The Ukranian Roots genealogy web ring begins at ukrcommunities .8k.com/ukrroots.html.

Eastern Slovakia, Slovak, and Carpatho-Rusyn Genealogy Research has articles, links, message boards and transcribed records at www .iarelative.com/slovakia.htm.

France   Besides the usual sites, such as Cyndi's List and WorldGenWeb, check out FrancoGene at www.francogene.com. Links to genealogy sites in former French colonies around the world, such as Quebec and Haiti, as well as to genealogy societies and institutions, can be found there.

Germany   Genealogy.net at www.genealogienetz.de/genealogy.html has how-tos, sample request letters, databases, translations of common terms, and many more tools for researching genealogy in Germany.

GermanRoots at www.germanroots.com offers tips, links, and research helps.

The Telephone Book for Germany can be found at www.teleauskunft .de/NSAPI/&BUAB = BUNDESWEIT.

Deutsche Bahn can be found at www.bahn.de.

Germany Genealogy Net can be found at www.genealogienetz.de/ gene/misc/geoserv.html.

Italy   The Italian Genealogy Homepage at www.italgen.com is the place to start. This page includes links to how-to articles, discussion groups, and history.

Spain   A personal site, Spanish Genealogy at Spain Genealogy Links (www.genealogylinks.net/europe/spa.htmwww.geocities.com/CapitolHill/ Senate/4593/geneal.html) has tips, data, and links about Spain, and more.

Portugal   LusaWeb is a site for Portuguese Ancestry at www.lusaweb.com/genealogy, and the Portuguese-American Historical & Research Foundation has a page for genealogy questions and answers at www.portuguesefoundation.org/genealogy.htm.

Scandinavia   Census records of Norway are being transcribed and posted by volunteers at:

♦ Norwegian Census and Bergen Emigration Information (http://digitalarkivet.uib.no/index-eng.htm)

♦ Norwegian Research Sources (http://www.rootsweb.com/ ~ wgnorway/NorLinks.htm)

♦ Ancestors from Norway (http://homepages.rootsweb.com/ ~ norway/index.html)

They all have a lot of how-to information for genealogy in Norway.

The National Archives of Norway (www.riksarkivet.no/english/about.html) covers the central administrative institutions and the eight regional state archives, including the local branches of the state administration.

Genealogy Research Denmark at www.ida.net/users/really is a personal page of one woman's collected research, plus links to other resources.

The Norwegian Emigration and Genealogy Center offers information for descendants at www.emigrationcenter.com/.

Martin's Norwegian Genealogy Dictionary at www.geocities.com/Heartland/Estates/5536/eidhalist.html can help you decipher words for relationships, occupations, and so on.

Swedish Genealogy Genealogical Society of Minnesota at www.rootsweb.com/ ~ mnsgsm/ has queries, data, a few transcriptions of records translated into English, and meeting dates of the Society.

United Kingdom   The United Kingdom (UK) and Ireland Genealogy site at www.genuki.org.uk is the best starting point. This site has transcribed data, such as parish records, plus links to individuals' pages where genealogy research (secondary material) is posted. Look at the index page (www.genuki.org.uk/mindex.html) for specific counties, surnames, and so forth.

The Free BMD (Free Birth, Marriage, and Death records) project at freebmd.rootsweb.com provides free Internet access to the Civil Registration Index information for England and Wales from 1837. The transcriptions are ongoing and the updates are posted once or twice a month. You can volunteer to help!

AncestorSuperSearch at www.ancestorsupersearch.com has 1.46 million English birth, marriage, and census events (1355–1891) that are searchable online.

The National Archives of Ireland at www.nationalarchives.ie has a genealogy how-to page.

The UK National Digital Archive of Datasets at ndad.ulcc.ac.uk has archived digital data from UK government departments and agencies. The system has been available since March 1998 and provides open access to the catalogs of all its holdings, as well as free access to open datasets following a simple registration process.

The National Archives of Scotland has records from the twelfth century. The family history fact sheet at www.nas.gov.uk/family_history_factsheet.htm has good how-to information. You can download PDF files of fact sheets on adoption, deeds, wills, and other topics.

South America

Genealogy.com has a good list of South American genealogy links at www.genealogy.com/links/c/c-places-geographic.south-america.html.

H. R. Henly, at his site Genealogical Research in Latin America (www.saqnet.co.uk/users/hrhenly/latinaml.html), has gathered the links that have helped him the most in his searches.

The South AmericanGenWeb Project (www.rootsweb.com/~sthamgw) is an online data repository for queries, family histories, and source records, as well as being a resource center to identify other online databases and resources to assist researchers.

Created by Rebecca R. Horne and maintained by Salena B. Ashton, the site at www.hfhr.com/websites.html is another good collection of links.

Australia and New Zealand

Australia is rich with genealogy websites. Start with Yahoo!'s category dir.yahoo.com/Regional/Countries/Australia/Arts_and_Humanities/Humanities/History/Genealogy, but don't miss the other pages, such as the Cyndi's List pages on Australia (www.cyndislist.com/austnz.htm) and New Zealand (www.cyndislist.com/newzealand.htm).

The Society of Australian Genealogists at www.sag.org.au offers materials, meetings, and special interest groups.

The Dead Person's Society, a site for genealogy in Melbourne, Australia, has a graphic of dancing skeletons at http://home.vicnet.net.au/ ~ dpsoc/ (see Figure 13-3). It has guides to searching Australian provinces, databases of cemeteries, census and other records, and general articles on Australian genealogy.

Convicts to Australia, a guide to researching ancestry during the time when Australia was used as a large prison, can be found at www.convictcentral.com/index.html.

The KiwiGen web ring has links to New Zealand genealogy at http://g.webring.com/hub?ring = kiwigen.

First Families of Australia 2001 is at www.firstfamilies2001.net.au/ sites.netscape.net/mgswebaus/firstfam.

National Archives of Australia, at www.naa.gov.au, has an entire section on family history and what records to look for.

Africa

Conrod Mercer's page at http://home.global.co.za/ ~ mercon is a personal collection of tips on doing South African (white) genealogy.

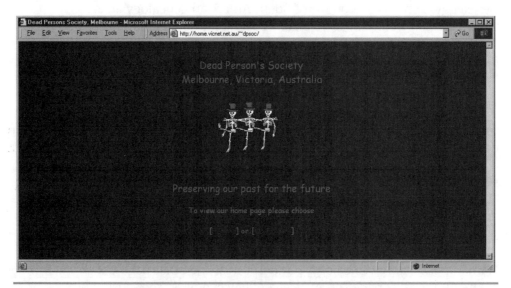

FIGURE 13-3.   *The Dead Person's Society is a nationwide Australian Genealogy organization.*

Check out Cyndi's List (search for the African nation of interest) and WorldGenWeb first.

The African Atlantic Genealogy Society, at www.africantic.com, has newsletters, queries, and census data to help you get started.

North America

The following sites are good places to start to search for information on ancestors from Canada and Mexico.

Canada   Canadian Genealogy and History at www.islandnet.com/ ~ jveinot/cghl/cghl.html lists online sites for vital records, genealogies, and general history, sorted by province.

Immigrants to Canada at http://ist.uwaterloo.ca/ ~ marj/genealogy/ thevoyage.html offers information extracted from various government records, as well as the odd shipping record (www.dcs.uwaterloo.ca/ ~ marj/genealogy/thevoyage.html).

The genealogy page of the National Archives of Canada is at www.archives.ca/02/020202_e.html. The National Archives of Canada publishes the free booklet, *Tracing Your Ancestors in Canada,* which describes the major genealogical sources available at the National Archives and makes reference to sources in other Canadian repositories. You can order a hard copy or access a PDF version online.

Mexico   Archivo Historico del Agua at http://www2.h-net.msu.edu/ ~ latam/archives/project4.html is the site of the national archives of Mexico.

Local Catholic Church History and Ancestors at http://home.att.net/ ~ Local_Catholic/Catholic-Mexico.htm has addresses to write for parish records in Mexico.

The Texas General Land Office has a page at www.glo.state.tx.us/ archives that describes records dating back to Spanish times. The page has how to write for these records, both the proper addresses and what is available.

The Genealogy of Mexico (http://members.tripod.com/ ~ GaryFelix/ index1.htm) is one genealogist's compilation of starting places.

The Hispanic Genealogical Society of New York at www.hispanicgenealogy.com includes Mexico, Puerto Rico, and other North American Hispanic genealogy.

A Success Story

Denzil J. Klippel had quite a bit of success in his international genealogy search, but it didn't happen overnight. Denzil started with what he knew, researched back to the boat, and finally found his family's village of origin. How he did this is fascinating.

Denzil only knew his parents, his grandmother on his mother's side, and her brother and sister.

"In the beginning, I didn't take advantage of the resources on the Net like DearMYRTLE, and so forth and ask questions (see Figure 13-4). But I soon learned everyone in the online genealogy community is willing to help answer questions. We don't need to reinvent the wheel—just ask if anyone has done this or that," Denzil says.

Denzil visited a local Family History Center (FHC) in New York City. There, he found his grandmother's family, but not his grandmother, on one of the microfilms. Requesting the name and address of the submitter, he

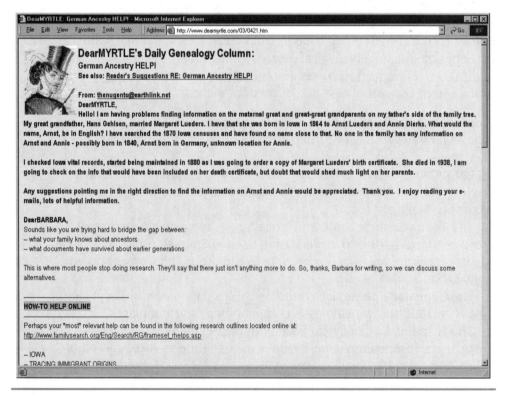

FIGURE 13-4. *Getting help from people who have done international genealogy is only one way the online world can make your quest easier.*

contacted him with a query, including his e-mail address. Soon, another researcher contacted him by e-mail, and everything began to fall together.

Denzil sent for his father's death certificate (New York) and found his place and date of birth (California), his father's place of birth (Upstate New York), as well as his mother's maiden name (Settle) and place of birth (California). He was able to order some of these records online through various vital records sites maintained by these states.

> ## Note
>
> *You can find where to write for many vital records at The National Center for Health Statistics page (www.cdc.gov/nchs/howto/w2w/ w2welcom.htm), which is shown in Figure 13-5.*

"After going back to my great-grandfather and finding he came from Germany, I hit a brick wall. Not knowing what to do, I went to one of the search engines—Yahoo!—and put in the name Klippel. It gave me

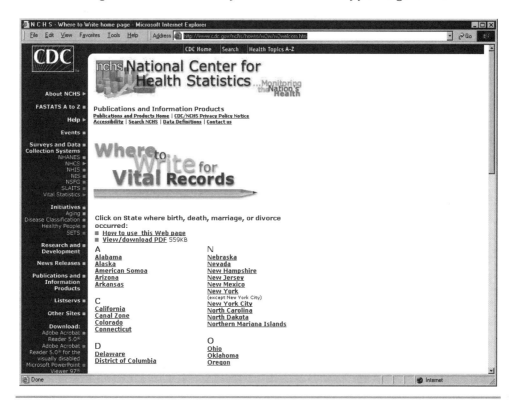

FIGURE 13-5.   *Where to Write for Vital Records is a very useful page.*

6,000 places where the name appeared on the Net, most of them regarding an illness discovered by a Klippel. I captured all of the Klippel e-mail addresses and sent them a message saying I was researching the Klippel family name, and if they were interested in working with me, perhaps we could find some common ancestors, or at least discover where the Klippels originated."

Denzil says he doesn't recommend this approach, however. "This shotgun approach never works," he said. What did work, though, was searching for the surname on www.google.com and looking for the genealogy sites.

After e-mailing people with Klippel genealogy sites, as opposed to every Klippel he could find online, Denzil heard from people who had been searching the line. Several were cousins he didn't know he had, and since that time he now calls all Klippels he comes in contact with "cousin."

"One of these cousins had the name of the town in Germany where my Klippel line came from (Ober-Hilbersheim). I found this village had a website (see Figure 13-6) and sent a letter to the mayor. He responded via e-mail and said he knew of my line and told me there were still Klippels living in the village," Denzil said.

"In the meantime, other Klippels in Europe contacted me and, before I knew it, I was planning a trip to visit some of them and Ober-Hilbersheim. When they heard I was going to visit, they all said I had to stay with them. I bought my airline tickets online via Priceline.com and my train pass online."

Now Denzil was really into the in-person, offline mode! Through electronic and surface mail, he made appointments at all the archives he planned to visit in Germany. When he arrived, they were ready for him and, in most cases, they'd already done all the lookups. As Denzil gathered the research material, he mailed it home to himself. This was important insurance against losing or misplacing any of the papers during his sojourn.

"My trip started in Ober-Hilbersheim, and I stayed with the mayor. He took me to all the archives and helped me get all the Klippel family history back to 1650! My distant cousins in the village welcomed me with open arms. I then went to the Netherlands and stayed with the Klippels there, and they took me to the Island of Tholen where the first Klippel came from

FIGURE 13-6.   *Denzil found his ancestors' village online.*

in the 1400s. Then on to Hamburg to visit Helmut Klippel and the archive there," Denzil said.

"And last, but not least, on to Sweden to stay with Alf Klippel, who had given me a wealth of information about the origins of the Klippel name via e-mail and did most of the translating of the old German documents I had been receiving over the Net."

It took some footwork and perseverance but, after seven years, Denzil feels he accomplished a lot in his international search, and the online resources made it possible (see Table 13-1 for some good sites to start your international search).

Site Name	URL
DearMYRTLE	http://www.dearmyrtle.com
Cyndi's List	http://www.cyndislist.com (search for the country of interest)
The International Internet Genealogical Society (IIGS)	http://www.iigs.org/
International Genealogy Meetup	http://genealogy.meetup.com/
GeneaSearch International	http://www.geneasearch.com/intl/internat.htm
Babel Fish Translation	http://babel.altavista.com/tr
Tracing Your Immigrant Ancestors	http://www.nysl.nysed.gov/genealogy/tracimmi.htm
Tracing Immigrant Ancestors Research Outline	http://www.familysearch.org/Eng/Search/RG/guide/Tracing_Immigrant_Origins4.asp

TABLE 13-1.   *Some Helpful General Links for Immigrant Ancestor Searching*

Wrapping Up

♦ Once you find your immigrant ancestor, you can use archives and ships' passenger lists to identify their home town.

♦ Many National Archives have web pages describing research techniques for that country.

♦ At FamilySearch, you can download and print research guides for immigrant origins and for specific countries, as well as word lists of genealogical terms in non-English languages.

♦ There are specific sites for genealogy of many nationalities.

Chapter 14

Ethnic Genealogy Resources

The international sources cited in Chapter 13 can also help you with ethnic research within the United States and Canada for well-documented ancestry such as Croatian or Chinese. For other groups, however, the search is a little more complex.

Special Challenges

As I described in the Introduction, sometimes you need to search unsuspected resources based on other genealogies, history, and, yes, the infamous "family legend." None of these things alone will solve your special challenges of ethnic research, but taken together, they might lead to that one document, vital record, or online resource that solves the puzzle. It worked for Bill Ammons, the success story in the Introduction, and it might work for you, too.

For example, African-American genealogy often presents special challenges. When researching the genealogy of a former slave, it's necessary to know as much about the slave owner's family as you do about the slave. Wills, deeds, and tax rolls hold clues to ancestry, as do legal agreements to rent slaves. Tracking down all these items can be difficult. You need to know the history of the region and the repositories of the records, and you need to consider family legends *clues*, not answers.

As another example, Native American genealogies are also difficult because in many cases, very little was written down in the eighteenth and nineteenth centuries. A genealogist must contact the tribe involved and look at many different kinds of records. Mixed ethnic heritages, such as Melungeon, are problematic to research because these mixed groups suffered from stigma for many years. If you are researching a Melungeon family line, the true genealogy may have been suppressed or even forgotten by your ancestors. These special cases have led to many online resources.

The sites mentioned in this chapter provide good information on how to begin to search for specific genealogy information, as well as the history and culture of different groups. The challenges you will face can be discussed in the forums and mail lists; you will often find tips on which records to seek and how to get them. Don't forget, however, that new pages are being added to the Web all the time. Search for "genealogy" plus the name of whatever ethnic group you're seeking on your favorite search engine about once a month to see if new information has come online.

And stay on the mail lists and newsgroups for the ethnic groups; when you hit a brick wall, perhaps someone on the list can help!

African-American

You will find many African-American resources in the "Caribbean" section later in the chapter, and you'll find plenty of Caribbean information among the African-American genealogy pages listed in this section.

To begin, the African-American Research area (www.archives.gov/research_room/genealogy/research_topics/african_american_research.html) on the National Archives and Records Administration (NARA) site provides a list of articles and other resources not to be missed.

AfriGeneas (see Figure 14-1) at www.afrigeneas.com is the best starting place for African-American research. Transcribed records, discussion groups, monthly articles, and more will help you get started.

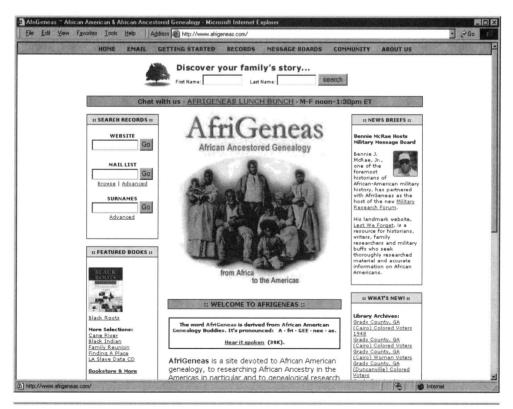

FIGURE 14-1. *AfriGeneas is the best starting place for African-American genealogy.*

The Afro-American Historical and Genealogical Society (AAHGS) is a group for the preservation of the history, genealogy, and culture of those with African heritage. The society's main emphasis is in recording research (as in transcribing sources and so on) and sharing completed genealogies. You'll find AAHGS at www.rootsweb.com/ ~ mdaahgs.

Slaves and the Courts (http://lcweb2.loc.gov/ammem/sthtml/) is an online collection of pamphlets and books about the experiences of African and African-American slaves in the United States and American colonies. It includes trial arguments, examinations of cases and decisions, and other materials concerning slavery and the slave trade. You can locate information by using the collection's subject index, author index, or title index, or you can conduct your own search by keyword. You can look at the items as transcriptions or as images of the original pages.

Cases from America and Great Britain are included with arguments by many well-known abolitionists, presidents, politicians, slave owners, fugitive and free territory slaves, lawyers and judges, and justices of the U.S. Supreme Court. Significant names include John Q. Adams, Roger B. Taney, John C. Calhoun, Salmon P. Chase, Dred Scott, William H. Seward, Theodore Parker, Jonathan Walker, Daniel Drayton, Castner Hanway, Francis Scott Key, William L. Garrison, Wendell Phillips, Denmark Vesey, and John Brown.

The African-American Genealogy Ring is a cooperative of sites linking different resources. Start at www.afamgenealogy.ourfamily.com.

Christine's Genealogy website (www.ccharity.com) has links to articles, census transcriptions, fugitive slave information, and more.

The Freedmen's Bureau Online (www.freedmensbureau.com) allows you to search many records. The Freedman's Bureau took care of education, food, shelter, clothing, and medicine for refugees and freedmen. When Confederate land or property was confiscated, the Freedman's Bureau took custody. Records include personnel records and reports from various states on programs and conditions.

The Alabama African-American Genealogy site is part of the AlaGenWeb. The opening page at www.rootsweb.com/ ~ alaag has links to The Village (a listing of resources online), Alabama Slave Project, Alabama Black Indians, Alabama Civil War Colored Troops, Alabama African-American Marriages, Slave Queries, and Slave Surnames.

The African-American Genealogical Society of Northern California is a local group, but its website has monthly articles, online genealogy charts, discussion groups, and more. It is worth a visit. Find it at www.aagsnc.org.

AAGENE-L is a moderated mail list for African-American genealogy and history researchers. Subscribe to the list by sending a message to aagene-l@upeople.com with SUBSCRIBE in the subject line. Details can be found at http://ftp.cac.psu.edu/ ~ saw/aagene-faq.html.

Here are two sites with no online resources but important nonetheless:

♦ **The National African American Archives Museum**   Located in Mobile, Alabama, this museum is dedicated to preserving the rich history contributed by African-Americans, particularly those born in greater Mobile. You can read details about the museum's holdings, events, and exhibits at http://community.al.com/cc/ nationalafricanamericanachivesmuseum. From the slave ship *Clotilde*, to baseball great Hank Aaron and U.S. Labor Secretary Alexis Herman, you can trace the history of famous African-Americans from Mobile. Admission is free to the public.

♦ **The Alabama A&M State Black Archives, Research Center, and Museum**   Located in Huntsville, Alabama, the Alabama A&M State Black Archives, Research Center, and Museum holds public programs and events on African-American family history. Details about upcoming exhibits, lectures, tours, and workshops are available at http://archivemuseumcenter.mus.al.us/activities/ index.html. The archives/center/museum is open to visitors Monday through Friday, 9:00 A.M. to 4:30 P.M. For information about exhibits, resources, programs, the museum, and tours, call (256) 372-5846 or fax (256) 372-5338, or you can write to the State Black Archives Research Center and Museum, P. O. Box 595, Normal, AL, 35762.

Arab

Genealogy.com has a discussion group for United Arab Emirates genealogy at www.genforum.genealogy.com/uae.

Australian Aborigines

The Aboriginal Studies WWW Virtual Library website, www.ciolek.com/ WWWVL-Aboriginal.html, has links to resources and articles concerning Australian Aborigines.

The National Library of Australia has a page on genealogy, www.nla.gov .au/oz/genelist.html, that includes links to many specific ethnic and family sites.

The Australian Institute of Aboriginal and Torres Strait Islander Studies has a page just for family historians at www.aiatsis.gov.au/lbry/fmly_hstry/fmly_hstry_hm.htm.

The Genealogy in Australia and New Zealand page has a link to the mail list for Australian/New Zealand genealogy at www.rootsweb.com/~billingh.

Caribbean

Caribbean Genealogy Resources, at www.candoo.comgenresources/index.html, lists links to archives, museums, universities, and libraries with historical and genealogical information for countries in the Caribbean. Another page from this site is www.candoo.com/surnames/index.html, which is a list of Caribbean surnames. The text files list surnames, places, and dates, as well as e-mail contact information for researchers looking for them.

SearchBeat, an Internet catalog (see Chapter 5), has a collection of links for Caribbean genealogy that isn't as extensive but includes some links that aren't in Candoo's, including some to Jewish Caribbean genealogy. Go to www.searchbeat.com and click Regional | Caribbean | Society and Culture | Genealogy.

The AOL Hispanic Genealogy Special Interest Group has many Caribbean links. The main page is at users.aol.com/mrosado007/index.htm.

RootsWeb, of course, has mail lists, WorldGenWeb pages, and transcribed records for most Caribbean countries. Go to www.rootsweb.com and search for the country of interest. Then go to www.rootsweb.com/~caribgw for the CaribbeanGenWeb pages.

Creole/Cajun

The Acadians/Cajuns were the French settlers ejected from Nova Scotia by the British in the mid-eighteenth century. Some went to Quebec, and some to Louisiana.

You may be aware that "Creole" means different things in different places. In Latin America, a Creole is someone of pure Spanish blood. In the Caribbean, it means a descendant of Europeans, whereas in the Guineas, it means someone descended from slaves, whether African or native to the islands. In the southern United States, the term refers to aristocratic landowners and slaveholders before the Civil War, part of the overall French/Cajun culture of the Gulf Coast. For almost all Creole research, parish records are your best bet—those and mail list discussions!

Acadian-Cajun Genealogy and History, at www.acadian-cajun.com, publishes records, how-to articles, history, mail lists, maps, genealogies, and more.

The Encyclopedia of Cajun Culture, at www.cajunculture.com, will give you good background information.

Vive La Cajun (www.vivelacajun.com) has information on how to research Cajun genealogy.

The Cajun and Zydeco Radio Guide also has a list of family histories posted to the Web at www.cajunradio.org/genealogy.html.

The Canada GenWeb has a section on Acadian Genealogy in Canada at www.geocities.com/Heartland/Acres/2162.

The St. Augustine Historical Society (Louisiana) has some church records online at www.caneriver.net.

The Louisiana Creole Heritage Center (see Figure 14-2) is located on the campus of Northwestern State University in Natchitoches, Louisiana and on the Web at www.nsula.edu/creole/default.asp.

The Confederation of Associations of Families Acadian (www.cafa.org) promotes the culture and genealogy of Acadian families in America.

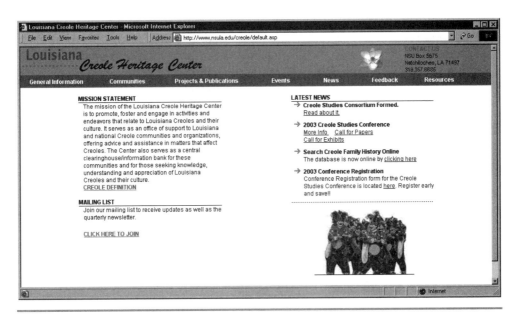

FIGURE 14-2. *The Creole Heritage Center has an online Family History database.*

From July 31 to August 15, 2004, Nova Scotia will host the Third World Acadian Congress; details are at acadien.com/2004. The Acadian Museum and Archives in Nova Scotia has many genealogies. A listing of them, plus hours of operation and so on, can be found at www.ccfne.ns .ca/ ~ museum/english.

Search RootsWeb's list of mail lists; there are several for Acadian/Cajun research and data in Louisiana and Canada. See lists.rootsweb.com/index/ usa/LA/misc.html for Louisiana mail lists and www.rootsweb.com/ ~ jfuller/ gen_mail_country-can.html for Canadian mail lists.

Cuban

Good pointers, tips, and exchanges on Cuban genealogy can be found at the Cuban GenWeb (www.cubagenweb.org).

Even as you read this, University of Florida researchers are working to preserve and copy about 10 million records in the Cuban National Archives. These records cover Cuban life, business, and shipping from 1578 to 1900, but they were sealed with the revolution of 1959. These records were collected by the Notaries of Cuba and stored by the government.

Called *The Notary Protocols*, these records document births, deaths, property, and slave ownership transactions—basically, data on everything and everybody who passed through Havana from Spain to America and back. Once they're made public, these records will enable slave descendants to trace their genealogy to the time their ancestors were first brought to the Americas.

This resource won't become available overnight, of course. The researchers still need to secure funding. Once they begin, the first stages of the project will take 12 to 18 months. Realistically, it will probably be 2004 or later before you can look at the indexes. The University of Florida will post a guide to the materials, and you will then be able to obtain copies of individual documents on CD-ROM. Read about it at www.uflib.ufl.edu/pio. Click the link Back Issues of Chapter One, then Spring 2001. The article is a PDF file, so you will need Acrobat Reader to view it.

Doukhobors

The history of this small sect of Russian pacifist dissenters is outlined in "Who are the Doukhobors?" at www.kootenay.org/Doukhobor.html.

Genealogy is covered at Doukhobors Saskatchewan Genealogy Roots at www.rootsweb.com/ ~ cansk/Saskatchewan/ethnic/doukhobor-saskatchewan.html.

The RootsWeb message boards at Ancestry.com have several topics on this group.

Gypsy, Romani, Romany, and Travellers

A list of links on Gypsy lore, genealogy, and images can be found at http://sca.lib.liv.ac.uk/collections/gypsy/links.htm.

Romani culture and history are covered at Patrin, www.geocities.com/Paris/5121/patrin.htm. Type **genealogy** in the search box at the bottom of the page and several past articles will come up in the results.

Learn about the Travellers at AllAboutIrish, http://allaboutirish.com/library/issues/travellers.htm.

Hmong

The Hmong people came to the United States from Laos at the end of the Vietnam War. The Hmong home page, at www.hmongnet.org, has culture, news, events, and general information. The Hmong Village (www.hmongvillage.com/geneology.htm) has information, as well.

Jewish

The first site to visit for Jewish genealogy is JewishGen.org (www.jewishgen.org). Mail lists, transcribed records, GEDCOMs, and more are at the site. You can also find links to special interest groups, such as geographic emphasis or genetics. Your next stop should be The Israel GenWeb Project website (www.rootsweb.com/ ~ isrwgw), which serves as a resource to those researching their family history in Israel.

Sephardic Genealogy (www.orthohelp.com/geneal/sefardim.htm) has links to articles and historical documents, as does Sephardim.org at www.sephardim.org, which has an article on Jamaican-Jewish history.

Canadian Jewish genealogists should begin at the Jewish Genealogical Society of Montreal (www.gtrdata.com/jgs-montreal), with a history of the first Jewish settlers there.

Native American

Indians/Native Americans on NARA is a reference page with links to various government records resources (www.archives.gov/research_room/alic/reference_desk/native_american_links.html). A good source on culture/heritage is Native Languages of America at www.native-languages.org.

Aboriginal Connections is a site that presents categorized links to Canadian Aboriginal, Native American Indian, and International Indigenous sites on the Web. The genealogy page is at www.aboriginalconnections.com/links/History_and_Culture/Genealogy. It lists links to eight genealogy pages and four language pages.

The African–Native American History & Genealogy web page at www.african-nativeamerican.com/ is mostly concerned with the history of Oklahoma and surrounding areas.

Access Genealogy's (www.accessgenealogy.com/native) Native American Genealogy page has transcribed records and a state-by-state list of online sites.

All Things Cherokee is a site about many aspects of Cherokee culture, genealogy included. The genealogy page is at www.allthingscherokee.com/genealogy.html.

The Potowami tribe has a site at www.potawatomi.org, with a history of the tribe.

The Cheyenne Genealogy site (www.cheyenneancestors.com) has a database of some ancestors, a bibliography for further study, and Montana links.

Many other tribes also have sites. Simply use any search engine for the tribe name, plus the word "genealogy," and you'll likely get a hit.

Metis

Metis is a name for those of Native American heritage, but mixed tribes. The Metis Genealogy Database (www.metisgenealogy.com) page lets you go directly to the database main page or check out other services and links.

Other Metis (www.othermetis.net/AboGene/genelink.html), shown in Figure 14-3, has links to resources and records.

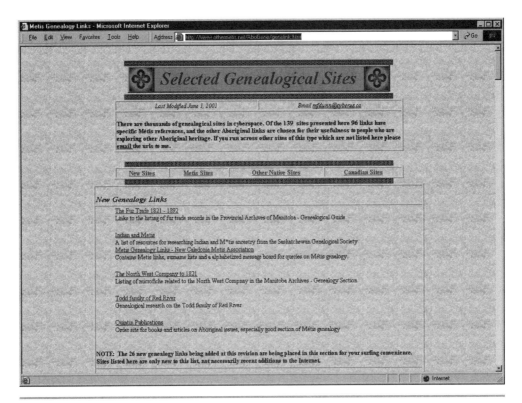

FIGURE 14-3. *Find Metis information from the links on the Metis Genealogy Links page.*

Melungeon

The origins of the people and even the name are controversial, but the Appalachian ethnic group called Melungeon seems to be of European, African, Mediterranean, and Native American descent. One legend is that Sir Francis Drake marooned Portuguese, Turkish, and Moorish prisoners on the North Carolina shore in the 1560s. The Melungeons may date as far back as 1657 in the Appalachian wilderness, possibly earlier.

Melungeons are found in the Cumberland Plateau of Virginia, Kentucky, North Carolina, West Virginia, Tennessee, and, some argue, North Alabama. Recently, Melungeon genealogy has taken on new and exciting relevance with the publication of *The Melungeons: The*

Resurrection of a Proud People, by Dr. N. Brent Kennedy (Mercer University Press, 1997).

Melungeons and other Mestee Groups (www.geocities.com/ mikenassau), by Mike Nassau, is an online book on the subject.

An informational page is "Avoiding Pitfalls in Melungeon Research," at http://pages.xtn.net/ ~ billiam/melungeon.html. This is the text of a talk presented by Pat Spurlock Elder at "Second Union, a Melungeon Gathering" held in Wise, Virginia, in July 1998.

The Melungeon Resource page includes an FAQ file at homepages (http://homepages.rootsweb.com/ ~ mtnties/melungeon.html).

The Appalachian Mountain Families page includes information on Melungeons (http://freepages.genealogy.rootsweb.com/ ~ appalachian).

Everton's site has an FAQ article on the "Black Dutch," who are often included in Melungeon genealogies, at www.everton.com/FHN/ weekly_index.php?show = yes&id = 566.

Some rare diseases are characteristic of Melungeons. The Melungeon Health Education and Support Network at www.melungeonhealth.org describes some of these diseases and has links to resources about them.

A Melungeon mail list exists for people conducting Melungeon and/or Appalachian research, including Native American, Portuguese, Turkish, Black Dutch, and other unverifiable mixed statements of ancestry or unexplained rumors, with ancestors in Tennessee, Kentucky, Virginia, North Carolina, South Carolina, Georgia, Alabama, West Virginia, and possibly other places. Details can be found at www.rootsweb.com/ ~ jfuller/gen_mail_states-gen.html#MELUNGEO.

Wrapping Up

- ◆ Many ethnic groups have started mail lists, newsgroups, and history sites.

- ◆ Once a month, use your favorite search engine to find new sites.

- ◆ Stay on mail lists to discuss your ethnic "brick walls."

Chapter 15

The National Genealogical Society

The National Genealogical Society (NGS) is one of the important genealogical societies in the United States. On its website (www.ngsgenealogy.org) you'll find announcements of NGS seminars, workshops, and programs, information on its home study course, youth resources, and other NGS activities. This is an excellent site for learning genealogy standards and methods.

NGS was organized in Washington, D.C., in 1903. The preliminary first meeting was held on the 24th of April, and the formal organization was effected on the 11th of November. Now, the NGS has over 17,000 members, including individuals, families, genealogical societies, family associations, libraries, and other related institutions.

National Genealogical Society

The NGS is one of the best umbrella organizations for family history. Its workshops, meetings, and publications are invaluable. You can see its home page in Figure 15-1.

On the home page, you'll find links to the newest and most relevant items on the site, including upcoming meetings, trips, courses, and competitions. And, on every page of the site, you'll find a navigation bar at the top that leads to the following sections:

- Home
- Learning Center
- Resources
- Conferences
- NGS Tech
- News and Events
- Bookstore
- Links

Home

Under the Home button on the navigation bar you'll find information about the Society itself, from how to join to competitions. You'll also

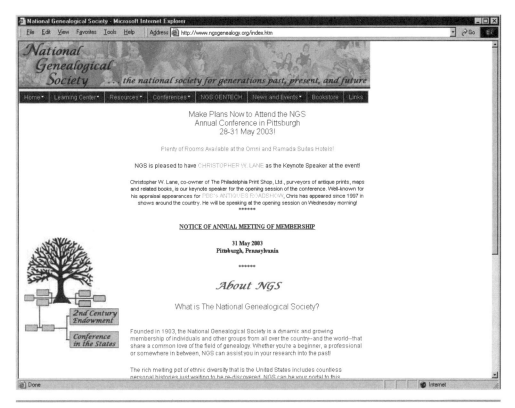

FIGURE 15-1. *The National Genealogical Society site has searchable data as well as information about the organization.*

find the headquarters' street address, phone numbers, a map to the NGS headquarters, e-mail addresses, and the hours of the library.

Programs include the Consumer Protection Committee, which maintains a page on how to recognize a scam, such as those described in Chapter 2. Another page in this section describes the activities of the Records Preservation and Access Committee of NGS, which is striving to develop a consistent and logical long-term strategy to deal with the preservation of records and access issues at all levels, from local to national. Because state and local governments are so strapped for cash, valuable records are being lost due to lack of funding and space to keep them. (People don't get excited about preservation when the budget gets cut!) The committee hopes to head off potential problems with solutions before they become issues. Another committee is the NGS

Family Health and Heredity Committee, which is promoting the value of researching and recording ancestral medical information in genealogy.

Under the Home button is a link to Member Benefits. In this section, you'll find the NGS guidelines for your genealogy research. The standards are listed on the page www.ngsgenealogy.org/comstandards.htm. You'll also find the standards at the end of this book in Appendix A. These standards give you a good roadmap to valid, ethical genealogical research.

Learning Center

The courses offered online, through correspondence, and through conferences, covered in Chapter 5, are listed here. You'll find the current costs as well as dates and times for in-person educational opportunities.

Resources

The NGS has a circulating library available to members. Reference material, records, and members' ancestral charts are among the holdings available online. Among the online services is the online card catalog (see Figure 15-2). You can also pay a fee to have research done

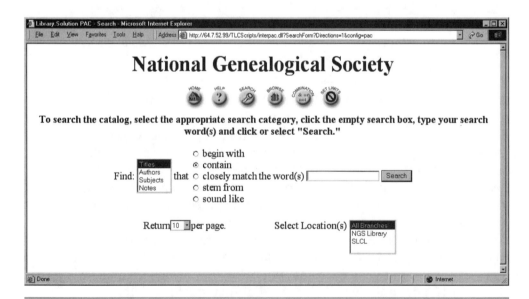

FIGURE 15-2. *Under Resources, you can find the card catalog to the NGS circulating library.*

for you in the Physician Data Base, a listing of AMA records of American physicians who died after 1905 and before 1965, and other sources held by the Society. The site also has a list of books by NGS members.

You'll also find information on their research trips, where you learn by doing at locations around the U.S. and abroad.

Resources that you can search online include the following:

- ◆ NGS library catalog

- ◆ Members ancestor charts (Mac file)

- ◆ Bible records

- ◆ Deceased physicians search

- ◆ Germans to America search

- ◆ Italians to America search

Conferences

Here you'll find links to information on the annual conference, regional conferences, research trips, competitions, and the NGS Hall of Fame. The conferences are excellent; experts from all over the world teach all levels of research techniques, from beginner to expert. You can also find many supplies and genealogy-related items from vendors at the conferences.

NGS Tech

This conference began as GENTECH in the early 90s as a separate enterprise from the Society. The NGS has become a partner in the endeavor; the next one will be in 2004 in St. Louis. The conference consists of two days of workshops and lectures on technical aspects of genealogy, from online research to modern archival techniques, with a special day of programs for librarians. It also has a vendor display.

News and Events

This section includes news about the organization and its members, news from the world of genealogy, articles from recent genealogy conferences, and press releases from other organizations. Of special interest are the online articles on aspects of genealogy and the queries.

Bookstore

From reference books and archival supplies, such as acid free paper, to NGS apparel and desk blotters, the NGS bookstore offers a wide variety of items for the genealogist.

Links

As with any good website, the NGS has a Links page (www.ngsgenealogy .org/links.htm). Here you'll find leads to sites for general genealogy; libraries and archives online; societies and organizations; ethnic and immigration resources and records, and miscellaneous information.

Wrapping Up

- ◆ The NGS is an umbrella institution for education and resources in genealogy.

- ◆ You can take online and at-home genealogy courses from NGS, take research trips, and attend NGS conferences to learn about genealogy.

- ◆ Certain databases can be searched online at the site; you can also pay a fee to have NGS staffers research for you.

- ◆ National and regional meetings also offer genealogy courses.

Chapter 16

RootsWeb

How would you like a place where you can search dozens of databases of genealogical materials, look through hundreds of genealogical web pages, and subscribe to thousands of mail lists? How about a place where you can publish your own page, upload your own data, and create your own mail list?

Welcome to "Online Genealogy Heaven," better known as *RootsWeb* (www.rootsweb.com). RootsWeb began as a site for a group of people working at the research center RAND who dabbled in genealogy on the side. Once upon a time, they had a little mail list, hosted by the University of Minnesota, and a little database on the RAND server. That was 13 years ago. Today, RootsWeb is the largest all-volunteer genealogy site on the Web.

Pro-Am

RootsWeb is sort of a Pro-Am site. It started as an all-volunteer effort. Then the costs of servers, disk space, and connections got so high that they had to merge with Ancestry.com. This means two things: First, people are no longer asked to contribute $25 a year to RootsWeb to help defray the costs the volunteers were incurring. Ancestry.com now subsidizes the hardware and software to keep RootsWeb up and running. Second, almost all the secondary information is free, but some of the primary source evidence is on Ancestry's site, and you have to subscribe. It's not a completely black-and-white situation; there are still plenty of transcribing projects that are free to access, such as ship's passenger lists, census transcriptions, and so on. And Ancestry hosts some of the free stuff, such as the message boards.

In the months immediately following the merger, many were concerned that RootsWeb's privacy and fair use policies would change, but so far they haven't. To date, if you submit data to RootsWeb, it won't be slapped onto a CD-ROM and sold by Ancestry (of course, you still need to be sure that data on living people isn't included in your submissions because anyone can copy publicly posted data and slap it anywhere). For the user, little has really changed.

The mission of RootsWeb is summed up in the following statement, published on its home page:

"The RootsWeb project has two missions:

To make large volumes of data available to the online genealogical community at minimal cost.

To provide support services to online genealogical activities, such as Usenet newsgroup moderation, mailing list maintenance, surname list generation, and so forth."

A quick guided tour of RootsWeb only scratches the surface of all the helpful and informative services available at this site. The following story gives you an idea of the unique possibilities RootsWeb offers.

Success Story: RootsWeb Leads to a Reunion

About three years ago, I started searching for my Powell ancestors (on my father's side), but about the only thing I knew how to do was search the surname and message boards.

One night, after having done nothing in about two months, I decided to get online and read the [RootsWeb] surname message boards. On a whim, I went into the Hubbard message boards (on my mother's side). The first message I read was about someone searching for descendants of my grandmother's parents.

When my grandmother was about three or four, her mother passed away and she went to live with an aunt and uncle. Eventually, my grandmother lost contact with her brothers. She did see her oldest brother once when she was about 15, but after that she never saw or heard from him again. That night, I found him, a person my grandmother had not seen in over 70 years.

We flew to Washington state and met all kinds of new cousins, aunts, and uncles. Over the next two years, my grandmother spoke with her brother many times. Unfortunately, he had passed away the summer before, but she did see him twice and was able to speak with him on numerous occasions.

We figured out that the message I responded to had been posted for about a minute before I discovered it. The surname message boards are a wonderful tool in searching for the ancestors and relatives you never knew you had, or those you had but didn't know who they were.

—Jennifer Powell Lyons

What You'll Find at RootsWeb

RootsWeb has more genealogical information than you can shake a stick at. Some of this is secondary source information, such as genealogies members have submitted. Some of this information is close to primary information—for example, transcripts of wills, deeds, census forms, and vital records, with citations of where exactly the original information can be found. Some of it is primary information (for example Ancestry's Census Images, which is covered in Chapter 17), and you have to pay a subscription fee to Ancestry to access that information.

At the top of all the RootsWeb pages, you'll see a navigation bar with these categories: Home, Searches, Family Trees, Mailing Lists, Message Boards, Web Sites, Passwords, and Help (see Figure 16-1).

Home and Help are self-explanatory, and the following text explains Searches, Family Trees, Mailing Lists, Message Boards, and Web Sites.

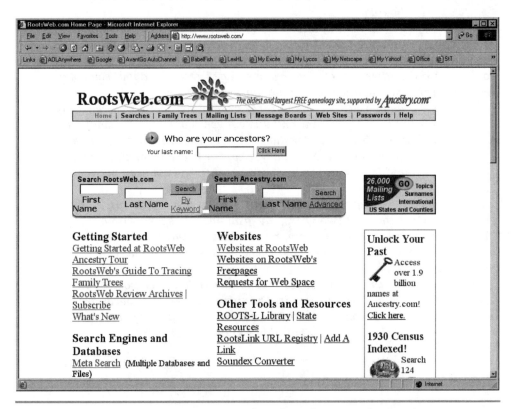

FIGURE 16-1. *The main page serves as an index; all RootsWeb pages have a navigation bar.*

The link to Passwords is a help page for retrieving lost passwords to mailing lists and websites.

When you look at the RootsWeb page in your browser, you'll find on the home page two search templates to input a surname, first name, or any keywords (see Figure 16-1). One searches RootsWeb's free information; the other searches Ancestry.com (see Chapter 17). The search will look in all the RootsWeb pages or Ancestry databases and show you the results. It's a great way to get started on your genealogy!

Finding information on RootsWeb can be that simple. However, you can use many different tools on the site to get more targeted results.

Getting Started at RootsWeb

On the Home page index is a section called "Getting Started." The sections there—Getting Started at RootsWeb; Ancestry Tour; RootsWeb's Guide to Tracing Family Trees; RootsWeb Review Archives | Subscribe; and What's New—will give the beginner a good grounding in RootsWeb.

Getting Started at RootsWeb is a short page on how to share, communicate, research, and volunteer with the site. Ancestry Tour is a multimedia overview of what the commercial side offers. The Guide to Tracing Family Trees is really a collection of guides sorted by general, sources, and countries. What's New lists the newest additions to the pages and databases on the volunteer side, and subscribing to *RootsWeb Review* will bring the same information to your e-mail box.

Available Files and Databases

ROOTS-L has tons of files and databases, which you can get by e-mailing the appropriate commands to the list server that runs ROOTS-L. You can search the ROOTS-L Library for everything from a fabulous collection devoted to obtaining vital records, to useful tips for beginners, to book lists from the Library of Congress, and more. Some of the available files are listed here:

♦ **Surname Helper (http://surhelp.rootsweb.com/)** Looks at the RootsWeb message boards and personal websites.

♦ **U.S. Town/County Database (http://resources.rootsweb.com/cgi-bin/townco.cgi)** Looks for locations. It's a sort of online gazetteer.

- **The WorldConnect Project (http://worldconnect.rootsweb .com/)**   Searches GEDCOMs of family trees submitted by RootsWeb members.

- **The USGenWeb Archives Search (http://www.usgenweb .org)**   Looks for pages posted across the United States in the GenWeb Project.

- **WorldGenWeb (http://www.worldgenweb.org)**   Searches for genealogy resources in nations outside the United States.

- **The Roots Location List (RLL; http://searches.rootsweb.com/ cgi-bin/Genea/rll)**   This list has locations of special interest to individual researchers, along with contact information for those researchers. This list is useful for trading research chores. For example, if you are in Colorado and need research in Ohio, you can try to find someone on the list in Ohio who needs Colorado research.

- **U.S. Civil War Units (http://www.ancestry.com/search/rectype/ military/cwrd/main.htm?rc = locale%7E&us = 0)**   A search engine for information about the military units that served in the United States Civil War. Muster rolls, histories, and more are included.

RootsWeb Surname List (RSL)

The RSL (http://rsl.rootsweb.com/cgi-bin/rslsql.cgi) is a registry of who is searching for whom, and in what times and places. The listings include contact information for each entry. When you find someone looking for the same name, in the same area, and in about the same time period, you might be able to help each other. That's the intent of the list. You don't have to pay to submit your own data or to search for data.

To search the list, you can use the form on the search page or go to the page rsl.rootsweb.com.

On the RSL page, you type in the surname you want to search for. You can narrow your search by including a location where you think the person you are looking for lives or lived, using the abbreviations you'll find at the link below the location box. Use the radio buttons to choose whether you want to search by surname (names spelled exactly as you've typed them) or by Soundex or Metaphone (names that sound like the one you've typed, though spelled differently). In future attempts, you can limit the search to new submissions within the last week, month, or two months. The list is updated once a month.

The Migration field shows you the path the family took. SC > GA, for example, shows migration from South Carolina to Georgia.

WorldConnect Project

The WorldConnect Project is one of several GEDCOM databases searchable through the Web. Searching it from the RootsWeb home page, you can only input first and last names. The results page has another input form at the bottom, enabling you to fine-tune the search by adding places and dates.

If you go to the WorldConnect page at worldconnect.rootsweb.com (see Figure 16-2), you can find links to tips and hints for using WorldConnect. Remember, all the data here is uploaded by volunteers, so errors might exist!

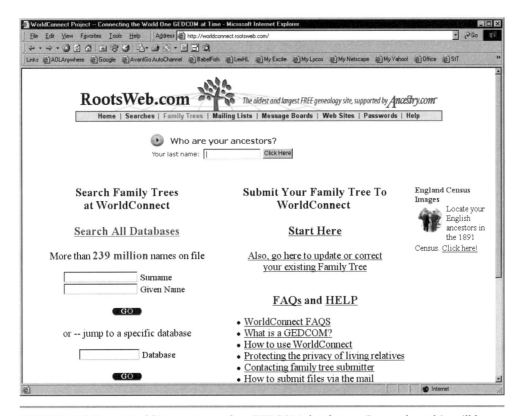

FIGURE 16-2. *WorldConnect searches GEDCOM databases. Remember, this will be secondary, not primary, evidence.*

Social Security Death Index (SSDI)

The Social Security Death Index (http://ssdi.rootsweb.com/) searches the federal records of deaths. Anyone who died before Social Security began in the 1930s won't be in this database.

Searching from the RootsWeb home page, all you can input is the first and last name, but the results page will let you link to the Advanced Search page, where you can narrow the search by location and date. This is an excellent tool for researching twentieth-century ancestors.

GenSeeker

GenSeeker looks for your search terms on the thousands of personal genealogy web pages at RootsWeb, plus any other registered documents, such as records transcriptions. You can also perform Boolean searches (see Chapter 6).

Other Search Engines

RootsWeb has several other ways for you to search both the site and the Web at large. GenSeeker (http://seeker.rootsweb.com/search.html), for example, enables you to search the contents of all the registered web documents at RootsWeb; SearchThingy (http://sitesearch.rootsweb .com/cgi-bin/search) looks at all the databases and text files; and MetaSearch (http://resources.rootsweb.com/cgi-bin/metasearch) looks for names across RootsWeb.

The Surnames search index, United States Counties/States index, and the Countries index all search different subsets of the RootsWeb information. All these are worth looking at, and all can be accessed from http://searches.rootsweb.com/.

These searches can be helpful in your research, but they assume you're a rank beginner with no more than a name or a place to launch your inquiries. Perhaps you know for sure you're looking for a land record in Alabama or a cemetery in Iowa. RootsWeb has several searchable resources for items such as these. You'll find the search engines for the RSL and the other databases at http://searches.rootsweb.com (see Figure 16-3).

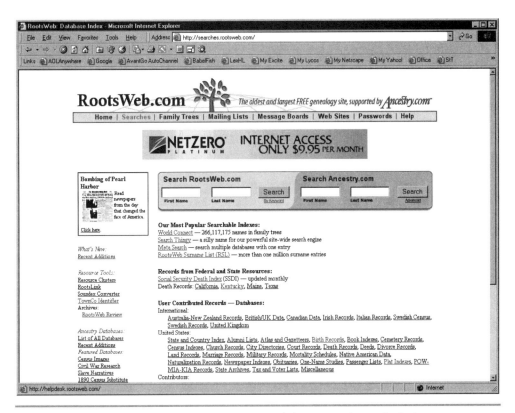

FIGURE 16-3. *The Searches page at RootsWeb has several search choices.*

Research Templates

This collection of links from the home page index will lead you to lists of pages for different subjects. The surname list, for example, leads you to first an alphabet list, then to all surnames under a certain letter, then to a page for a specific surname. The Spencer Research Template page is shown in Figure 16-4.

Other research templates are for geographic locations such as states in the U.S. or a whole country such as France.

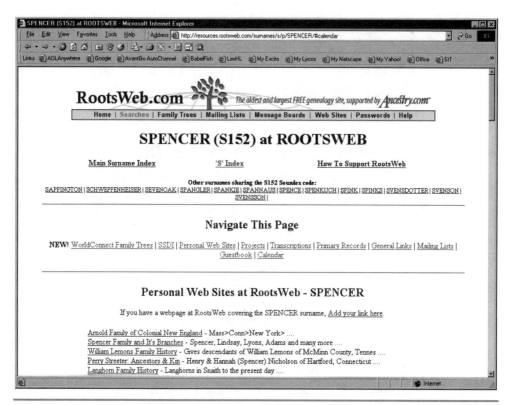

FIGURE 16-4. *The Spencer Research Template leads you to resources on RootsWeb that have Spencer information, from personal genealogy pages to a calendar of Spencer events.*

Message Boards and Mailing Lists

Among the best resources on RootsWeb are the mail lists and message boards, now hosted at Ancestry. A *message board* is a place where messages are read, sent, and answered on the Web, using a browser to read them. A *mail list* is where messages are e-mailed to and from the members. A mail client is used to read them. Both the message boards and the mail lists are archived and searchable. Figure 16-5 shows a typical message board on RootsWeb since the Ancestry merger.

Click the bottom of any message board's page to read the FAQs, request a new board, read the rules, or get help.

The mail lists at http://lists.rootsweb.com cover many topics, such as the RootsWeb newsletters, described later in this chapter. Lists exist for specific surnames, every state in the United States, other countries

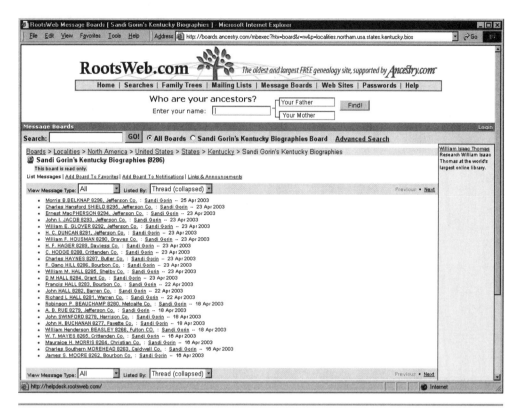

FIGURE 16-5.   *Message boards on RootsWeb are hosted by Ancestry.*

(from Aruba to Zimbabwe), and lists for topics such as adoption, medical genealogy, prisons, and heraldry. From the Mailing Lists page, you can click a link to each one and you'll get instructions on how to use the list, including subscribing, unsubscribing, sticking to the topic, and so on. The page for the Heraldry mail list on RootsWeb is shown in Figure 16-6.

Besides ROOTS-L, which is the grandparent of genealogy mail lists on the Internet, RootsWeb hosts literally thousands of mail lists. As mentioned in Chapter 8, you can find lists for surnames and family names, regions, and topics being researched. The index at www.rootsweb .com/~maillist has thousands of lists you can join, along with instructions explaining how to subscribe. It won't include all the mail lists at RootsWeb, however, because it's a voluntary listing, and not all list owners choose to be featured.

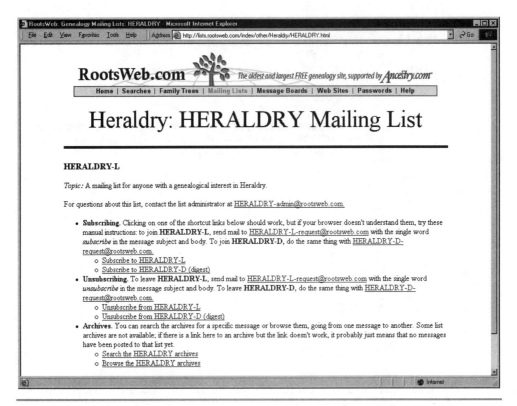

FIGURE 16-6. *Each mail list has an information page with instructions for subscribing.*

A good rule of thumb: Be choosy in joining lists! Take on only a few at a time. Read the lists for a while, sign off if they don't prove useful, and then try some others. Some lists are extremely active—sometimes overwhelmingly so. One RootsWeb user who signed up for every possible mail list for the United Kingdom had 9,000 e-mails in his inbox within 24 hours! Be careful what you wish for....

And remember, some lists are archived, so you needn't subscribe to see if that list is talking about subjects of interest to you. Just search the archive for your keywords and save the important messages.

You might even want to start a mail list of your own someday, which contributors can do. You can learn more about what's required of a list owner by going to the Help page and clicking the Request a Mailing List link or by going to http://resources.rootsweb.com/adopt/.

GenNewbie

GenNewbie is an electronic mail list for people who are new to computers and/or genealogy. It is the place to ask questions, help others, and generally share information, research techniques, brick walls, and computer/genealogy woes. It began on October 31, 1996 as an offshoot of the renowned ROOTS-L. Subscribing is as simple as clicking one of the buttons at the bottom of the page at www.rootsweb .com/~newbie. The GenNewbie archives include a six-part course in genealogy by Jean Legreid, a Certified Genealogical Records Specialist.

GENMTD-L

Genealogical methods and resources are the topics for GENMTD-L. This isn't a queries list. Instead, it's a list about the nuts and bolts of genealogy research. You can participate through e-mail or through Usenet news. The discussions are archived, searchable, and retrievable.

GENMTD-L is a moderated group intended for helpful discussions of the research methods, resources, and problems genealogists have in common, regardless of the different families or different cultural groups they study. The exception is methods relating to computing, databases, and online research. Often a problem is presented to the group, which then discusses possible solutions. Also, useful research strategies and resources might be posted. Like most RootsWeb mail lists, you send a message with SUBSCRIBE in the body to the list's subscribe address. In this case, it's GENMTD-L-request@rootsweb.com for single-message format, GENMTD-D-request@rootsweb.com for digests of messages, and GENMTD-I-request@rootsweb.com for index format. A complete explanation of how to manage your subscription can be found at www.rootsweb.com/~genmtd.

Newsletters

A newsletter, like a mail list, comes straight to your e-mail inbox. Unlike the lists discussed previously, however, they are not for discussion; the communication is one-to-many. Like a print magazine, a newsletter will have news, notes, stories, and the occasional (text) advertisement. RootsWeb has several e-mail newsletters, all of which are worth reading. Here are some descriptions of them.

RootsWeb Review

RootsWeb is always growing, and you can't depend on luck to find out about the latest and greatest sites! *RootsWeb Review* is a free weekly newsletter sent to subscribers with the news about RootsWeb. You'll find announcements of programs and services for RootsWeb users, new mail lists, GenConnect boards, and websites, plus success stories from other online genealogists.

If you're interested in reading through previous issues, go to http://e-zine.rootsweb.com/rwr-issues.html. You can subscribe by sending an e-mail to RootsWeb-Review-L-request@rootsweb.com with only the word "subscribe" in the subject line and message area.

Missing Links and Somebody's Links

Missing Links is a weekly compilation of articles about genealogical research methods and sources from all parts of the world. You can subscribe at www.petuniapress.com. *Somebody's Links* is a monthly collection of uncovered genealogical treasures, such as photographs, diaries, letters, and family bibles. The contributors describe each item as accurately as possible, hoping someone out there is looking for it. Back issues of the newsletter are available as plain-text files at www.petuniapress.com. Files are named according to the date of the issue (for example, 19991201.txt).

Note

All back issues of RootsWeb Review *and* Missing Links *are searchable at www.petuniapress.com.*

Web Pages at RootsWeb

RootsWeb hosts thousands of genealogy websites. Some, such as Cyndi's List at www.cyndislist.com and the USGenWeb Project's main site at www.usgenweb.com, you've already read about in this book. RootsWeb also hosts the WorldGenWeb Project at www.worldgenweb.org and a majority of the country sites. Some examples follow.

RootsWeb-Sponsored Pages

Books We Own (www.rootsweb.com/ ~ bwo) is a list of resources owned/accessed by volunteers who are willing to look up genealogical information and then e-mail or snail mail it to others who request it. This is a free service, and volunteers might ask for reimbursement of copies and postage if information is provided via snail mail. The project began in 1996 as a way for members of the ROOTS-L mail list to share their resources with one another. Today, over 1,500 volunteers exist. Resource owners are volunteers with a limited amount of time and resources to spend looking up information. Jenny Tenlen has served as the Webmaster of Books We Own since February 1997 and is the third Webmaster since this project began.

Cemetery Photos (www.rootsweb.com/ ~ cemphoto/Cemetery_Photos .html) is the same sort of idea, applied to cemeteries. Volunteers will go to a cemetery and take pictures of tombstones for you if you know the exact names, dates, and locations for them to look for. Cemetery Photos is a project designed to help people obtain photos of headstones in areas they can't get to themselves. Over 3,500 volunteers cover 24 countries. Some ask to be reimbursed for the film and postage. You can volunteer to be part of this effort, too!

FreeBMD (England and Wales), at http://freebmd.rootsweb.com, stands for *Free Births, Marriages, and Deaths*. The FreeBMD Project's objective is to provide free Internet access to the Civil Registration index information for England and Wales. The Civil Registration system for recording births, marriages, and deaths in England and Wales has been in place since 1837. This is one of the most significant single resources for genealogical research back to Victorian times.

Immigrant Ships Transcribers Guild (http://istg.rootsweb.com) is a group of volunteers dedicated to making the search for our ancestors' immigration easier. The page is shown in Figure 16-7. The aim is to make as many ship's passenger lists as possible available online—and not just for U.S. ports. There are databases for Australia, Canada, Irish passengers to Argentina, and more. This group would also be happy to have your help!

Random Acts of Genealogical Kindness (www.raogk.org) is a cooperative effort. Once a month, the volunteers of this movement agree either to videotape cemeteries or to visit county courthouses in the county (or an area of a country) they live in to transcribe records.

FIGURE 16-7. *ISTG is a volunteer project sponsored by RootsWeb.*

The cost to you would be reimbursement of costs incurred in granting your request (videotape, copying fees, and so forth).

State Resource Pages, one of the main areas of RootsWeb, is at www.rootsweb.com/roots-l/usa.html. It offers a wealth of information to those researching in the United States.

Freepages

Freepages are genealogy pages by volunteers. These pages must fit the RootsWeb mission, cannot contain copyrighted, commercial, or multimedia material, and cannot redirect to another site. If you meet these and all the other rules stated on http://accounts.rootsweb.com/index.cgi?op = show&page = freagree.htm, you can have free web space at RootsWeb. The freepages include sites of major RootsWeb projects, such as USGenWeb and WorldGenWeb, as well as genealogical or historical organizations.

You can find kids' pages, lessons and help pages, memorials and timelines among these pages. If you already have a genealogy-related website and want it linked from RootsWeb, you can register it as well.

The HelpDesk

The HelpDesk (http://helpdesk.rootsweb.com/) maintains a page to help you find an FAQ file about RootsWeb and its services. If you have a question or problem, check here first. If you can't find an answer here, you can follow the links from this site to the message board, where you can post a question for the HelpDesk team to answer.

More and More

This quick tour is just enough to whet your appetite. Spend some time getting to know RootsWeb. Then get acquainted with Ancestry.com, the subject of Chapter 17.

Wrapping Up

- ◆ The RootsWeb site is a great place to begin your family history research.

- ◆ Message boards are now hosted on Ancestry.com.

- ◆ Newsletters from RootsWeb help you stay on top of the latest in genealogy.

- ◆ Online files at RootsWeb have transcribed primary-source records.

- ◆ RootsWeb mail lists cover a broad range of topics.

- ◆ Search engines on RootsWeb make using the site easier.

- ◆ You can get free space for your genealogy-related web page at RootsWeb.

Chapter 17

The MyFamily.com Network

MyFamily.com, based in Salt Lake City, Utah, is a wide-ranging collection of genealogy resources. Besides supporting RootsWeb .com, its genealogy empire includes the following sites:

- ♦ **MyFamily.com**   An interactive site where you can post your genealogy, interact with family members, and store your backup files. You can do some things for free, but fees apply for additional disk space and some other services.

- ♦ **Ancestry.com**   Publishes books, magazines, and other genealogy materials and has subscription-based research materials on their website, with mostly U.S. material.

- ♦ **Ancestry.com.uk**   A website with research for Canada, Australia, and the United Kingdom, based on subscription.

- ♦ **Genealogy.com**   A website recently acquired by MyFamily.com that has subscription-based resources as well as free material and news. Genealogy.com also owns Family Trees software and GenForum message boards. It shares a cross-marketing agreement with A&E's The History Channel.

As mentioned in the previous chapter, Ancestry.com (whose parent company is now called MyFamily.com), a commercial venture, and RootsWeb, a volunteer cooperative, have merged. The two sites are still different from each other, however, except in the area of the message boards. The files, chats, and other online functions are different among the MyFamily.com family of sites.

MyFamily.com also publishes magazines and books. *Genealogical Computing* magazine covers technology issues and breakthroughs in genealogy; *Ancestry* magazine covers general topics such as research techniques, success stories, and historical topics. *Ancestry's Red Book: American State, County, and Town Sources, Finding Answers in U.S. Census Records,* and *The Source: A Guidebook of American Genealogy* are just three of the well-respected publications under the Ancestry imprint.

RootsWeb, covered in Chapter 16, still has free downloads of files and information. The MyFamily.com sites have some free areas and other areas to which you must pay a monthly, quarterly, or yearly subscription to access.

Ancestry.com

Ancestry.com, which was the first website among the MyFamily.com empire, has two main parts. The research side has databases of transcribed and secondary material, much of which is accessible for a fee. The exchange side includes uploaded GEDCOMs, messages boards, and original articles on genealogy, accessible for free. Features include the following:

♦ A large online genealogy library, searchable from the Web. The library includes such records as land, birth, marriage, death, census, and immigration records, as well as the Periodical Source Index (PERSI), Daughters of the American Revolution Lineage Books, the 1790 Census Collection, and the Early American Marriages Collection, to name just a few. Of note is the recent addition of the *London Times* (editions from 1786 to 1833) and the U.K. Census of 1891, with every name indexed for both.

♦ Name-indexed GEDCOM databases, which are updated frequently, so future searches may turn up what today's search did not.

♦ Regular genealogy columns by writers such as George G. Morgan, Dick Eastman, Kip Sperry, Juliana Smith, Elizabeth Kelley Kerstens, and Drew Smith are available free of charge.

The opening page is shown in Figure 17-1.

Subscription Areas

You can choose from several different levels of subscription to Ancestry .com: A "super subscription," with access to standard data and the U.S. Federal Census images, for about $190 a year; access to standard data for $119 a year; access to the U.S. Federal Census images for $80 a year; and access to message boards and articles free of charge. Sometimes the company will run free access specials, especially around Christmas time, to encourage people to give subscriptions as gifts. Their free daily newsletter (you sign up on the Learning page at www.ancestry.com/ learn/main.htm?lfl = m) has alerts on when the free offers begin and end.

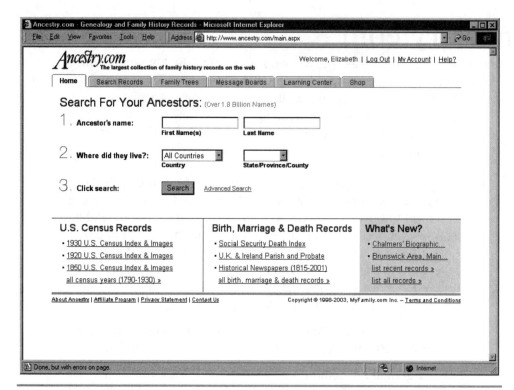

FIGURE 17-1. *Ancestry.com's opening page has a quick search form, so you can determine whether your ancestors' names are in the databases on the site.*

Note

Check out the new Beginner's Membership, with access to selected databases most likely to help someone just starting to research family history.

Free Areas

Even if you don't sign up for a paid subscription, you can find loads of useful information in the free sections of Ancestry.com. The most popular part of the site is its searchable database of the free Social Security Death Index (SSDI). If you're looking for someone who died after the 1930s, this is a good place to start.

Another popular free area is the Ancestry.com World Tree database. Visitors to the site are welcome to submit what data they have for this database, the largest collection of its kind on the Internet. It's all-volunteer, and Ancestry.com has pledged to keep the searches free. Be aware, however, that Ancestry.com, as with most other sites that accept an individual's data, doesn't check the data submitted. These genealogies must all be considered secondary material at best. Nevertheless, it can give you some good clues.

To use the Ancestry.com World Tree database, click the tab labeled Family Trees or open the page www.ancestry.com/trees/main.htm and simply enter a name and that person's parents' names, if you have them. The matches in the databases are presented in a table, as shown in Figure 17-2.

You can click the links to view the person's pedigree, look at data for that individual, e-mail the submitter, and download the GEDCOM.

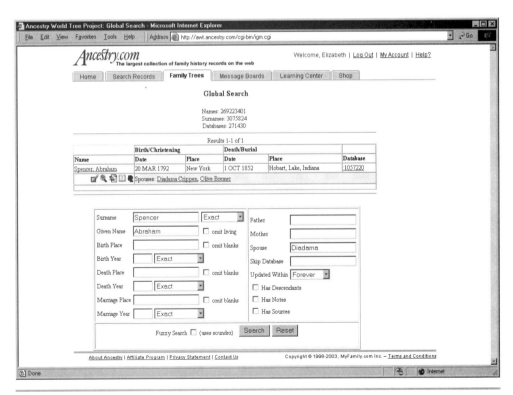

FIGURE 17-2. *Find names in submitted GEDCOMs at World Tree by clicking the Family Trees tab and typing in at least one name.*

Some of the links will be to the pay areas, as described earlier. For example, putting in Marvin Wayne Crowe, I had no hits in World Tree but had six hits in the Periodicals and Newspapers databases, which are only available to paid subscribers (see Figure 17-3).

You also might want to check out the software Ancestry Family Tree, which is free. You can load your GEDCOM into it and it will search Ancestry.com automatically for matches to each name in your database. You can also add names, dates, and places as you find them, add sources and connect specific facts to them, and handle divorces and other records.

Other good links in the free area include articles on genealogy techniques, genealogy lessons, phone and address searches, Juliana's Links, a searchable database of websites, and maps and gazetteers. The site also features a chat area, bookstore, and sample articles from *Ancestry* magazine, the print version.

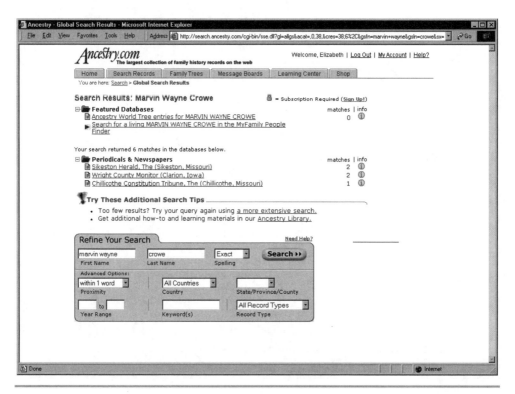

FIGURE 17-3.   *The subscription areas include scanned newspapers and periodicals, indexed by the names that appear in the text.*

Success Story: Proving a Family Legend

I smashed a brick wall recently using Ancestry.com. I have a basic subscription to Ancestry.

There has been a family story in my husband's family for as long as anyone can remember that the name Flynt isn't really the family surname, that it is really Damon. No one knew any more than that.

Ancestry.com put an index to Maine court records online. I did a search for the great-great-grandfather Daniel Flint/Flynt. I was rewarded with "Daniel Flint (Alias)." I copied down the book and page numbers and contacted the State of Maine Archives for copies of the court records. The records showed a conviction for bigamy and included marriage records for the first marriage as Delafayette Damon to Esther Damon in Reading, Massachusetts in 1805 and his second, unlawful marriage as Daniel Flint to Lydia Anne Williams in Farmington, Maine in 1812. He appealed the conviction on the grounds that the first marriage took place in Massachusetts, and Maine didn't have jurisdiction. He was granted a new trial, but the Attorney General didn't pursue the matter, and Daniel Flint went home to Abbot, Maine to raise his second family, from which my husband was descended.

With this information I was able to find his ancestors through his mother back to Thomas Flint, one of the early settlers of Reading, Massachusetts, and his first wife's family, as well as their three children. This has all been from secondary sources and not yet proved, but at least now I know where to look for proof.

—Alta Flynt

MyFamily.com

The free MyFamily.com site is a portal. Portals are good places to start when you log on to the Internet. Also, portals might be the last place you visit online before you log off because they offer so many features and activities—you might never need to surf anywhere else.

MyFamily.com's portal is a family history/community portal. The tools on the MyFamily.com site include a family calendar, family chat, family history features, message boards, a photo album, and more. Access to each family's site has both private, password-only areas and public areas. You can use up to 5MB of free space per site you create. To use more space, you have to pay a yearly fee of about $25 up to about $200, depending on the amount of space you need. You can also get a package that includes a domain name (for example, www.CroweFamily.com). The details are at www.myfamily.com.

Still, 5MB of space is ample room to create a site for your family, with a short family tree. You can store photos, sounds, and video clips in your album, and you can upload games or shareable applications to the file cabinet.

Other features are on the MyFamily.com site (they have much less to do with genealogy), but for this book I will only cover those areas related to genealogy.

At the My Sites link (on the MyFamily.com home page), you can create a private message board, calendar, and file cabinets. You can also put together online scrapbooks of image, sound, and video files, upload your genealogy, and host private chats among members of your family you choose to invite. Once you create the site, your MyFamily home page will look similar to the one shown in Figure 17-4.

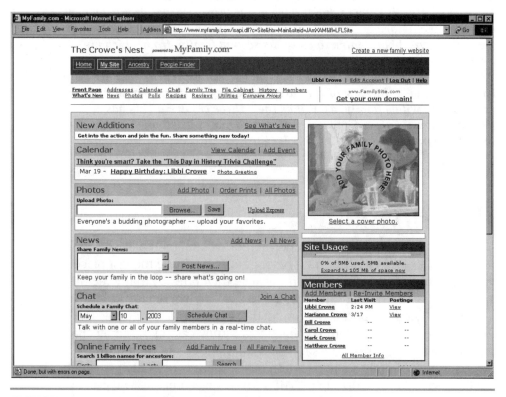

FIGURE 17-4. *Your family page can include pictures, birthdays, chat schedules, and more.*

Creating a site is just a matter of a few clicks. You define a name and login, and then you draw up a list of relatives. You input their birthdays, anniversaries, and other important calendar dates and then invite family members to join you by creating a list of their e-mail addresses. Everyone on the list is e-mailed a specific logon name and password for that site (no one can access your site without them). You can also create an address book with phone numbers and so forth for you to access when you're online.

Family Tree

Now it's time to begin constructing your online family tree. To do this, use the Family Tree link in the navigation bar at the top of every page on your MyFamily site. You can create a family tree by typing in entries online or by uploading a GEDCOM (by far the most recommended method!). I uploaded a GEDCOM, and one view is shown in Figure 17-5.

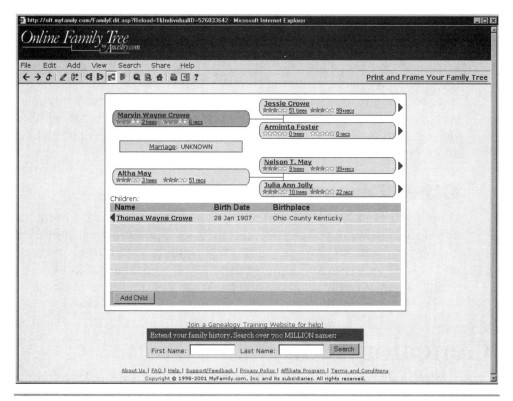

FIGURE 17-5. *You can view, edit, and print your genealogy in several different views on MyFamily.com.*

This is the Family View; you can also see your information in Ancestry, Descendent, and Family Story (modified outline) views.

Updates are simple: You can do them offline and then upload them to overwrite the old tree, or you can click any individual's name in the display in Figure 17-5 and correct the data on the fly. Those who have logon privileges to your site can download the data and submit trees of their own.

History

A nice feature is Our Family History (listed as "History" on the navigation bar). Every family member you've invited to participate can log on, click Add History, and contribute memories of events, stories, and experiences. By clicking List History, the members can view all the contributions. When reading one, they can "reply" and add their perspectives, ask questions, and so on. Remember, all this information is available only to those people you've invited to join your family site.

Chats

Whenever you like, all the members of your family site can sign on together for a private, real-time chat. To do this, scroll down the first page of your site to the Chat listing and pick a day and time. Everyone who is a member of your site will then be e-mailed regarding when to sign on. This is good for planning family reunions, interviewing relatives about family history, or swapping genealogical data.

Other Features

Other features include news (where you can post current family events), photo albums (where you can post pictures), a recipe-swap area, a reviews area (where you can share opinions on current movies, music, and art), and utilities for maintaining the website you created. Furthermore, the site offers a gift center, channels on health and parenting, contests, and so on. All these are fun, even if they aren't related to genealogy!

Genealogy.com

This recently acquired site has many resources that are similar in type to the MyFamily and Ancestry sites but differ in specifics. For example, both Ancestry.com and Genealogy.com have marriage index databases in the subscription area, but one might have marriages from Indiana in the 1880s while the other might have Michigan and Wisconsin. The cross-promotion agreement with The History Channel continues after Genealogy.com's merger with MyFamily.com, and the site itself has changed very little.

Learning Center

Under the Learning Center link in the navigation bar at the top of every page, you can find articles, self-paced lessons on organization and other topics, as well as references such as a glossary, a relationship chart, and tips on reunions. The beginner can learn a lot from this free information.

Community

Under the Community link in the navigation bar, you'll find the message boards, where you can post queries, ask and answer questions, and exchange information. The boards are sorted by surname, location, and general topics.

Under Community, you can also create a home page or search through those already there. Home pages are free. You can simply fill out a form with the information you want to appear or upload a page you have created with an HTML editor such as FrontPage. You can add a family tree by uploading a GEDCOM or by entering each individual in a JavaScript window on the site. The pages can be simple (see Figure 17-6), or you can add pictures, links, and other features.

The Community area also includes celebrity genealogies, from royal families to artists and musicians. Finally, under Community, check out the Virtual Cemetery, where volunteers post tombstone pictures and information on where the cemeteries are located. This saves travel and helps create a resource for other genealogists. Contributing to and searching the database are both free.

MyGenealogy.com

The MyGenealogy.com area includes your home page (mentioned earlier) as well as access to a storage area of about 10MB. This can hold the text, HTML, graphics, and other files you would like to display, and it can serve as a backup point for your genealogy information. (Remember, I urged you to do backups in Chapter 2; this is one way to do them!)

FIGURE 17-6. *Genealogy.com offers free web pages you can build with simple forms.*

Search

The Search page has several forms to use for different searches. The first form lets you input a name, a place, and a date to search all the Genealogy.com data—both the free stuff and the subscription area—for any matches. It also searches a pay-per-view site of U.K. records called Origins.net. This site has records of vital statistics as well as apprentice records, wills, and witness depositions. These records cover the years from about 1538 to about 1900.

The Site Search allows you to type in a keyword, say "wills" or "Kentucky," and find pages within the Genealogy.com site that match. I found, however, that it will show links to pages that have been removed or renamed.

The last search on the page is the SSDI, a search of the Social Security Death Index. This area has recently gone over to the "subscription" side. As of this writing, the SSDI search is still free on RootsWeb (see Chapter 16).

Shop

In the Shop area, you'll find books, CD-ROMs of databases (from vital records to GEDCOMs submitted by Family Tree Maker users), videos, and genealogy supplies. The software Family Tree Maker (FTM) is available here, as are paid memberships to the online databases. Memberships range from $70 to $150 a year, and all include a copy of the FTM software.

Note

Your genealogy information entered into FTM and uploaded to Genealogy.com will appear on some of the CD-ROMs the site sells.

A Nice Collection of Sites

The MyFamily.com collection of sites, which now includes RootsWeb, is a great place to start your genealogical quest. RootsWeb allows you more creativity in your website design than MyFamily, but the MyFamily sites are more interactive. Either way, both sites can be useful in continuing and sharing your genealogy research.

Wrapping Up

♦ MyFamily.com has several different sites: Ancestry.com for research, MyFamily.com for interaction, and the message boards of RootsWeb.

♦ Many Ancestry.com features are free, but the bulk of the data is only available to paying customers.

♦ MyFamily.com allows you to create a family site with genealogy data, messages boards, and so on. Recently, this portal started charging for members' sites over 5MB in size.

Chapter 18

Everton Publishers

Oﬀne of the most respected publishing companies in genealogy, Everton Publishers produces books, CD-ROMs, a print magazine, and an excellent website (www.everton.com).

The New Look

The website has been reorganized and renamed the Family History Network. Figure 18-1 shows the opening page. The Everton web page offers several free features, although you do have to register your name, address, and e-mail address to access them.

> *Note*
>
> *The venerable* Everton's Genealogical Helper, *started in 1947, is now called* Family History Magazine, *and you can subscribe to it from the site.*

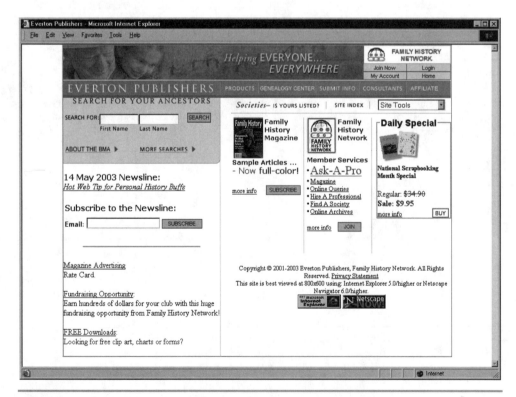

FIGURE 18-1. *Everton Publishers has been producing genealogy materials since 1947.*

Free Side Features

The Everton site has had many upgrades since the last edition of this book. When you register for the free features, you are a "guest." The free area is now called On-Line Search. What used to be called the Root Cellar, The Pedigree File, and The Family File are now all combined in an area called The Bureau of Missing Ancestors (www.everton.com/submit/bma.form1.php?magtype = 1), which is available at the lowest level of subscription.

As a guest, you can make unlimited searches on the 60 million ancestor names for matches in the free and the paid areas. You can also receive the free, daily e-mail called Family History Newsline, and you can access selected articles on genealogy and family history. The free area also contains a database of professional genealogists (www .everton.com/network/pros.php) willing to be hired for family history research.

The free side also allows you to read the daily genealogy article, read the current table of contents of *Family History Magazine*, and search to see whether your ancestor is in any of the databases accessible by subscription. The result of a search in the free area is shown in Figure 18-2. The small locks indicate that the information is available to paid members only.

As a guest, you also have access to some of the Genealogy Center. Here you'll find an abbreviated "5 Steps to Research" page, the Daily Quiz (which enters you for a monthly drawing), free downloads, links to local and surname-based genealogy societies, a sorted catalog of genealogy sites, and a way to search for a professional genealogist in your area.

One of the free downloads is a handy relationship chart, with a clear explanation of cousins, "once-removed," and other relationship terms.

The "5 Steps to Research" page (see Figure 18-3) in the free area has selected articles from the archives, free forms to help you keep organized, and links to online sites for your research. On the paid side are more detailed articles and tips.

The Subscription Side

The subscription side includes the FHN, magazine subscribers, society and library memberships, and professional members. Memberships range from about $28 for a one-year magazine subscription to about $150 for a two-year professional membership.

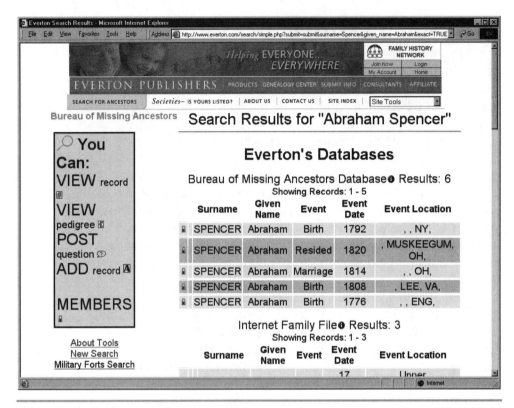

FIGURE 18-2. *As a guest, you can check to see if your ancestors are included in the paid area databases.*

One free "entry," which is essentially a query, in the Bureau of Missing Ancestors in the printed version of the magazine comes with a subscription to the magazine.

With a membership in the FHN for about $80 a year, you can submit unlimited entries in the new online Bureau of Missing Ancestors, get a one-year subscription to the magazine, receive unlimited access to the online article archives of *Family History Magazine*, obtain access to professional genealogists for Q&As, and receive detailed genealogy tips and lessons. Paid membership also lets you in on discounts in the online store.

Other Features

Family History Magazine has several departments to which readers and site users can contribute. These departments sometimes pay for

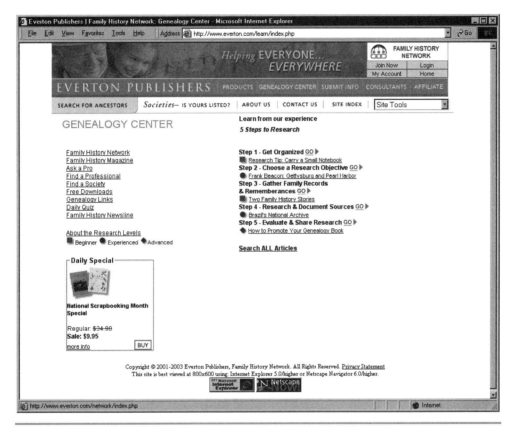

FIGURE 18-3.   *The short, free version of "5 Steps to Research." A longer, more detailed version is available for FHN subscribers.*

submissions; sometimes you pay to have the information included in an issue. In other departments, your submissions are voluntary, and no money is exchanged either way. You'll find these listed on the page at www.everton.com/submit/index.php.

All Annual Directories

The annual directories include listings of websites and databases, genealogical libraries, and locality periodicals. You can submit sites for inclusion in each of these areas for free. Each directory appears in the magazine once a year.

The directory of family associations appears each spring, and each listing costs $7.50. The listing of professional genealogists also costs

$7.50 per submission, and the list appears on the website as well as in the magazine (see Figure 18-4).

Bureau of Missing Ancestors

This is the name of the queries department, and publishing a query costs $1 a word, excluding your contact information. Then the query appears in the magazine, as well as in the paid part of the website. Missing Folk Finder is the department for queries about living people, and the same rules apply.

Our Readers Write, Questions & Answers, News to Peruse, and Bureau of Missing Persons Short Story

These sections are free to submit to. Letters to the editor, questions for experts, and news briefs all appear in the magazine and are submitted

FIGURE 18-4. *Professional genealogists are listed in the site and in an annual directory in the magazine.*

by the readers. You can submit a story about finding your ancestors to be published in the magazine for free.

Your Story

This section contains stories written by readers for which the magazine will pay $75. The 1,000-word articles describe personal research experiences.

Relatively Speaking

This section contains shorter success stories written by readers, and the magazine will pay $50 for each one published.

Roots Cellar

This is where queries are uploaded to the website, searchable by paid subscribers. You pay $5.50 to submit a query.

Wrapping Up

- ◆ The resources and how-to articles in the Everton website's free area are good for the beginner and intermediate genealogist.

- ◆ *Family History Magazine* is one of the most respected journals in genealogy and worth subscribing to, and it now includes some access to the online areas.

- ◆ Other databases are available for subscription.

- ◆ Try the site at least once. You might find many treasures to take away with you.

Chapter 19

Proprietary Content

Online genealogy resources are sometimes buried treasures within proprietary services. This chapter will show you how to find resources on online services.

Limited Access Resources

Most national ISP providers offer at least some proprietary content, as well as resources that are available by web access. Generally, you will find articles, message boards, and sometimes chat rooms available on the Web. Some ISPs (for example, AOL) also have respectable file exchanges of transcribed material and GEDCOMs in the areas accessible only to paying customers.

Note

Remember that when you find a GEDCOM, an article, or published genealogy on the Web, it is secondary information. You must locate the primary documents in order to prove the genealogy.

This chapter will simply hit the highlights of some of the better known ISPs.

MSN Genealogy

MSN's proprietary content has never been very broad nor deep. Nevertheless, you might want to at least check out the message boards (called *groups* on MSN) and the chats. Go to http://family.msn.com and click the link Family Roots, and you will see the page in Figure 19-1. Much of what is on the page comes repackaged from Ancestry.com (see Chapter 17). You will usually find a feature story or two on celebrity genealogies and lots of links to ads for everything from travel agents to help for planning your family reunion to horoscopes so you can look up your ancestors' star signs.

MSN Groups: Genealogy

Click the People & Chat link from any MSN.com page navigation bar, and you can find the groups. MSN has over 3,000 genealogy message boards at http://groups.msn.com/, and it's easy to start one of your own. Simply click the link Create a Group on the genealogy groups' page and then fill out the form.

FIGURE 19-1. *MSN's web genealogy page is mainly links to ads for products, sometimes tenuously related genealogy.*

It's not so easy to find just the group you want on MSN, because the list is not searchable or categorized. You just have to page through the alphabetized list of them, and that's a real pain.

GenPals is one active, worthwhile group on MSN, located at www.geocities.com/genpals2002 (see Figure 19-2). Despite the terribly annoying background music to almost every page, you will find some useful beginners' tips, regular chats, and more.

Another MSN genealogy group is A Genealogy Experience, at http://groups.msn.com/AGenealogyExperience. As with GenPals, you'll find tips for beginners, query message boards, and chats. This group

FIGURE 19-2.   *GenPals is more than just a surname-query board, offering several categories.*

also has an area where you can swap lookup chores with other genealogists, in addition to a newsletter, a social side, success stories, and a resource center to help you find good genealogy information.

MSN Chats: Genealogy

These chat rooms are not moderated and therefore are not very useful. Even those that claim to be about genealogy have mostly teenagers (or people pretending to be) typing idiocies to each other. MSN chats are a waste of your time, and they expose you to spammers. Skip them.

AOL Genealogy and Golden Gate

Like most commercial online services, AOL's proprietary content is available only through its proprietary front-end software. AOL's network has local access numbers throughout the world, but not necessarily in rural areas. The software package will find the phone number closest to you during the setup procedure, but every now and then this list is expanded. It's a good idea to go to keyword ACCESS to see whether you're using the best and closest connection.

The Genealogy Forum (keyword ROOTS) is the center of genealogical activity on America Online. From the Beginners' Center to the Genealogy Chat Rooms and the Resource Center, this forum is an incredibly rich resource. The Genealogy Forum's tens of thousands of members make it the largest genealogical society in the world, online or off. Figure 19-3 shows the Golden Gate Genealogy Forum main window in AOL 8.

Don't forget to add the Genealogy Forum to your list of Favorite Places. To do this, just click the heart on the top-right side of the forum main window. You can also add it to the toolbar of AOL 5.0 and later versions. Just click and drag the heart up to the toolbar area. A window will pop up asking you to choose a picture and a name for the link. Make your choices, and you have a quick way to get to the genealogy area of AOL.

The opening screen has links to several areas of the forum.

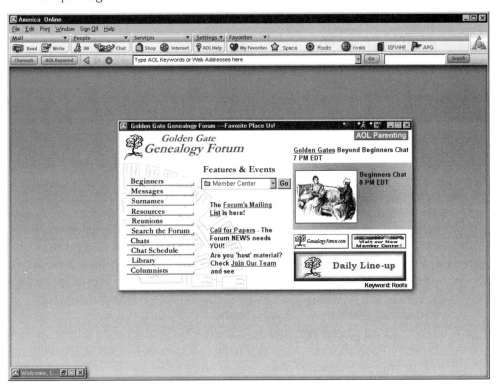

FIGURE 19-3. *You can reach the Golden Gate Genealogy Forum on AOL at keyword ROOTS.*

Beginners

To reach the Beginners' Center, you click the Beginners button on the Genealogy Forum main window. This takes you to the Beginners' Center on the www.genealogyforum.com website. Here you'll find the Beginner's Took Kit, which is a collection of links to answer the most basic questions about genealogy. These include Information on Getting Started, Making Sense of It All, Obtaining Information, Organizational Ideas, Organizing Information, Other Genealogy Forum Centers, Other Related Forums, and DearMYRTLE. After you've paged through all these, especially DearMYRTLE's Beginners' Lessons, you'll be ready to begin your quest.

The Beginners' Center has many useful files and articles. A few of them are listed next.

Beginners' Library   This area includes downloadable text and graphic files on several topics such as occupations listed in censuses and transcripts of chats.

Beginning Chat Schedule   This area lists moderated chats aimed at those new to genealogy. You must be an AOL member to participate in the chats, which are held several times a day, Monday through Saturday.

Introduce Yourself Message Board   This is a link to the message board where the topic is member introductions: Who you are, and where and what you're searching. Everyone who posts here will get personal e-mail with tips on how to use the forum.

Messages

The message boards in the Genealogy Forum are the place to post messages when you need information you can't find elsewhere in the forum. The boards operate on a volunteer basis. You're invited to post any questions you might have and are encouraged to post a reply to anyone else's question if you have information. Also, don't forget to post the family names you're looking for in the message board under the Surname category.

To reach the message boards, click the large Messages button in the Genealogy Forum main window. Using the Message Board Center, you can post messages in any of six major subject areas:

- **Computer and General**   Post messages here about topics that don't fit into the other message board.

- **U.S.**   A place for messages about genealogy in the United States.

- **International**   Post messages in this area about research in countries other than the United States.

- **Surnames**   Post messages here asking about specific family names you're researching.

- **Ethnic and Special Groups**   Post messages here about your research into ethnic or other special groups.

- **Internet Message Boards**   These messages are posted on the Genealogy Forum website and therefore reach people who are nonmembers of AOL.

Surnames

The Surnames Center is another collection of message boards organized by surname. Here, individual surnames have their own boards, as opposed to the surname boards you can reach from the Quick Start Guide, which group surnames alphabetically.

Resources

Click the button marked Resources and you'll find The Resource Center, which is chock-full of information meant to save you lots of trial and error. Articles, help texts, and tips under subject headings such as Regions of the World, Ethnic Resources, and Vital all can make your research more productive.

Reunions

The Reunions button on the AOL Genealogy Forum main window will take you to www.genealogyforum.rootsweb.com/gfaol/reunion. Here you'll find archives of discussions, tips, and articles to help you plan and execute a successful family reunion, either online or in the real world.

Search the Forum

Clicking the Search the Forum button on the Genealogy Forum main window opens the Genealogy Search window. When you enter a search term in this window, the program will search the file libraries in the forum (the program doesn't search the messages). The result is a list of files that contain the search term.

Chats and Chat Schedule

The Chat Center is where you go to hold online, real-time conversations with other genealogists. To get to the Chat Center, click the Chats button on the forum's main window. Chat rooms exist for many different topics: Beginning Genealogy Chat, Southern Chat, and War Between the States Chat are three examples.

The Chat Schedule is the latest list of topics, hosts, times, and dates for scheduled chats on AOL.

Library

Under this link, you'll find text and graphics files on all sorts of topics. Uploaded GEDCOM files, articles on history, and more can be found here. You'll also find software ranging from trial versions of popular genealogy software to GEDCOMs and other genealogy information from members. You can use the Library Sort feature to make finding specific files in the libraries easier, or you can click Search the Forum on the main Genealogy Forum window to use the Search Genealogy Forum feature.

Columnists

Under the Columnists button, you will find links to regular columns by hosts in the AOL Golden Gate forum. Some are daily, some weekly, and some monthly. They include:

- **The Genealogy Forum News**   A monthly collection of articles and information around a certain theme, such as "The American Revolution" or Father's Day.

- **DearMYRTLE's Daily Column**   As described in other parts of this book, this column will have notes, news, tips and techniques.

- **Bits of Blue and Gray**   A column on researching genealogy in the American Civil War era, by different genealogists.

- **Pilgrims, Pioneers & Aliens**   By Diana L. Smith, this column concentrates on finding the original immigrant in a family line.

- **Adventures in Genealogy**   By "Uncle Hiram" (William Hocutt), this is a weekly look at genealogy from a wry perspective.

- **Genealogy Mailing Lists**   This is a monthly update of John Fuller's collection of mailing lists.

Software Search

Start with AOL's Software Center (keyword FIND SOFTWARE). Here you have four choices: search for shareware (try-before-you-buy programs such as Brother's Keeper), search for commercial software (such as Family Tree Maker), check out the recommended Daily Download (usually a general purpose program), or visit the Computing Superstore.

To search for shareware, click the link. You'll get the Software Search window (keyword FILESEARCH). You can limit your search according to the time (all dates, past month, or past week) the file was uploaded, and by categories (applications, operating system, and so on). Then type your keywords (genealogy programs, for example). In a few seconds, you have a list of matches. You can select one, read its description, and then decide whether to add it to your Download Manager (the list of files to be downloaded). When you have your list complete, you can choose Download Manager from the window that pops up when you choose Download Later and tell it to start.

GenealogyForum.com on the Web

Some, but not all, of the AOL Genealogy Forum content is at www.genealogyforum.rootsweb.com (see Figure 19-4).

In addition, the web version has some resources you won't find by simply clicking links in the AOL keyword ROOTS area. The website has the Genealogy Forum News, a monthly update on the newest files, features, and chats. It also has an area called Military Resources, a collection of articles and links for using military records for genealogy research, and several similar resources. You should explore both the AOL side and the web side to get the most out of this site.

CIS

AOL acquired CompuServe Information Service (CIS) a few years back. You can still sign up for a membership, but if you have an AOL membership or a screen name with AOL Instant Messenger, you can access the CompuServe forums from a web interface, without having to sign up with CIS.

The essence of CompuServe is still there. Despite sporting quite a few AOL-like features in the new interface, it's still the premier service for serious, mature users ("adult" in the good sense). CompuServe users tend to be those who work for a living and use CompuServe to do their

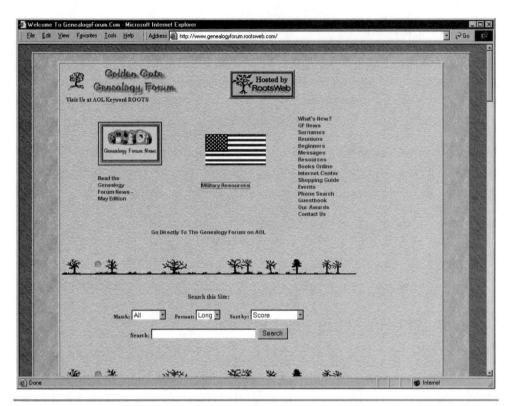

FIGURE 19-4. *GenealogyForum.com has materials you can reach from AOL links, as well as materials not mentioned on AOL.*

work and their hobbies faster, better, and cheaper. CompuServe has little nonsense and lots of common sense.

To get to the genealogy forums, point your web browser at http://forums.compuserve.com and sign in with your CompuServe, AOL, or AIM name and password. CompuServe has four different genealogy forums, each useful for a different type of genealogical research.

Genealogy Techniques Forum

The oldest genealogy forum on CompuServe is the Genealogy Techniques Forum. This is the place for beginners to share successes and to ask about how to get beyond a brick wall in their research. You can access it from within CompuServe with the GO word ROOTS on the Web at http://forums.compuserve.com/vlforums/default.asp?SRV = Genealogy Forum&loc = us&access = public (see Figure 19-5 for the Web version).

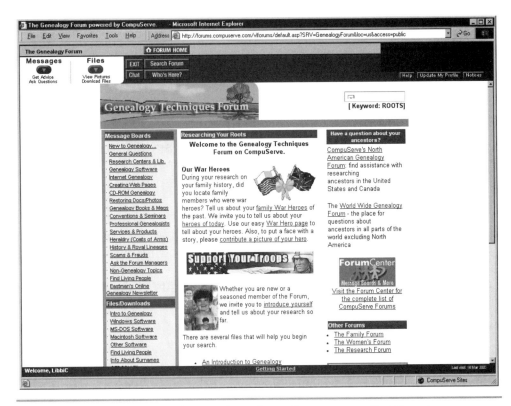

FIGURE 19-5. *The original CompuServe Roots Forum, now called Genealogy Techniques Forum, is available on the Web.*

You can also find links to all the messages, files, and chat rooms of the other genealogy forums here. Click Messages, Library Files, or Chat Rooms in the navigation bar to the left.

In the Genealogy Techniques Forum, you can learn how to use your computer for genealogy, how to use the Web, and where to find professional genealogists. You can also learn about coats of arms, how to conduct adoption searches, and more.

Eastman's Genealogy Newsletter (see Chapter 8), from Dick Eastman, is part of this forum, and has a page at www.rootsforum.com. You can subscribe, read the current issue, and search an archive of previous issues from this site.

North American Genealogy Forum

The North American Genealogy Forum is for queries about ancestors in Canada, the United States, and Mexico. To get there, use the GO word

NAROOTS or, on the Web, go to http://forumsb.compuserve.com/vlforums/ default.asp?SRV = NAGenealogy. This forum covers specific states and provinces in Canada, Mexico, and the United States; societies and organizations (including their workshops, meetings, and seminars); and ethnic groups, such as Native Americans.

World Wide Genealogy Forum

For queries about ancestors anywhere but North America, check the World Wide Genealogy Forum. Use the GO word WWROOTS or the URL http://forums.compuserve.com/vlforums/default.asp?SRV = WWGenealogy.

Other Forums

You can also find genealogy discussed on other forums. For example, genealogy is often discussed in the Civil War and History Forums. The Civil War Forum is at http://forums.compuserve.com/vlforums/ default.asp?SRV = CivilWar&Loc = US&Access = Public; the History Forum is at http://forums.compuserve.com/vlforums/default.asp?SRV = History.

Other ISPs

Other ISPs, such as Prodigy (www.prodigy.net) have similar offerings, with message boards, moderated chats, and articles. If you have a national ISP, poke around in the home page to see if there is a genealogy area.

Wrapping Up

- ◆ National ISPs often offer resources available only to paying customers.

- ◆ MSN has genealogy message boards, chats, and some repackaged Ancestry.com resources.

- ◆ AOL has boards, moderated chats, resources uploaded by volunteers, articles, and newsletters.

- ◆ CompuServe has resources similar to AOL, but with different content.

- ◆ Your ISP may also have a special genealogy area.

Chapter 20

Genealogy Database Sites

GEDCOM files are to genealogists what trading cards are to kids. GEDCOM files can be uploaded to databases with lineage indexing and links. GEDCOM files can be shared with others in an e-mail attachment or on a disk. GEDCOM files can be converted for use in genealogy companion software programs and utilities that will create specialty charts, books, scrapbooks, and websites. GEDCOM files can be uploaded to genealogy sites for searching and swapping.

GEDCOM files can also be adjusted for privacy and copyright concerns (see Chapter 4). Also, you should always remember to remove data on living people as well as give proper credit to all your sources in your GEDCOM files.

Note

When you look at someone's GEDCOM file, remember that this is secondary source material. You must contact the GEDCOM file's owner to determine the primary sources used.

GEDCOMs 101

GEDCOM is a generic, database format designed to allow users to share family history database files between different genealogy software programs and platforms. In other words, with a GEDCOM you can take your genealogy information from Family Tree on a Mac and share it with your cousin's Brother's Keeper on a PC.

The name is an abbreviation of "**GE**nealogical **D**ata **COM**munication." GEDCOM is a defined, specific structure for a file of genealogy data. The file format is a standard ASCII text file, so it can be read by or written to virtually any computer and/or any genealogy program.

The GEDCOM Standard was written by the Family History Department of The Church of Jesus Christ of Latter-day Saints (LDS or Mormon Church) back in the mid-1980s to have a standard for sharing genealogical information electronically. The GEDCOM Standard has been through several versions, but the current standard (version 5.5) is over seven years old.

Note

When you export a GEDCOM, be sure to turn on any privacy features your genealogy software may have, to protect data on living people.

To create a GEDCOM file (in most programs), go to File | Export to GEDCOM and create a new file with a ".ged" file extension after the name. To read another person's GEDCOM file (in most programs), go to File | Import from GEDCOM and create a new database file that can be opened in your genealogy software program. This will not merge with your existing database file unless you indicate that you wish for the two files to be merged.

Note

A new program called GEDMARK allows you to mark each entry in your GEDCOM file with your name as the source for that information. That way, if someone merges your GEDCOM file with theirs, you remain as the source of the information on each record.

It's not perfect, of course. The GEDCOM standard is very complicated and programmers sometimes do not take the time to read it in detail and understand all the features. It has been said that no program on the market correctly implements every aspect of the standard—even Personal Ancestral File (PAF), the program from the LDS church! Some deviations are minor and merely are a nuisance. Others are major problems, resulting in loss of data or even crashes when a file is imported into a different program. It depends both on the source and destination programs. Some do better than others.

For this reason, when you get a GEDCOM from someone, *always* import it to a *new* database in your genealogy program. Do not merge it to your current genealogy database until you have determined whether it has the data you need and performs well enough with your software to work. Even then, before you merge, *make a backup of your original database*.

Caution

Never *merge a new GEDCOM to your current program's database before you have made a backup.*

Once you get the hang of creating, swapping, and collecting GEDCOMs, you can have some real fun!

GEDCOM Database Sites

Sites where you can search, download, and upload GEDCOMs abound. I've already discussed the GEDCOM databases at Family Search (Chapter 10), RootsWeb (Chapter 16), Ancestry (Chapter 17), and proprietary sites such as AOL (Chapter 19). This chapter will look at some sites for searching GEDCOMs beyond those well-known sites. Check Cyndi's List Surname Database Sites at www.cyndislist.com/database.htm#Surname often for new and updated sites.

Note

Most of these sites require you to remove data on living people before contributing your GEDCOM.

GenServ

GenServ (www.genserv.com) is a GEDCOM-exchange system you can search via e-mail or on the Web, and it is a cooperative genealogy data exchange. You can query the system through commands sent by e-mail, and you also receive the results by e-mail. Web-based queries are also supported. The opening page is shown in Figure 20-1.

This ten-year-old project is a GEDCOM exchange and search site. People upload their GEDCOMs (which, of course, are secondary source information), and then members can search the different databases for matches on names, dates, and locations. The data in these databases is accessible through commands sent to the system via a regular e-mail message and also via web access. The system then formats the results and e-mails a report back to the user who sent the request. GenServ can generate several different kinds of reports from these e-mail requests.

Submitting your GEDCOM data file is required for a 60-day free trial to this system, and the system has data from over 50 countries. Membership costs from $12 to $35 a year. More money gets you more queries to the databases. The money goes toward disk drives and computers to run the system, and volunteers do all the work.

Dave Wilks' Free GEDCOM Server

This site, at www.my-ged.com, is a database server designed for genealogy research on the Internet. Dave Wilks welcomes both those who wish to upload and those who wish to search.

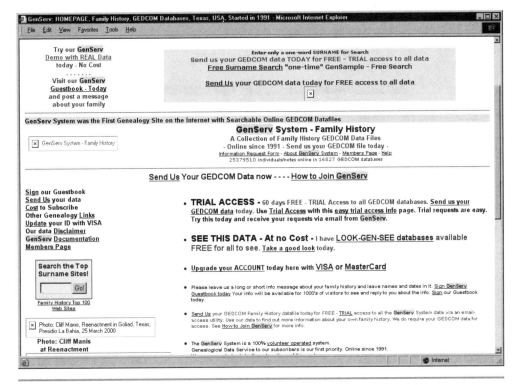

FIGURE 20-1. *GenServ is the oldest GEDCOM exchange on the Web, dating back to 1991.*

You can publish to the site by creating a GEDCOM file and attaching it to an e-mail. Include the text and title you'd like to have on the cover page to the GEDCOM. You can even include pictures if you like. The GEDCOM is then turned into HTML, as shown in Figure 20-2, and the cover page will link to the HTML pedigree chart.

This site has over 7 million individual data pages, each indexed on Gene Stark's GENDEX server (see the following section). The search engine is based on Google's search technology. This means a search for a name in quotation marks will look for those words, in that order, together. It's extremely fast.

You do not download GEDCOM files from this page; instead, you only read the matches and the cover pages, and decide if you need to correspond with someone based on the data displayed. There is no privacy requirement; that is, you are not required to remove data on living persons before you submit.

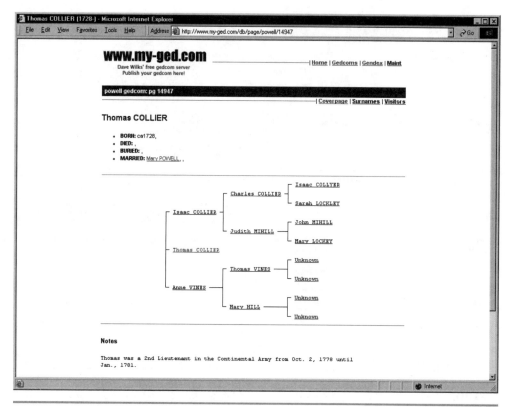

FIGURE 20-2. *My-GED.com converts your GEDCOM file into a searchable HTML page.*

GENDEX

GENDEX (www.gendex.com) is the home site of the GENDEX and GED2HTML software. When you use GED2HTML to post your genealogy on the Web, you can register to be part of the worldwide GENDEX, a search engine for all such genealogy sites. The GENDEX site does not store the genealogical data; instead, it searches the registered websites with a fast, sophisticated search engine.

Users can be registered or unregistered. You can be a registered user by contributing a minimum of $10 per 1,000 hits. Unregistered access is the default mode of accessing the GENDEX server. Whenever you are accessing the server in unregistered mode, a "login" button will appear near the bottom of each screen. Registered users get a more

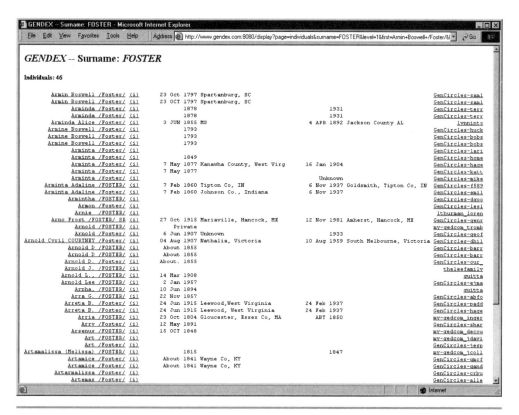

FIGURE 20-3. *GENDEX searches GEDCOMs on many different websites to find the surnames you want.*

powerful search engine, can control how the results are displayed, and receive priority access to the server.

Unregistered searches are easy: Input any part of a surname and all close spellings are found. Alternatively, you can put in the surname and use the Soundex search. A list of names, sorted, will appear, as shown in Figure 20-3. How many names on the list depends on how many hits you get on your search. You may have to drill down the sorted lists until you come to the web page that has that information.

GenCircles

This site, at www.gencircles.com, is the invention of Cliff Shaw, who also created GenForum. Registration is free, as are the searches and the message boards. You upload your GEDCOM file to the Global Tree,

FIGURE 20-4. *GenCircles is a free site for uploading GEDCOM files and searching them.*

taking out data on living people, and a page is created. The displays include family group sheets and pedigree charts. The home page, with the search input box, is shown in Figure 20-4.

The site uses a proprietary search engine called SmartMatching that compares the individuals in your file against all the individuals in the rest of the Global Tree. The matches are displayed on your page within the site within hours of your upload.

There is no copying or downloading of GEDCOM files on the site, only uploads and searches.

OneGreatFamily

This is a for-fee site, much like MyFamily.com. The difference is, they aim to replace your desktop genealogy software with their site software.

If you already have a GEDCOM file, you upload it and then add new data to it as you find it. If you don't have one, you can start creating one with their site software.

Meanwhile, if another member's data matches something in your data in date, name, and place, a light bulb symbol appears on your page to alert you so that you can exchange information. Once you are a member, you can also search through the submitted GEDCOM files.

Other Sites

If you use a good search engine site (see Chapter 6) and input GEDCOM as a search term with the surname or full name you're looking for, you will probably come up with some personal genealogy sites with published ancestries, as shown in Figure 20-5.

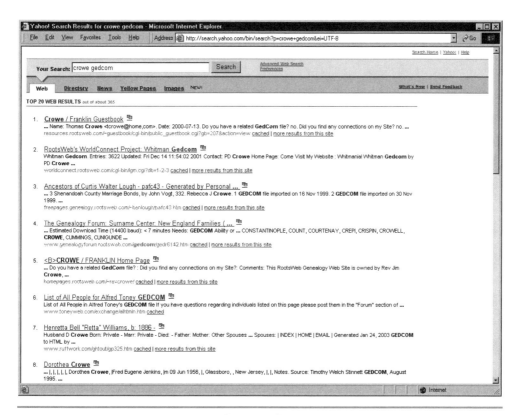

FIGURE 20-5. *Use search sites to find specific GEDCOM files uploaded to HTML pages.*

Wrapping Up

- ◆ GEDCOM files can be swapped like baseball cards, with precautions.

- ◆ Don't post or export a GEDCOM file with data of living people in it.

- ◆ Don't merge a GEDCOM file to your existing genealogy database without checking it out with your program first.

- ◆ Some sites collect GEDCOM files for searching.

- ◆ GENDEX indexes GEDCOM files that have been turned into web pages.

Chapter 21

Around the Web
in 80 (or so) Sites

As you've no doubt noticed while reading this book, genealogy websites come in all categories. You will find portals that aim to be your web home. You will find sites with images of original documents or transcribed records, and sites with completed, annotated genealogies. You will find sites where folks have slapped up any data they found, regardless of accuracy or relevancy. You will find primary records, secondary records, family legends, and scams. It's truly an embarrassment of riches out there.

As discussed in Chapter 1, you must remember to judge each source you find critically and carefully. Compare it to what you have proven with your own research. Look for the original records cited in an online genealogy to see if they have been interpreted correctly (remember the lesson about census records in Chapter 1!). Most of all, look for application to your genealogy. How helpful is it?

This list of websites reflects what I've found to be valuable. Some of these sites are portals and will link you to sites I haven't found or that didn't exist at press time. Other links may be "dead" (as they say in web parlance) by the time you read this. Don't be discouraged by this. That's part of the fun of online genealogy: There's always something new!

Note

Most online genealogists have at least these five links bookmarked:
Cyndi's List (www.cyndislist.com)
DearMYRTLE (www.dearmyrtle.com)
FamilySearch.com (www.familysearch.com)
NARA (www.archives.gov)
RootsWeb (www.rootsweb.com)

Golden Needles in the World Wide Haystack

In the manner of websites everywhere, these sites will all lead you to other sites, where (I hope) you'll find the information you need. Note that this isn't even close to an exhaustive list. For that, see Cyndi's List and Genealogy Resources on the Internet. I have sorted these sites by topic.

Adoption

The following are places that concentrate on reuniting birth families:

- **Adoptee/Birth Family Connections (www.birthfamily.com)**
  This site's motto is, "You existed before you were adopted." The site has articles on topics such as activism and reform of adoption laws, birth family registry, and warnings about scams.

- **Adoptees Internet Mailing List (www.aiml.org)**   This is a mail list to discuss adoption search and reunion issues, as well as social, media, and legal issues related to adoption.

- **Adoption Search and Reunion (www.nmia.com/ ~ rema2/)**
  This site has a search index (for the entire site), information about all 50 states, lists of mail lists and registries, and over a thousand links to other sites.

- **AdoptionForum.com (www.adoptionforums.com/f200.html)**
  This is a discussion board for adoptees, including birth mother searches.

- **PeopleFinder UK Adoption Section (www.peoplefinders.co.uk/ adoption.html)**   This site explains laws in the United Kingdom concerning finding birth mothers by adoptees.

- **Reunite.com (www.reunite.com)**   This site has a birth-family search guide and other free resources. The opening page is shown in Figure 21-1.

Beginners' "Classes," How-to Articles, Tips, Etc.

These sites feature articles, lessons, helpful hints, and columnists:

- **About.com Genealogy (genealogy.about.com/hobbies/ genealogy)**   This site has tips, discussion groups, and weekly articles on genealogy.

- **Ancestors Series Teacher's Guide (www.pbs.org/kbyu/ ancestors/firstseries/teachersguide)**   This site is a set of pages

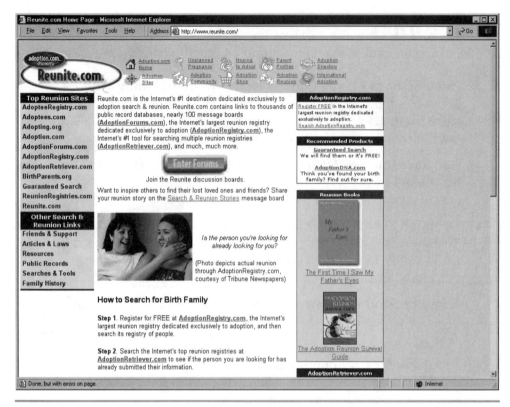

FIGURE 21-1. *Reunite is part of a suite of adoptee resource pages.*

designed to help teachers and students in grades 7–12 use the ten-part Ancestors series to create their genealogies as a school project.

♦ **Branching Out Online (www.didian.com/branch)** This is one of many sites that have "Branching Out" in the title, but this site is special. It's a tutorial on learning about online techniques and genealogy sites, and it's great for beginners.

♦ **Cybertree Genealogy Database (www.kuhnslagoon.net/ cybertree/howto/index.html)** This site has a list of some words and phrases whose early meanings were different from today's. This site also contains obscure nicknames and abbreviations, as well as certain genealogical tools that might seem mysterious at first.

♦ **Eastman's Online Genealogy Newsletter (www.rootsforum.com)**
This is a weekly all-text newsletter on genealogy topics. A typical issue will cover reviews of genealogy computer programs, news items of note to genealogists, a list of websites to visit, reviews of books, CD-ROMs, TV programs, and more. Eastman publishes a short, free version and a "Plus Edition" for $10 a year.

♦ **Family History, How Do I Begin? (www.familysearch.org)** Go to the Family Search site, then click Search | Research Guidance | How Do I Begin? This is The Church of Jesus Christ of Latter-day Saints' basic tutorial (see Figure 21-2).

♦ **Genealogy Dictionary (home.att.net/ ~ dottsr/diction.html)**
This site gives you definitions for all those confusing terms such as "cordwainer" and "primogeniture."

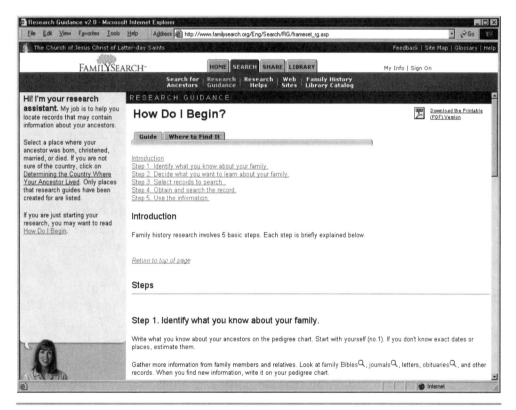

FIGURE 21-2. *The LDS guide to genealogy, "How Do I Begin?" can be read online, downloaded as a PDF file, or ordered in hard copy.*

- **Genealogy Lesson Plan (www.teachnet.com/lesson/misc/familytrees040199.html)** Located at TeachNet.com, this site has a lesson plan on family history for different curriculum areas.

- **Genealogy for Teachers (earth.execpc.com/~dboals/geneo.html)** This site lists resources, organizations, guides, and tutorials. Aimed at educators, this site should help any beginner.

- **Genealogy Today (www.genealogytoday.com)** This site announces and rates genealogy sites, has news updates and links to databases, lets readers vote for their favorite sites, and so forth.

- **Internet Tourbus (www.tourbus.com)** This is Patrick Douglas Crispen's e-mail course on how to use every part of the Internet. This site taught my mom everything she knows about the Net.

- **Janyce's Root Digging Dept. (www.janyce.com/gene/rootdig.html)** This is yet another good place for beginners to start their online genealogical research.

- **Kindred Trails (www.kindredtrails.com)** This site has links, a kinship calculator, articles, message boards, and more.

- **Lineages, Inc. (www.lineages.com)** This is the website for a group of professional genealogical researchers who, for a fee, will help you find your roots. Many of them hold professional certification. In addition, their site includes some free information, such as "First Steps for Beginners," a free genealogical queries page, and more.

- **Personal History Help (www.personalhistoryhelp.com)** This is a step-by-step guide to writing a personal history and keeping your memorabilia organized, and it just happens to sell a kit for personal historians.

- **SBt Genealogy Resources (www.cswnet.com/~sbooks/genealogy)** This is a collection of articles, links, and graphics for the genealogist. Especially interesting is the article "Comparison of Four Search Engines for Online Genealogy Research."

- **StateGenSites (www.stategensites.com)** This site has monthly and weekly columnists on all aspects of genealogy. Uncle Hiram's weekly column is especially good!

- **Treasure Maps, the How-to Genealogy Site (www.amberskyline.com/treasuremaps)** This is one of the best sites on the Web for novices. To keep track of the latest news on Treasure Maps, you might want to subscribe to its monthly newsletter.

Birth, Death, Marriage, and Other Records

Here are just a few of the sites where volunteers are uploading data. Be sure you visit RootsWeb and Cyndi's List often for updates and new pages:

- **Cemetery Junction: The Cemetery Trail (www.daddezio.com/ cemetery/index.html)**   This site has transcriptions of tombstones found in cemeteries across the U.S., collected and uploaded by volunteers.

- **Census Bureau Home Page (www.census.gov)**   This site has a list of frequently occurring names in the United States for 1990, a Spanish surname list for 1990, an age search service, and a frequently asked questions (FAQ) file on genealogy.

- **FreeBMD (freebmd.rootsweb.com)**   FreeBMD stands for *Free Births, Marriages, and Deaths*. The FreeBMD Project is made up of volunteers transcribing the Civil Registration Index information for England and Wales from the years 1837 to 1898 onto the Internet. Progress is sporadic; volunteer if you can. The opening page is shown in Figure 21-3.

- **Headstone Hunter (www.headstonehunter.com)**   This site is all about cemetery research. Here, people volunteer to find headstones for each other.

- **The Bureau of Land Management Land Patent Records (www.glorecords.blm.gov)**   This site is a searchable database. It's invaluable, especially for information in the western states when they were territories and when local records were scarce.

DNA

DNA research is becoming part of online genealogy. These are sites you can explore for this topic:

- **Chris Pomery's DNA Portal (freepages.genealogy.rootsweb.com/ ~allpoms/genetics.html)**   This is a scholarly article and set of links on the topic.

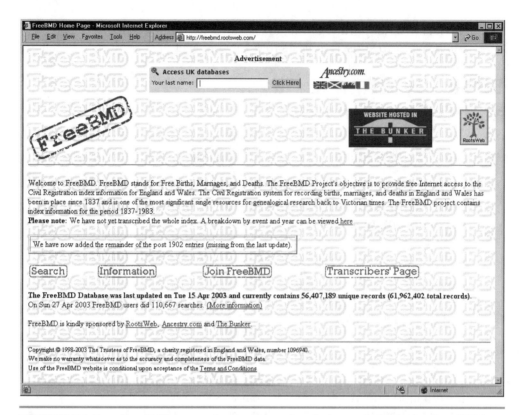

FIGURE 21-3. *FreeBMD is a project to transcribe vital records in England and Wales.*

- ◆ **Family Tree DNA (www.familytreedna.com/index.html)** This is a company you can pay to look for matches with people you suspect are relatives. In searching my mother's genealogy, we had long suspected that our Abraham Spencer was related to a certain Abner Spencer. Using this site, my uncle and another man submitted saliva samples. The other man (who wishes not to be named) was a proven descendant from that Abner. The results showed that he and my uncle have an ancestor in common. Many professional genealogists scoff at such proof (for example, the white descendants of Thomas Jefferson), but we feel this has finally solved our 30-year brick wall on Abraham's parents.

- **Genealogy DNA Mail List (lists.rootsweb.com/index/other/ Miscellaneous/GENEALOGY-DNA.html)** This is a discussion group about the topic of DNA, hosted by RootsWeb.

- **Oxford Ancestors (www.oxfordancestors.com)** This is a company that does the same thing as Family Tree DNA, but in the U.K.

- **Sorenson Molecular Genealogy Foundation (www.smgf.org/ index.jsp)** Brigham Young University has a site explaining its DNA genealogy research. You can learn how this project is progressing and how you can participate in your area at the site. You can also read about how BYU hopes to use the data to further the Mormons' quest to have a family history for all mankind.

Ethnic/National

Here's a list of some important ethnic pages:

- **Australian National Library (www.nla.gov.au/oz/genelist.html)** The genealogy page has links to resources, organizations, military service records, and so on, as well as an online card catalog.

- **AfriGeneas Home Page (www.afrigeneas.com)** This is the starting place for African-American family history. Don't miss the in-depth profile of this site later in the chapter.

- **Center for Basque Studies (basque.unr.edu)** This site, at the University of Nevada, Reno, covers history, anthropology, and other aspects of Basque culture.

- **Center for Jewish History (www.cjh.org/indexresponsibility .cfm)** This site has a special section on family history.

- **Christine's Genealogy Website (ccharity.com)** This is an excellent site about African-American history and genealogy.

- **Byzantines.net (www.byzantines.net/genealogy/index.htm)** This site is for persons of Ruthenian—Carpatho-Rusyn—ancestry and those of the Byzantine Catholic/Orthodox faiths who came from the former Austro-Hungarian Empire.

♦ **Family History in India (members.ozemail.com.au/ ~ clday/)**
This site is for tracing British, European, and Anglo-Indian families
with marriage records, church records, and other databases (see
Figure 21-4).

♦ **The National Huguenot Society (www.huguenot.netnation
.com/general/)** This site is for the study and preservation of
the history of the sixteenth- and seventeenth-century Huguenots,
especially those who immigrated to the United States.

♦ **New Zealand Genealogy Search Engine (www.downtown.co.nz/
genealogy/)** This site has searchable ships' passenger lists,
uploaded genealogies, a mail list, and more.

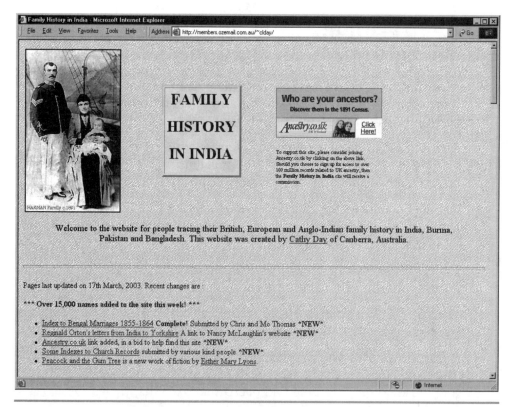

FIGURE 21-4. *If your ancestors lived in South Asia during the British Empire period,
Family History in India can be a big help.*

♦ **Federation of East European Family History Societies (www.feefhs.org)**   This site has databases, maps, and directories to help with genealogy in this region.

♦ **Gathering of the Clans Home Page (www.tartans.com)**   This site describes itself as a reference for people researching the Scottish clans. It includes information on 65 clans, as well as certain genealogical resources (specifically Scottish).

♦ **Hungarian Genealogy (www.rootsweb.com/ ~ wghungar)**   This is a good place to start if your research leads you to Hungary.

♦ **JewishGen (www.jewishgen.org)**   This is a comprehensive resource for researchers of Jewish genealogy worldwide. Among other things, it includes the JewishGen Family Finder, a database of towns and surnames being researched by Jewish genealogists worldwide, and it can be searched on the Web or via e-mail (you simply e-mail the server commands, and results are e-mailed back to you).

♦ **History and Genealogy of South Texas and Northeast Mexico (vsalgs.org/stnemgenealogy/)**   This is an interesting source if you're looking for relatives from the South Texas/Northeast Mexico area. The database has over 11,000 names, all linked as lineages.

♦ **Spanish Heritage Home Page (members.aol.com/shhar)**   This is an AOL-based site that's the home of the Society of Hispanic Historical and Ancestral Research.

Historical Background

Certain historical events may have an impact on your genealogy. The following sites can give you some information on the people in history:

♦ **American Civil War Home Page (sunsite.utk.edu/civil-war)**   This site has links to fantastic online documents from many sources, including those of two academics who've made the Civil War their career.

♦ **Ancient Faces (www.ancientfaces.com/cgi-bin/index.cfm)**   This site adds a personal touch to genealogy research by including photographs, documents, stories, recipes, and more—all located under individual surnames.

- ◆ **British Civil War, Commonwealth, and Protectorate (www.skyhook.co.uk/civwar/)** This site offers timelines, biographies, and military history on the United Kingdom, from 1638 to 1660.

- ◆ **British Heraldic Archive (www.kwtelecom.com/heraldry)** This site is dedicated to increasing interest in heraldry, genealogy, chivalry, and related topics. You can register to get an e-mail when the page is updated.

- ◆ **Calendars Through the Ages (www.webexhibits.org/ calendars)** This site explores the fascinating history of how we have tried to organize our lives in accordance with the sun and stars (see Figure 21-5).

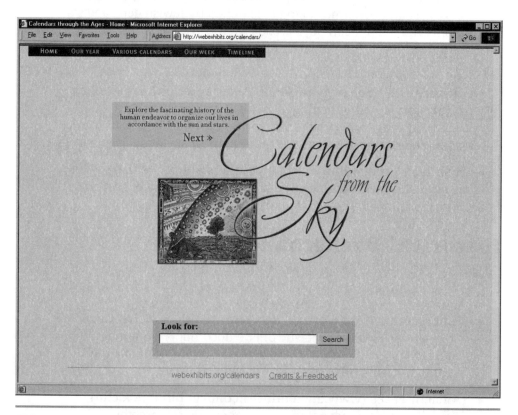

FIGURE 21-5. *Calendars and dates in genealogy can get tricky. This site helps you decipher them.*

◆ **Dan Mabry's Historical Text Archive (historicaltextarchive .com)**   This is a compilation of articles and documents on various topics. Of special interest are the collections on African-American history and genealogy.

◆ **Daughters of the American Revolution (www.dar.org)**   This is the organization for those who can prove an ancestor fought in the American Revolution. A free lookup in the DAR Patriot Index is just one of the site's many features.

◆ **Directory of Royal Genealogical Data (www.dcs.hull.ac.uk/ public/genealogy/royal/catalog.html)**   This is a database with the genealogy of the British Royal family and many other ruling families of the Western world—they all seem to be interrelated somehow. It contains over 18,000 names.

◆ **Genealogy of the Royal Family of the Netherlands (www.xs4all.nl/ ~ kvenjb/gennl.htm)**   This is a detailed genealogical history of the House of Orange-Nassau. It covers from Heinrich the rich of Nassau (born 1180) to Juliana Guillermo (born 1981).

◆ **Hauser-Hooser-Hoosier Theory: The Truth about Hoosier (www.geocities.com/Heartland/Flats/7822)**   This site explains how genealogy solved the mystery of "What is a Hoosier?"

◆ **HistorySeek! History Search Engine & Historical Information (www.historyseek.com)**   This is a directory search engine specifically made for historians, genealogists, scholars, and history enthusiasts (see Figure 21-6).

◆ **Immigration: The Living Mosaic of People, Culture & Hope (library.thinkquest.org/20619)**   This is a student project about immigration in the United States.

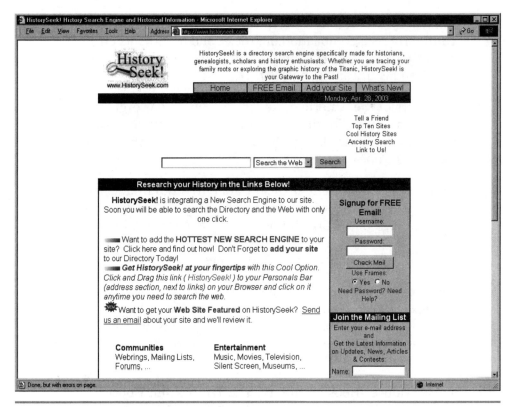

FIGURE 21-6.   *HistorySeek! is a search engine designed for genealogists.*

♦ **Mayflower Web Pages (www.mayflowerhistory.com)**   These pages contain the passenger lists of the *Mayflower,* the *Fortune,* and the *Anne,* plus many related documents.

♦ **Medal of Honor Citations (www.army.mil/cmh-pg/moh1.htm)**   This site contains the names and text of the citations for the more than 3,400 people who've been awarded the Congressional Medal of Honor since 1861.

♦ **Migrations (www.migrations.org)**   This site has two separate parts. First is a database of migration information submitted by volunteers (secondary source information, of course!), searchable by name and place. Second is a list of links to resources on migration.

- **Olden Times (theoldentimes.com/newsletterpage.html)**   This site has historic newspapers online.

- **Pitcairn Island Website (www.lareau.org/genweb.html)**   This is the place to go for information on over 7,500 descendants of the crew of the *H.M.S. Bounty,* of *Mutiny on the Bounty* fame.

- **Sons of the American Revolution (www.sar.org)**   This site has information on this organization's genealogical library, articles from its quarterly magazine, the history of the American Revolution, and more.

- **United States Civil War Center (www.cwc.lsu.edu)**   This site publishes book reviews, research tips, and articles about studying the War Between the States.

Libraries

Search the web catalogs (Yahoo!, Lycos, Google, and so on) for "library" plus "State" or "National" or the region you need. Some state libraries also have special genealogical collections, which you might find with a search such as "Michigan State library genealogy". These are some of the best library sites for genealogy:

- **Abrams Collection, Library of Michigan (www.michigan. gov/hal/)**   Click the "Genealogists" link at the bottom of the page. The Abrams Collection Genealogy Highlights lists what the researchers can find at this wonderful library. From assistance on specific genealogy topics to an online newsletter, this page lists resources at the Library of Michigan and at other libraries and research centers. The Abrams Foundation Historical Collection of genealogy materials covers more than just Michigan.

- **Allen Public Library Genealogy Division (www.acpl.lib.in.us/ genealogy/)**   This is one of the leading genealogy departments in a public library in the United States (see Figure 21-7).

- **Connecticut State Library History and Genealogy Unit (www.cslib.org/handg.htm)**   This page explains the special collections and services the state library has for genealogists.

- **Elmer's Genealogical Library (www.elmerslibrary.com)**   This library is in Madison, Florida and was founded to be a place for

FIGURE 21-7.   *The Allen County (IN) public library has outstanding genealogy resources.*

folks to share documented family histories and records for present and future generations.

♦ **Gateway to Northwestern Ontario History (www.nextlibrary. com/tbpl/home.html)**   This site has more than 1,000 photographs and drawings as well as the full text of several books.

♦ **Genealogy and Local History Library (www.mcpl.lib.mo.us/ branch/ge/)**   This is a branch of the Mid-Continent Public Library, based in Independence, Missouri. The branch has its own page, building, card catalog and participates in interlibrary loans.

♦ **Indiana State Library Genealogy Division (www.statelib.lib.in.us/ www/www_old/indiana/genealogy/genmenu.html)**   This site has searchable databases and an online card catalog.

♦ **Library of Virginia Digital Collections (image.vtls.com)**   A starting point where you can search Virginia colonial records, as well as bible records, newspapers, court records, and state documents.

♦ **OPLIN Genealogy Gleanings (www.oplin.lib.oh.us)**   Click "Genealogy" in the navigation bar to the left. This page archives all issues of Ohio Public Library Information Network's monthly, online column on genealogy issues by contributing editor for genealogy, Donovan Ackley. You'll find tips about how to find reliable genealogical information on the Internet as well as in the library (see Figure 21-8).

♦ **Repositories of Primary Sources (www.uidaho.edu/special-collections/Other.Repositories.html)** This is a listing of over 2,500 websites describing holdings of manuscripts, archives, rare books, historical photographs, and other primary sources. This site is worth a look.

♦ **South Carolina Library (www.sc.edu/library/socar/books.html)** This is the online card catalog for the South Carolina Library, which houses an extensive collection of genealogy holdings.

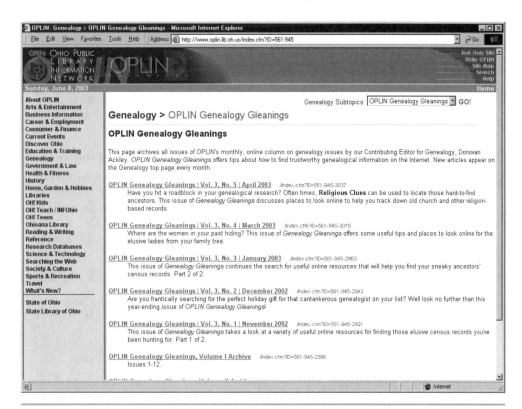

FIGURE 21-8. *The Ohio Public Library Information Network (OPLIN) has a monthly genealogy newsletter called Genealogy Gleanings.*

- **Texas State Library and Archives (www.tsl.state.tx.us/ arc/genfirst.html)**   This site lists available resources, including microfilm of the federal census schedules for all states through 1910, selected states from the 1920 and 1930 censuses, printed family and county histories, and a variety of Texas government records.

Maps, Geography, Etc.

"Where is that township?" is sometimes a hard question to answer. It can be even harder to find a community that no longer exists, or where county or state lines were moved. Searching for "Historical Maps" and the name of the county, state, province, or nation in question may turn up a hit in Google, Yahoo!, or other search sites. An excellent article on this topic can be found at www.rootsweb.com/ ~ srgp/articles/place.htm. It's titled "You Gotta Know the Territory—The Links between Genealogy, Geography and Logic." Some good sites to help with maps:

- **Deed Platter (genealogy.bearnip.com/deeds/deed_platter.html)**
  If the deed with your ancestor has the metes and bounds, you can have this site draw a map. As mentioned in Chapter 5, learning to do this can sometimes help you see a connection you didn't see before.

- **The Hargrett Rare Book and Manuscript Library, at the University of Georgia (scarlett.libs.uga.edu/darchive/hargrett/ maps/maps.html)**   This library has a collection of over 800 historic maps spanning five centuries.

- **Global Gazetteer (www.calle.com/world/)**   This is a directory of over a quarter-million of the world's cities and towns, sorted by country and linked to a map for each town.

- **GEONET Name Server (www.nima.mil/gns/html/)**   This site lets you search for foreign geographic feature names, and it responds with latitude and longitude coordinates.

- **U.S. Census Bureau Gazetteer (www.census.gov/cgi-bin/ gazetteer)**   This is where you can search by entering the name and state abbreviation (optional), or the five-digit ZIP Code.

- **Great Britain Historical GIS Project (www.geog.port.ac.uk/ gbhgis/)**   This project started in 1994, and it's creating a major

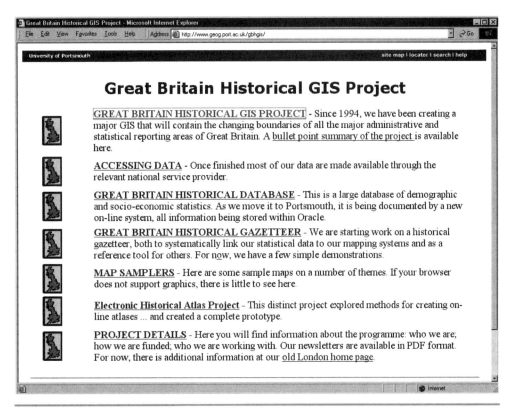

FIGURE 21-9.   *Find historical geographical information at the Great Britain Historical GIS Project.*

Geographical Information System (GIS) to map the boundary changes of all the major administrative and statistical reporting areas of Great Britain (see Figure 21-9).

♦ **Historical Maps of the United States, from the University of Texas at Austin (www.lib.utexas.edu/maps/histus.html)**   This site has dozens of maps under the headings Early Inhabitants, Exploration and Settlement, Territorial Growth, Military History, Later Historical Maps, and Other Historical Map Sites.

♦ **Old Maps, UK (www.old-maps.co.uk/)**   This site lets you search online and order hard copies.

Regional

If you need a regional resource, first go to Google, Yahoo!, Lycos, or another web catalog and search for "archives." For example, this search

on Google brings you to the catalog page directory.google.com/Top/
Reference/Archives/, which has over 100 links for government archives.
The following links are good examples of what you can expect to find:

♦ **Alabama Department of Archives and History Genealogy Page
(www.archives.state.al.us/ge.htm)**　This is a specific genealogy
page with links to what records are available. The site accepts
credit cards for reference requests and is shown in Figure 21-10.

♦ **Alabama Genealogy Sources (www.genealogyforum.rootsweb
.com/gfaol/internet/Alabama.htm)**　This is just an example of
the lists of links available at the Genealogy Forum Internet Center.
There is one for each state.

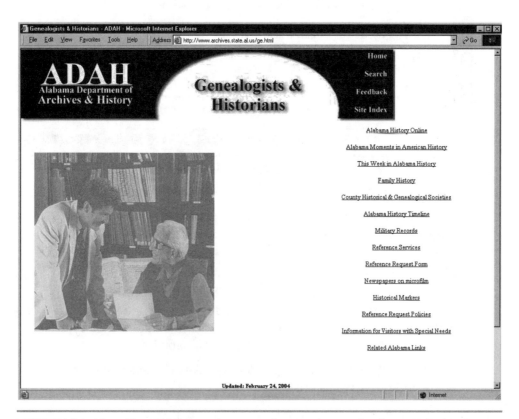

FIGURE 21-10.　*The ADAH Genealogy page is a good example of a state archive's
website.*

- **Canadian Heritage Information Network (www.chin.gc.ca)**
  This is a bilingual—French or English—guide to museums, galleries, and other heritage-oriented resources in Canada.

- **European Archival Network (www.european-archival.net/archives/)**   This page lists national archive sites by alphabet and region.

- **Filson Historical Society (www.filsonhistorical.org)**   This is a library, manuscript collection, and museum, concentrating on Kentucky history and genealogy. It has a searchable, online library card catalog of materials.

- **GENUKI (www.genuki.org.uk)**   This site is all about genealogy in the U.K. and Ireland.

- **Local Ireland: Genealogy (www.local.ie/genealogy)**   This is a portal with message boards, transcribed records, surname origins, and a newsletter.

- **National Archives of Singapore (www.museum.org.sg/NAS/nas.shtml)**   This site offers relatively recent records.

- **New England Historic Genealogical Society (www.nehgs.org)**
  This site is designed to be a center for family and local history research in New England. The Society owns 200,000 genealogy books and documents. If you're a New England genealogist, you should check it out.

- **Surnames.com (www.surnames.com)**   This site discusses general genealogy, with some focus on the Arizona area. It includes a surname search and a map of genealogical organizations in the United States. The site also has a useful beginner's section.

- **Traveller Southern Families (misc.traveler.com/genealogy/)**
  This site has information about Civil War web pages, government web servers, genealogy software companies, family societies and/or associations pages, books for sale, and genealogy newsgroups.

- **Utah State Archives (www.archives.state.ut.us)**   Here you can access the research center for the Archives' public services. This site includes research, places where questions can be answered, and places where records can be ordered. Not everything here is free, but it's very convenient!

Software

As noted in Chapter 2, software can help you gather, analyze, store, and compare information you find online and offline. Some good ones to investigate are:

♦ **Clooz (www.clooz.com)** This is a program to organize your genealogy research by name, source, family line, and other categories.

♦ **David Eppstein's home page (www.ics.uci.edu/~eppstein/gene)** This page has information on Eppstein's shareware program, Gene for the Macintosh.

♦ **Family Tree Maker Online (www.familytreemaker.com)** This site boasts the FamilyFinder Index, which has genealogy data from users of their programs. It includes 153 million names you can search, the Internet FamilyFinder, and a 1,200-page guide to genealogy titled "Genealogy How-To."

♦ **GEDmark (www.progenysoftware.com)** GEDmark adds your name and contact information as a source citation on each record of your GEDCOM file. GEDmark is a free program.

♦ **GEDStrip (freepages.genealogy.rootsweb.com/~hotrum/ gedstrip.htm)** This program takes the living out of your GEDCOM file for privacy, if your genealogy database program doesn't already do so.

♦ **GENDEX (www.gendex.com)** This is the home site of the GENDEX and GED2HTML software.

♦ **GENTRACER (www.crazyfox.net/GenTracer.htm)** This free Access database template is designed to track genealogical research data.

♦ **RootsMagic (www.rootsmagic.com)** This is a new genealogy database program.

Starting Places

Here are some good places to begin your search for people, places, and pages:

- **Cyndi's List of Genealogy Sites on the Internet (www.cyndislist.com)**   The best-organized and annotated list of WWW genealogy sites on the Internet. A must-see!

- **Distant Cousin (distantcousin.com)**   This site has several online databases, including marriages, military rosters, tombstone transcriptions, and ships' passenger lists, which you can search for free, as well as a large human-edited directory of genealogical websites, organized by surname, ethnicity, and geographical location.

- **Everton's Guide to Genealogy on the World Wide Web (www.everton.com)**   This site has links to online resources and a tutorial for genealogy beginners. Test-drive their genealogical database On-Line Search.

- **Genealogy Home Page (www.genhomepage.com)**   This page offers a wide-ranging index of genealogy resources on the Internet. It includes links to maps, libraries, software, and societies.

- **Genealogy Links.Net (www.genealogylinks.net)**   This site includes over 9,000 links, most of them to online searchable databases, such as ships' passenger lists, church records, cemetery transcriptions, and censuses for England, Scotland, Wales, Ireland, Europe, USA, Canada, Australia, and New Zealand.

- **Genealogy Pages (www.genealogypages.com)**   This site provides a collection of links to free genealogical services, as well as to over 29,000 online resources.

- **Genealogy and Native American Bulletin Boards (genealogy .bb.prodigy.net)**   This is part of the Prodigy.net/SBC website. It's a good place for beginners' questions.

- **Genealogy Resources on the Internet (www.rootsweb.com/ ~jfuller/)**   This site provides you with a quality-sorted list for finding the exact genealogical information you're looking for.

- **Genealogy Spot (www.genealogyspot.com)**   This is a free portal with links to online genealogy resources for beginners and experts alike. Sites featured here are hand-selected by an editorial team for quality, content, and utility.

- **GeneaNet (www.geneanet.org)**   Based in France, this is a genealogy database site you can search by name or geographic location. It is not based on GEDCOM but rather has its own database format. Other resources are available, such as a list of genealogy books, genealogy news briefs, and more. Much of the emphasis is on French history, genealogy, and research, but there are other resources, too.

- **GENSUCK.com (www.gensuck.com)**   This is where the web hosts and their readers post dialogues about controversies and rants about online genealogy. If you want to find out what sucks about online genealogy, check out this site.

- **Marston Manor (www.geocities.com/Heartland/Plains/1638)** This personal genealogy site offers numerous useful items for online genealogists, including a chart for calculating family relationships, and a detailed discussion of the terms "proof" and "evidence" as they relate to genealogy.

- **The USGenWeb Project (www.usgenweb.com)**   This is a noncommercial project with the goal of providing websites for genealogical research in every county and every state of the United States.

- **Yahoo! Genealogy Page (www.yahoo.com/Arts/Humanities/ History/Genealogy/)**   A huge collection of links to guides, resources, and personal genealogies on websites. It also includes links to related resources.

Supplies, Books, Forms, Etc.

There are several good sources of free forms and supplies (see Chapter 1). Check out DearMYRTLE's page (www.dearmyrtle.com/bookshelf/ supplies.htm) for some downloadable ones. The Ancestors series Teacher's Guide has several PDF files of research forms for downloading, too. You can buy supplies from Ancestry.com (see Chapter 17) and Everton.com (see Chapter 18) as well. Here are a few other sites:

- **Heritage Quest (www.heritagequest.com/genealogy/microfilm/ html/order_info.html)**   This site has books, microfilm, and other materials you can rent as well as purchase. It also has a database of information accessible from public libraries that subscribe to the service.

♦   **Global: Everything for the Family Historian (www.globalgenealogy.com)**   This is the Global Genealogy Supply website. Shop online for genealogy supplies—maps, forms, software, and so forth—and subscribe to the Global Gazette, a free e-mail newsletter covering Canadian genealogy and heritage.

♦   **Family Chronicle (www.familychronicle.com)**   The website for the *Family Chronicle* magazine, which is dedicated to families researching their roots. Check out their offerings and request a free sample of the magazine.

♦   **Genealogical.com (www.genealogical.com)**   This site has genealogy supplies, articles about research, as well as books and CD-ROMs.

A Closer Look

Although one of the most exciting things about genealogy and web browsing is the joy of discovery, some sites deserve a guided tour. The sites featured here are particularly interesting or useful to online genealogists, and each one has something special to offer. If you want to discover everything yourself, however, you have more than enough information to spend years researching online. Just skip past the rest of this section and be on your way.

AfriGeneas

AfriGeneas (www.afrigeneas.com) is a site for researching families of African ancestry (see Figure 21-11). The AfriGeneas website at www.afrigeneas.com has a mailing list that gathers and presents information about families of African ancestry and is a guide to genealogical resources around the world. Members of the mail list are invited to contribute information and resources, sometimes going as far as taking responsibility for information for a certain area.

AfriGeneas has a searchable database of surnames (in addition to slave data) from descendants of slaveholding families, as well as from other sources both public and private. Tips and topics to help people in

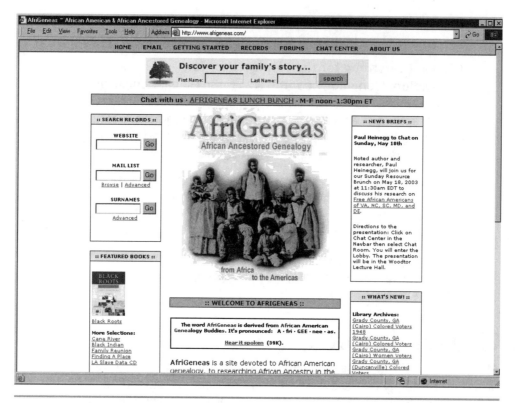

FIGURE 21-11. *AfriGeneas is a genealogy cooperative for African-American genealogy.*

their search for family history are distributed through mail lists, chats, newsletters, and the Internet. Volunteers do all of this; they extract, compile, and publish all related public records with any genealogical value. The site also maintains an impressive set of links to other Internet resources to help African-Americans in their research:

♦ **Beginner's Guide**   This slideshow-like presentation steps you through online genealogy. It's a no-nonsense approach, showing what can and can't be done online. It also includes some success stories.

♦ **Mailing List**   This is the discussion list. You'll find the rules and the archives, plus information about how to subscribe and unsubscribe to the mail list.

- **State Resources**   With a clickable map, this page links to sites for each state in the United States with history, links to state resources, and queries.

- **World Resources**   This is along the same lines as State Resources, but only the United States and the Bahamas are up at press time. Volunteers are actively being sought for other countries.

- **Surnames**   This is a set of queries with names, dates, and places of known ancestors. You can search the ones there as well as post your own.

- **Slave Data**   This area will help you find the last owned slave in your family. Records kept by the slave owner are frequently the only clue to African-American ancestors, particularly during the period 1619–1869. The site is also designed to help descendants of slaveholders and other researchers, as well. Users share information they find containing any references to slaves, including wills, deeds, and other documents. This site also houses a search engine and a form for submitting any data you might have. To use the database, click the first letter of the surname you're interested in. This takes you to a list of text files with surnames beginning with that letter. Now, click a particular file name. The text file may be transcribed from a deed book, a will, or some other document. The name and e-mail address of the submitter will be included, so you can write to that person for more information, if necessary.

- **Census Records**   These are transcribed census records. As a file is submitted, it's listed at the top of the What's New list on this page. Not all states have volunteers transcribing right now, so you can only click those states that show up as a live link.

- **Library**   This contains guides, articles, chat transcripts, and images for you to look at online or download to your computer. Among the titles are "Researching in Southwest Louisiana" and "Cherokee Freedmen in Indian Territory."

- **Community**   This page shows how you can get involved, where and how to sign up as a volunteer, and testimonials about how much AfriGeneas has helped the people who use it.

- ◆ **Newsletter** The monthly newsletter looks at genealogy news from the African-American perspective.

- ◆ **Forum and Chat** Chats on specific topics meet on a scheduled basis, and open discussions are usually available 24 hours a day. The forum is a web-based list of messages sorted by date, with the most recent at the top.

- ◆ **AfriGeneas Links** This page offers hundreds of fascinating links, sorted by topic, from good starting points such as Christine's Genealogy website (see the earlier listing) to WPA Slave Narratives to Canadian Black History.

AfriGeneas has come a long way from its beginnings as a mail list, and it keeps getting better and better.

Cyndi's List

Cyndi Howell's list of genealogy links is on everyone's list of top-five genealogy places on the World Wide Web. With over 180,000 links, sorted into over 150 categories, it is the best place to start looking for genealogy sites. The links are categorized, alphabetized, and searchable, and the list has links to sites large and small, from national archives to personal genealogies.

The Main Index, from the home page, lists each category in alphabetical order—from "Acadian, Cajun and Creole" to "Writing Your Family History." The Topical Index (www.cyndislist.com/topical.htm) rearranges those topics into about a dozen different groupings. The "No Frills" index (www.cyndislist.com/nofrills.htm) has every single category page, with no icons for the newest or latest update.

The Main Index page also has the FAQs about Cyndi's List, as in how she collects, verifies, and updates the links, and how to submit a link for her consideration. You will also find on the main page the newest links, sorted by month, and Cyndi's speaking schedule.

Cyndi's List is indispensable for finding pages on genealogy.

DearMYRTLE

For the beginning-to-intermediate genealogist, there's no better spot than DearMYRTLE's Place at www.dearmyrtle.com. DearMYRTLE has helped hundreds of genealogists with her daily columns, weekly chats, newsletters, and online courses. Her site will help you learn and grow as a genealogist.

The first page of DearMYRTLE's site (see Figure 21-12) is her list of favorite things to do on the Internet for family history.

The choices range from listening to her Internet radio talk show (see Chapter 7) to her "step-by-step" guides.

Her "Best of the Internet for Genealogists" is a frequently updated list of helpful sites, especially for beginners. The Bookshelf is a collection of book reviews, and the Events page is her schedule of speeches, workshops, and guided tours on genealogy. DearMYRTLE has a message board hosted by RootsWeb and Ancestry, and you can subscribe to get her daily genealogy column delivered to your e-mail box.

Bookmark DearMYRTLE's site. You'll be coming back often!

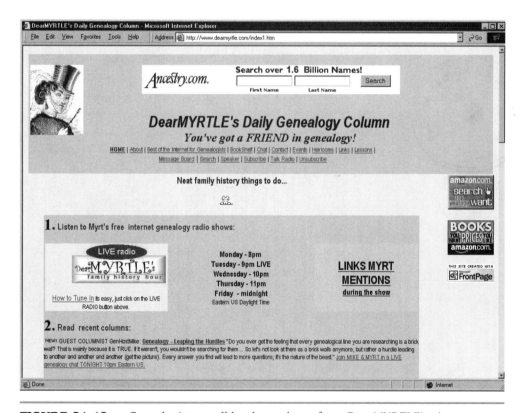

FIGURE 21-12.   *Genealogists at all levels can learn from DearMYRTLE's site.*

Wrapping Up

- ◆ Thousands of websites exist to help with genealogy.

- ◆ Some of the most useful websites are collections of links to other sites, such as Cyndi's List and the RootsWeb.

- ◆ A number of websites are more specific with genealogies submitted from users (for example, GenServ).

- ◆ Several websites have data such as land records, family bible entries, and transcribed census data (for example, AfriGeneas, The Library of Virginia, and the Bureau of Land Management).

- ◆ Other pages have good information on how to proceed with your research (for example, DearMYRTLE and the Adoptee Search Resource page).

Part IV

Appendixes

Appendix A

Genealogical Standards from the National Genealogical Society

Often, a beginning genealogist's first problem is how to proceed. As with any endeavor, you can go about gathering your family history in good ways and in bad ways.

The National Genealogical Society (NGS; covered in Chapter 15) has a committee on sound genealogical standards. The guidelines are intended to make the genealogist's task somewhat easier by giving a roadmap, so to speak, of how to navigate the collection of data, as well as preserve, interpret, and share genealogical data. Study and follow these guidelines, and your quest for ancestry will be a rewarding one.

These standards are revisited at NGS meetings and may be updated in the future. Check the web page at www.ngsgenealogy.org/comstandards .htm for updates.

Standards for Sound Genealogical Research

Recommended by the National Genealogical Society

Remembering always that they are engaged in a quest for truth, family history researchers consistently—

- ♦ record the source for each item of information they collect.

- ♦ test every hypothesis or theory against credible evidence, and reject those that are not supported by the evidence.

- ♦ seek original records, or reproduced images of them when there is reasonable assurance they have not been altered, as the basis for their research conclusions.

- ♦ use compilations, communications and published works, whether paper or electronic, primarily for their value as guides to locating the original records, or as contributions to the critical analysis of the evidence discussed in them.

- ♦ state something as a fact only when it is supported by convincing evidence, and identify the evidence when communicating the fact to others.

- ♦ limit with words like "probable" or "possible" any statement that is based on less than convincing evidence, and state the reasons for concluding that it is probable or possible.

- avoid misleading other researchers by either intentionally or carelessly distributing or publishing inaccurate information.

- state carefully and honestly the results of their own research, and acknowledge all use of other researchers' work.

- recognize the collegial nature of genealogical research by making their work available to others through publication, or by placing copies in appropriate libraries or repositories, and by welcoming critical comment.

- consider with open minds new evidence or the comments of others on their work and the conclusions they have reached.

©1997, 2002 by National Genealogical Society. Permission is granted to copy or publish this material provided it is reproduced in its entirety, including this notice.

Guidelines for Using Records, Repositories, and Libraries

Recommended by the National Genealogical Society

Recognizing that how they use unique original records and fragile publications will affect other users, both current and future, family history researchers habitually—

- are courteous to research facility personnel and other researchers, and respect the staff's other daily tasks, not expecting the records custodian to listen to their family histories nor provide constant or immediate attention.

- dress appropriately, converse with others in a low voice, and supervise children appropriately.

- do their homework in advance, know what is available and what they need, and avoid ever asking for "everything" on their ancestors.

- use only designated work space areas and equipment, like readers and computers intended for patron use, respect off-limits areas, and ask for assistance if needed.

- treat original records at all times with great respect and work with only a few records at a time, recognizing that they are irreplaceable and that each user must help preserve them for future use.

- ◆ treat books with care, never forcing their spines, and handle photographs properly, preferably wearing archival gloves.

- ◆ never mark, mutilate, rearrange, relocate, or remove from the repository any original, printed, microform, or electronic document or artifact.

- ◆ use only procedures prescribed by the repository for noting corrections to any errors or omissions found in published works, never marking the work itself.

- ◆ keep note-taking paper or other objects from covering records or books, and avoid placing any pressure upon them, particularly with a pencil or pen.

- ◆ use only the method specifically designated for identifying records for duplication, avoiding use of paper clips, adhesive notes, or other means not approved by the facility.

- ◆ return volumes and files only to locations designated for that purpose.

- ◆ before departure, thank the records custodians for their courtesy in making the materials available.

- ◆ follow the rules of the records repository without protest, even if they have changed since a previous visit or differ from those of another facility.

©1997, 2001 by National Genealogical Society; includes material ©1995 by Joy Reisinger, CG. Both copyright owners grant permission to copy or publish these standards, provided they are reproduced in their entirety, including this notice.

Standards for Use of Technology in Genealogical Research

Recommended by the National Genealogical Society

Mindful that computers are tools, genealogists take full responsibility for their work, and therefore they—

- ◆ learn the capabilities and limits of their equipment and software, and use them only when they are the most appropriate tools for a purpose.

- do not accept uncritically the ability of software to format, number, import, modify, check, chart or report their data, and therefore carefully evaluate any resulting product.

- treat compiled information from on-line sources or digital databases in the same way as other published sources--useful primarily as a guide to locating original records, but not as evidence for a conclusion or assertion.

- accept digital images or enhancements of an original record as a satisfactory substitute for the original only when there is reasonable assurance that the image accurately reproduces the unaltered original.

- cite sources for data obtained on-line or from digital media with the same care that is appropriate for sources on paper and other traditional media, and enter data into a digital database only when its source can remain associated with it.

- always cite the sources for information or data posted on-line or sent to others, naming the author of a digital file as its immediate source, while crediting original sources cited within the file.

- preserve the integrity of their own databases by evaluating the reliability of downloaded data before incorporating it into their own files.

- provide, whenever they alter data received in digital form, a description of the change that will accompany the altered data whenever it is shared with others.

- actively oppose the proliferation of error, rumor and fraud by personally verifying or correcting information, or noting it as unverified, before passing it on to others.

- treat people on-line as courteously and civilly as they would treat them face-to-face, not separated by networks and anonymity.

- accept that technology has not changed the principles of genealogical research, only some of the procedures.

Standards for Sharing Information with Others

Recommended by the National Genealogical Society

Conscious of the fact that sharing information or data with others, whether through speech, documents or electronic media, is essential to family history research and that it needs continuing support and encouragement, responsible family historians consistently—

- ◆ respect the restrictions on sharing information that arise from the rights of another as an author, originator or compiler; as a living private person; or as a party to a mutual agreement.

- ◆ observe meticulously the legal rights of copyright owners, copying or distributing any part of their works only with their permission, or to the limited extent specifically allowed under the law's "fair use" exceptions.

- ◆ identify the sources for all ideas, information and data from others, and the form in which they were received, recognizing that the unattributed use of another's intellectual work is plagiarism.

- ◆ respect the authorship rights of senders of letters, electronic mail and data files, forwarding or disseminating them further only with the sender's permission.

- ◆ inform people who provide information about their families as to the ways it may be used, observing any conditions they impose and respecting any reservations they may express regarding the use of particular items.

- ◆ require some evidence of consent before assuming that living people are agreeable to further sharing of information about themselves.

- ◆ convey personal identifying information about living people— like age, home address, occupation or activities—only in ways that those concerned have expressly agreed to.

- ◆ recognize that legal rights of privacy may limit the extent to which information from publicly available sources may be further used, disseminated or published.

- communicate no information to others that is known to be false, or without making reasonable efforts to determine its truth, particularly information that may be derogatory.

- are sensitive to the hurt that revelations of criminal, immoral, bizarre or irresponsible behavior may bring to family members.

Guidelines for Publishing Web Pages on the Internet

Recommended by the National Genealogical Society, May 2000

Appreciating that publishing information through Internet web sites and web pages shares many similarities with print publishing, considerate family historians—

- apply a title identifying both the entire web site and the particular group of related pages, similar to a book-and-chapter designation, placing it both at the top of each web browser window using the < TITLE > HTML tag, and in the body of the document, on the opening home or title page and on any index pages.

- explain the purposes and objectives of their web sites, placing the explanation near the top of the title page or including a link from that page to a special page about the reason for the site.

- display a footer at the bottom of each web page which contains the web site title, page title, author's name, author's contact information, date of last revision and a copyright statement.

- provide complete contact information, including at a minimum a name and e-mail address, and preferably some means for long-term contact, like a postal address.

- assist visitors by providing on each page navigational links that lead visitors to other important pages on the web site, or return them to the home page.

- adhere to the **NGS "Standards for Sharing Information with Others"** regarding copyright, attribution, privacy, and the sharing of sensitive information.

- include unambiguous source citations for the research data provided on the site, and if not complete descriptions, offering full citations upon request.

- label photographic and scanned images within the graphic itself, with fuller explanation if required in text adjacent to the graphic.

- identify transcribed, extracted or abstracted data as such, and provide appropriate source citations.

- include identifying dates and locations when providing information about specific surnames or individuals.

- respect the rights of others who do not wish information about themselves to be published, referenced or linked on a web site.

- provide web site access to all potential visitors by avoiding enhanced technical capabilities that may not be available to all users, remembering that not all computers are created equal.

- avoid using features that distract from the productive use of the web site, like ones that reduce legibility, strain the eyes, dazzle the vision, or otherwise detract from the visitor's ability to easily read, study, comprehend or print the online publication.

- maintain their online publications at frequent intervals, changing the content to keep the information current, the links valid, and the web site in good working order.

- preserve and archive for future researchers their online publications and communications that have lasting value, using both electronic and paper duplication.

Guidelines for Genealogical Self-Improvement and Growth

Recommended by the National Genealogical Society

Faced with ever-growing expectations for genealogical accuracy and reliability, family historians concerned with improving their abilities will on a regular basis—

◆ study comprehensive texts and narrower-focus articles and recordings covering genealogical methods in general and the historical background and sources available for areas of particular research interest, or to which their research findings have led them.

◆ interact with other genealogists and historians in person or electronically, mentoring or learning as appropriate to their relative experience levels, and through the shared experience contributing to the genealogical growth of all concerned.

◆ subscribe to and read regularly at least two genealogical journals that list a number of contributing or consulting editors, or editorial board or committee members, and that require their authors to respond to a critical review of each article before it is published.

◆ participate in workshops, discussion groups, institutes, conferences and other structured learning opportunities whenever possible.

◆ recognize their limitations, undertaking research in new areas or using new technology only after they master any additional knowledge and skill needed and understand how to apply it to the new subject matter or technology.

◆ analyze critically at least quarterly the reported research findings of another family historian, for whatever lessons may be gleaned through the process.

◆ join and participate actively in genealogical societies covering countries, localities and topics where they have research interests, as well as the localities where they reside, increasing the resources available both to themselves and to future researchers.

◆ review recently published basic texts to renew their understanding of genealogical fundamentals as currently expressed and applied.

◆ examine and revise their own earlier research in the light of what they have learned through self-improvement activities, as a means for applying their new-found knowledge and for improving the quality of their work-product.

Appendix B

Forms of Genealogical Data

One of the reasons to get involved in the online genealogy world is to share the information you have—and to find information you don't have. To do this, standards have been set up for transmitting that information.

GEDCOMs, Ahnentafels, and Tiny Tafels

GEDCOMs, ahnentafels, and tiny tafels are all designed to put information in a standard format. GEDCOMs and tiny tafels can be used by many different genealogical database programs, and many utilities have been written to translate information from one to another.

GEDCOMs

In February 1987, The Church of Jesus Christ of Latter-day Saints (Mormon church) approved a standard way of setting data for transfer between various types of genealogy software, including its own Personal Ancestral File (PAF). The standard is a combination of tags for data and pointers to related data. Most major genealogy programs, such as MacGene, The Master Genealogist, Family Tree Maker, Family Ties, Brother's Keeper, Legacy, and so on, use at least some form of the standard.

However, the implementation from one program to another can vary slightly. If the GEDCOM data from one program doesn't fit precisely into the new one, the genealogy program will often save the extraneous data to a special file. A good program can use this data to help you sort and search to determine whether it has what you're looking for. This is why so many people upload GEDCOMs to sites: It is the hope that someone somewhere can use the data. But because GEDCOMs tend to be large, some sites have a policy against uploading them. Instead, you upload a message that you're willing to exchange the data for the price of the disk, or some other arrangement.

The current release of the GEDCOM standard is 5.5. At the page www.gendex.com/gedcom55/55gctoc.htm, you will find the standard spelled out in detail.

Ahnentafels

Ahnentafels aren't big tiny tafels. The word means *ancestor table* in German, and the format is more than a century old. An *ahnentafel* lists all known ancestors of an individual and includes the full name of each, as well as dates and places of birth, marriage, and death. It organizes this information along a strict numbering scheme.

Once you get used to ahnentafels, reading them becomes easy, moving up and down from parent to child, and then back again. The numbering scheme is the key to it all. Consider this typical pedigree chart:

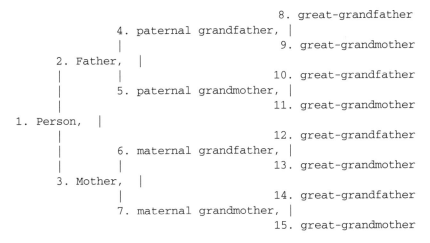

```
                                          8. great-grandfather
                    4. paternal grandfather, |
                    |                         9. great-grandmother
        2. Father,  |
        |           |                         10. great-grandfather
        |           5. paternal grandmother, |
        |                                     11. great-grandmother
    1. Person,  |
        |                                     12. great-grandfather
        |           6. maternal grandfather, |
        |           |                         13. great-grandmother
        3. Mother,  |
        |                                     14. great-grandfather
                    7. maternal grandmother, |
                                              15. great-grandmother
```

Study the numbers in this chart. Every person listed has a number, with a mathematical relationship between parents and children. The number of a father is always double that of his child's. The number of the mother is always double that of her child's, plus one. The number of a child is always one-half that of its parent (ignoring any remainder).

In this example, the father of person #6 is #12, the mother of #6 is #13, and the child of #13 is #6. In ahnentafel format, the chart reads like this:

1. person

2. father

3. mother

4. paternal grandfather

5. paternal grandmother

6. maternal grandfather

7. maternal grandmother

8. great-grandfather

9. great-grandmother

10. great-grandfather

11. great-grandmother

12. great-grandfather

13. great-grandmother

14. great-grandfather

15. great-grandmother

Notice the numbers are exactly the same as in the pedigree chart. The rules of father = 2 × child#, mother = 2 × child# + 1, child = parent/2, ignore remainder, and so forth remain the same. This is an ahnentafel chart.

In practice, ahnentafels are rarely uploaded as text files, but it's one way to show what you do know about your tree quickly, and in few characters. Just clearly state that it's an ahnentafel. Some websites list genealogies as ahnentafels.

Tiny Tafels

Despite the similar name, a tiny tafel (TT) is a different animal. A *TT* provides a standard way of describing a family database, so the information can be scanned visually or by computer. It was described in an article titled "Tiny-Tafel for Database Scope Indexing," by Paul Andereck in the April-May-June 1986 issue (vol. 5, number 4) of *Genealogical Computing*.

The concept of TTs was adopted by COMMSOFT first in its popular program, Roots-II, and later in Roots-III. TT has since been adapted by other genealogical programs, such as Brother's Keeper and GED2TT.

A TT makes no attempt to include the details contained in an ahnentafel. All data fields are of fixed length, with the obvious exceptions of the surnames and optional places. A TT lists only surnames of interest (with Soundex), plus the locations and dates of the beginning and end of that surname. TTs make no provision for first names, births, marriages, deaths, or multiple locations.

In the COMMSOFT TT, the name of the database, the version of the database, and any special switches used when the TT was generated are shown on the line of data called the *Z line*. The definitions of the special switches are shown next:

♦ **D DATEFILLDISABLED**   When data for birth dates is missing (unknown), then the tiny tafel format can skip that field. When this switch is on, the TT generator has estimated missing dates. The TT program applies a 30-year per generation offset wherever it needs to reconstruct missing dates.

♦ **N NOGROUPING**   TT normally "groups" output lines that have a common ancestor into a single line containing the most recent birth date. Descendants marked with an interest level greater than zero, however, will have their own line of output. Alternatively, when this switch is enabled, one line of output is created for every ultimate descendant (individual without children).

♦ **M MULTIPLENAMES**   TT normally lists a surname derived from the descendant end of each line. Specifying this option lists all unique spellings of each surname (up to five) separated by commas.

♦ **P PLACENAMES**   TT includes place names for family lines when this switch is enabled. Place names will be the most significant 14 to 16 characters of the birth field. When this option is enabled, the place of birth of the ultimate ancestor and the place of birth of the ultimate descendant of a line of output, respectively, are added to the end of the line.

♦ **S SINGLEITEMS**   TT normally suppresses lines of output that correspond to a single individual (that is, in which the ancestry and descendant dates are the same). This switch includes single-person items in the output.

♦ **#I INTERESTLEVEL**   TT normally includes all family lines meeting the previous conditions, no matter what its interest level. An interest level may be specified to limit the lines included to those having an interest level equal to or greater than the number specified. For example, with the interest level set to 1, all lines that have an ancestor or descendant interest level of 1 or higher will be listed.

The Soundex code for any given line is obtained from the end of the line that has the highest interest level. But, if the interest level is the same at each end, the name at the ancestor end will be used. If the application of these rules yield a surname that cannot be converted to Soundex, however, the program will attempt to obtain a Soundex code from the other end of the line.

Interest flags are as follows:

Interest flag	Codes for interest level are
[space]	No interest (level 0)
.	Low interest (level 1)
:	Moderate interest (level 2)
*	Highest interest (level 3)

Up to five surnames can be on one line where the surname has changed in that line. If more than five surnames are found in a line, only the latest five will be shown. The inclusion of additional surnames is enabled by the *M* switch.

Place names for the birth of the earliest ancestor and the latest descendant may be included by using the *P* switch. If a place name isn't provided for the individual whose birth year is shown, the field will be blank. The place for the ancestor is preceded by a backslash (\) and for the descendant by a slash (/).

The final line is called a Terminator. It shows the date of the file in this format:

W Date Tiny Tafel file was generated, DD MMM YYYY format.

That's how you build a TT manually. Most genealogical software packages now have a function to create and accept either a TT or a GEDCOM, or both, from your information in the database. Always be certain a downloaded GEDCOM or TT has verified information before you load it into your database, because taking it back out isn't fun.

Check out the Roots and Branches website at www.srcomm.com/ryan/gen/TafelHowTo.htm for a list of sites where you can search and swap TT files.

Glossary

A

a. (or c.)   *About* (or *circa*, in Latin). Often used in front of uncertain dates.

AF (Ancestral File)   A searchable collection of genealogical data submitted to the LDS archives, to help genealogists coordinate their research, in GEDCOM format.

AG   Accredited Genealogist. A designation conferred by the LDS church.

ahnentafel   The word means "ancestor table" in German, and the format is more than a century old. The ahnentafel lists all known ancestors of an individual and includes the full name of each ancestor, as well as dates and places of birth, marriage, and death. It organizes this information along a numbering scheme. Any individual's father is twice that individual's number in the table; any individual's mother is twice plus one that individual's number in the table. Therefore, all males in the table are even numbers and all females odd numbers. If you are #1 in the table, your father is #2 and your mother is #3. Your father's father is #4, your father's mother #5, and so on.

anonymous FTP (File Transfer Protocol)   The process of connecting to a remote computer, as an anonymous or guest user, to transfer public files back to your local computer. (See also: *FTP* and *protocol.*) Anonymous FTP is usually read-only access; you often cannot contribute files by anonymous FTP.

B

backbone   A set of connections that make up the main channels of communication across a network.

BCG   Board for Certification of Genealogists.

browser   An Internet client for viewing the World Wide Web.

bulletin board   A way of referring to online message systems where you must log on to the site or ISP to read and post messages. Also called a *message board.*

C

catalog A search page for the Web within an edited list, not the whole Internet.

CG Certified Genealogist, by the Board for Certification of Genealogists (BCG).

CGI Certified Genealogical Instructor, by the Board for Certification of Genealogists (BCG).

CGL Certified Genealogical Lecturer, by the Board for Certification of Genealogists (BCG).

CGRS Certified Genealogical Record Specialist, by the Board for Certification of Genealogists (BCG).

chat When people type messages to each other across a host or network, live and in real time. On some commercial online services, this is called a *conference*.

client A program that provides an interface to remote Internet services, such as mail, Usenet, telnet, and so on. In general, the clients act on behalf of a human end-user (perhaps indirectly).

collateral line A family that is not in your direct line of ancestry but of the same genealogical line.

compression A method of making a file, whether text or code, smaller by various methods. This is so the file will take up less disk space and/or less time to transmit. Sometimes the compression is completed by the modem. Sometimes the file is stored that way. The various methods to do this go by the names (followed by the system that uses it) PKZIP (DOS), ARC (DOS), tar (UNIX), StuffIt (Macintosh), and so forth.

conference A usually large gathering with discussions, lectures, exhibits, and perhaps workshops. Genealogy conferences are held around the country every year.

D

database A set of information organized for computer storage, search, retrieval, and insertion.

default In computer terms, the "normal" or "basic" settings of a program.

directory **1**. A level in a hierarchical filing system. Other directories branch down from the root directory. **2**. A type of search site where editors choose the websites and services in the catalog, instead of a robot collecting them indiscriminately.

domain name The Internet naming scheme used to locate an organization or other entity's pages on the World Wide Web. A machine on the Internet is identified by a series of words from more specific to more general (left to right), separated by dots: microsoft.com is an example. (See also: *IP address.*)

domain name server (DNS) A machine with software to translate a domain name into the corresponding numbers of the IP address. "No DNS entry" from your browser means a name such as first.last.org wasn't in the domain name server's list of valid IP addresses.

downloading The process of getting information from another computer to yours. (See also: *uploading.*)

E

e-mail An electronic message, text, or data sent from one machine or person to another machine or person.

F

family group sheet A one-page collection of facts about one family unit, including husband, wife, and children, with birth and death dates and places.

FHC Family History Center. A branch of the Family History Library in Salt Lake City, Utah, found in a local LDS parish.

firewall Electronic protection against hackers and other unauthorized access to your files while you're connected to a network or the Internet. This protection is especially important with broadband, "always-on" connections to the Internet.

flame A message or series of messages containing an argument or insults. This is not allowed on most systems. If you receive a flame, ignore that message and all other messages from that person in the future.

forum A set of messages on a subject, usually with a corresponding set of files. This can be on an open network, such as ILINK, or restricted to a commercial system, such as CompuServe.

French Revolutionary Calendar The French Revolutionary Calendar (or Republican Calendar) was introduced in France on 24 November 1793 and abolished on 1 January 1806. It was used again briefly during the Paris Commune in 1871.

FTP (File Transfer Protocol) Enables an Internet user to transfer files electronically between remote computers and the user's computer.

G

gateway Used in different senses (for example, mail gateway and IP gateway) but, most generally, means a computer that forwards and routes data between two or more networks of any size or origin. A gateway is never, however, as straightforward as going through a gate. It's more like a labyrinth to get the proper addresses in the proper sequence.

GEDCOM The standard for computerized genealogical information, which is a combination of tags for data and pointers to related data.

Gregorian Calendar This calendar was introduced by Pope Gregory XIII in 1582 and adopted by England and the colonies in 1752, by which time it was 11 days behind the solar year, causing an adjustment in September of 1752.

H

hacker Originally, someone who messed about with computer systems to see how much could be accomplished. Most recently, a computer vandal.

host computer In the context of networks, a computer that directly provides services to a user. This is in contrast to a network server, which provides services to a user through an intermediary host computer.

HTML (Hypertext Markup Language) A coding language used to format and link documents on the World Wide Web and intranets.

hub A site that collects connections from other computers regionally and distributes the information up to the next level.

I

IGI The International Genealogical Index. A database of names submitted to the LDS church.

IM (instant message) A type of chat program that requires users to register with a server. Users build "buddy lists" of others using the same program and are notified when people on their buddy list are available for chat and messages.

institute A week-long set of courses on a specific area, usually held at the same site every year, with class size ranging from 15–30 students, allowing personalized instruction. Genealogical Institutes are held yearly in many sites in the United States and other countries.

Internet The backbone of a series of interconnected networks that includes local area, regional, and national backbone networks. Networks in the Internet use the same telecommunications protocol (TCP/IP) and provide electronic mail, remote login, and file-transfer services.

intranet A local network set up to look like the World Wide Web, with clients such as browsers, but self-contained and not necessarily connected to the Internet. Makes use of web technologies for communications and collaboration within a certain group, such as a corporation.

IP address The alphabetic or numeric address of a computer connected to the Internet. Also called *Internet address*. Usually the format is user@someplace.domain, but it can also be seen as ###.##.##.##.

IP (Internet Protocol) The Internet standard protocol that provides a common layer over dissimilar networks, used to move packets among host computers and through gateways, if necessary.

IR (Internet Relay Chat) Used to send real-time chat messages typed over an open, public server.

ISP (Internet service provider) A company that has a continuous, fast, and reliable connection to the Internet and sells subscriptions to the public to use that connection. These connections may use TCP/IP, shell accounts, or other methods.

J

Julian calendar The calendar replaced by the Gregorian calendar, because it had fallen behind the solar year.

L

LDS Accepted abbreviation for The Church of Jesus Christ of Latter-day Saints, also known as the Mormons.

list (Internet) Also called "mail list." Listserv lists (or listservers) are electronically transmitted discussions of technical and nontechnical issues. They come to you by electronic mail over the Internet using LISTSERV commands. Participants subscribe via a central service, and lists often have a moderator who supervises the information flow and content.

lurk To read a list or echo without posting messages yourself. It's sort of like sitting in the corner at a party without introducing yourself, except it's not considered rude online. In fact, in some places, you're expected to lurk until you get the feel of the place.

M

mail list Same as *list*.

MNP (Microcom Networking Protocol) Data compression standard for modems.

modem A device to modulate computer data into sound signals and to demodulate those signals to computer data.

moderator The person who takes care of a message list, newsgroup, or forum. This person takes out messages that are off topic, chastises flamers, maintains a database of old messages, and handles the mechanics of distributing the messages.

Mozilla A nickname for Netscape Navigator, and recently, an open-source browser project. In the early days, Netscape's mascot was a little dragon-like creature called Mozilla.

N

navigation bar A set of words and/or images that appears on every page of a website, with links to other sections or pages of the same website.

NGS National Genealogical Society, U.S.

NIC (Network Information Center) Provides administrative support, user support, and information services for a network.

O

offline The state of not being connected to a remote host.

online To be connected to a remote host.

OPAC (Online Public Access Catalog) A term used to describe any type of computerized library catalog.

P

PAF (Personal Ancestral File) A free genealogy program for use by members of the LDS church for submittal to the Temple in Salt Lake City.

PDF (Portable Document Format) A file format that allows a document to be saved to look a certain way, no matter what machine is used to display it. The machine, however, must use Adobe's Acrobat reader (a free program) to display the file.

pedigree chart The traditional way to display a genealogy. This is the familiar "family tree," where one person's ancestors are outlined. Other formats are the fan chart, the descendency chart (starts with the ancestor, comes down to the present), and the timeline.

plat *v.* To draw a map of a piece of land by the description of a deed. *n.* The map of a piece of land as defined by the deed.

PPP (Point-to-Point Protocol) A type of Internet connection. An improvement on SLIP (see the definition later in this glossary), PPP allows any computer to use the Internet protocols and become a full-fledged member of the Internet, using a high-speed modem. The advantage to SLIP and PPP accounts is you can usually achieve faster connections than with a shell account.

PRF (Pedigree Resource File) Genealogical information submitted by users of FamilySearch.com.

protocol A mutually determined set of formats and procedures governing the exchange of information between systems.

Q

query A request for genealogical information. To be effective, a query must include at least one name, one date, one geographical location, and your contact information.

R

RAM (random access memory)   The working memory of a computer. RAM is the memory used for storing data temporarily while working on it, running application programs, and so forth. "Random access" means any area of RAM can be accessed directly and immediately, in contrast to other media, such as a magnetic tape, where data is accessed sequentially. RAM is called *volatile memory;* information in RAM will disappear if the power is switched off before it's saved to disk.

remote access   The capability to access a computer from outside another location. Remote access requires communications hardware, software, and actual physical links, although this can be as simple as common carrier (telephone) lines or as complex as telnet login to another computer across the Internet.

ROM (read-only memory)   A chip in a computer or a peripheral that contains some programs to run the unit. The memory can be read but not changed under normal circumstances. Unlike RAM, ROM retains its information even when the unit is turned off.

S

search engine   A program on the World Wide Web that searches parts of the Internet for text strings. A search engine might search for programs, for web pages, or for other items. Many claim to cover "the whole Internet," but that's a physical impossibility. Getting more than 50 percent of the Internet is a good lick.

seminar   An educational event highlighting interaction and exchange of information, typically among a small number of participants. Genealogy seminars (sometimes called *workshops*) are often held by local organizations.

server   A computer that allows other computers to log on and use its resources. A client (see the earlier definition) program is often used for this.

shareware The try-before-you-buy concept in microcomputer software, where the program is distributed through public domain channels, and the author expects to receive compensation after a trial period. Brother's Keeper, for example, is shareware.

shell account A method of connecting to the Internet. You dial an Internet service provider with regular modem software and connect to a computer that's connected to the Internet. Using a text interface, usually with a menu, you use the Internet with this shell, using commands such as telnet. In this system, the Internet clients don't reside on your computer but rather on that of the ISP.

signature A stored text file with your name and some information, such as names you're researching or your mailing address, to be appended to the end of your messages. Your signature should contain only ASCII characters, no graphics.

SLIP (Serial Line Internet Protocol) A system allowing a computer to use the Internet protocols with a standard telephone line or a high-speed modem. Most ISPs now offer PPP or SLIP accounts for a monthly or a yearly fee.

Soundex An indexing system based on sound rather than the spelling of a surname.

spider A program that gathers information on web pages for a database, usually for a search engine.

SSDI (Social Security Death Index) A searchable database of records of deaths (reported to the Social Security Administration) of Americans with Social Security numbers. The index runs from the 1960s to the present, although a few deaths prior to the 1960s are in it. The records give full name, place and date of death, where the card was issued, and birth date. Many websites have online searches of the SSDI, some with Soundex (see definition).

sysop The *system operator* (manager) of an online community, forum, or echo. The sysop sets the rules, maintains the peace and operability of the system, and sometimes moderates the messages.

T

tagline A short, pithy statement tagged on to the end of a BBS e-mail message. Example: "It's only a hobby, only a hobby, only a...." Taglines are rarely seen on commercial networks, such as AOL, MSN, and CompuServe.

TCP/IP (Transmission Control Protocol/Internet Protocol)
A combined set of protocols that performs the transfer of data between two computers. TCP monitors and ensures correct transfer of data. IP receives the data from TCP, breaks it up into packets, and ships it off to a network within the Internet. TCP/IP is also used as a name for a protocol suite that incorporates these functions and others.

telnet An Internet client that connects to another computer, making yours a virtual terminal of the remote computer. Among other functions, telnet enables a user to log in to a remote computer from the user's local computer. On many commercial systems, you use telnet as a command (for example, telnet ftp.cac.psu.edu). Once there, you are using programs and, therefore, commands from that remote computer.

terminal emulation Most communications software packages will permit your personal computer or workstation to communicate with another computer or network, as if it were a specific type of terminal directly connected to that computer or network. For example, your terminal emulation should be set to VT100 for most online card catalog programs.

terminal server A machine that connects terminals to a network by providing host telnet services.

thread (message thread) A discussion made up of a set of messages in answer to a certain message and to each other. Sometimes worthwhile threads are saved into a text file, as on CompuServe's Roots Forum. Some mail readers will sort by thread (that is, according to subject line).

Trojan horse A type of malicious code. This is usually a program that seems to be useful and harmless. In the background, however, it might be destroying data or breaking security on your system. It differs from a virus in that it rarely propagates itself as a virus does.

TT (tiny tafel)   A TT provides a standard way of describing a family database so the information can be scanned visually or by computer. All data fields are of fixed length, with the obvious exceptions of the surnames and optional places. Many TTs are extracted from GEDCOMs.

U

uploading   The process of sending a file or message from your computer to another. (See also: *downloading.*)

USB (universal serial bus)   A connection to a computer. Unlike a parallel port (where your printer probably plugs in) or a serial port (where your modem probably plugs in), a USB port enables you to "daisy chain" peripherals. If you have a USB printer, modem, and CD-ROM drive, you could plug only one into the USB port and the rest connect by USB cables in a chain (in theory, say, computer to modem to printer to CD-ROM). In practice, sometimes it's a little tricky to get them in an order that makes all the peripherals happy.

Usenet   A set of messages and the software for sending and receiving them on the Internet.

V

virus   A program that installs itself secretly on a computer by attaching itself to another program or e-mail. This program then duplicates itself when it is executed or when the e-mail is opened. Some viruses are harmless, but most of them intend to do damage, such as erasing important files on your system.

vital records   The official records of birth, death, marriage, and other events of a person's life.

W

workshop   See *seminar.*

worm   A computer program that makes copies of itself and spreads through connected systems, using up resources in affected computers or causing other damage.

WWW or the Web (World Wide Web) A system to pull various Internet services together into one interface, called a browser. Most sites on the Web are written as pages in HTML.

Smiley (Emoticon) Glossary

Because we can't hear voice inflection over e-mail, a code for imparting emotion has sprung up. These punctuation marks, which are used to take the place of facial expressions, are called *Smileys* or *emoticons*. Different systems have variations of these symbols. Two versions of this "Unofficial Smiley Dictionary" were sent to me by Cliff Manis (Internet: cmanis@csf.com), and I've edited and combined them. Several versions are floating around, but I think this one sums up the symbols you're most likely to see.

:-) Your basic Smiley. This Smiley is used to show pleasure, or to indicate a sarcastic or joking statement.

;-) Winky Smiley. The user just made a flirtatious and/or sarcastic remark. It's somewhat of a "don't hit me for what I just said" Smiley.

:-(Frowning Smiley. The user didn't like the last statement or is upset or depressed about something.

:-I Indifferent Smiley. Better than a frowning Smiley, but not quite as good as a happy Smiley.

:-/ Smiley showing puzzlement or consternation.

:-> The user just made a biting, sarcastic remark. Worse than a happy Smiley.

>>:-> The user just made a devilish remark.

>>;-> The winky and devilish Smileys combined.

Those are the basic symbols. Here are some less common ones:

Note ——————————————————————————————

A lot of these can be typed without noses to make midget Smileys.

- -:-)	Smiley is a punk rocker.
- -:-(	Real punk rockers don't smile.
;-)	Wink.
,-}	Wry and winking.
:,(	Crying.
:-:	Mutant Smiley.
.-)	Smiley only has one eye.
,-)	Ditto, but he's winking.
:-?	Smiley smoking a pipe.
:-/	Skepticism, consternation, or puzzlement.
:-\	Ditto.
:-'	Smiley spitting out its chewing tobacco.
:-~)	Smiley has a cold.
:-)~	Smiley drools.
:-[	Un-Smiley blockhead.
:-[	Smiley is a vampire.
:-]	Smiley blockhead.
:-{	Mustache.
:-}	Wry smile or beard.
:-@	Smiley screaming.
:-$	Smiley with its mouth wired shut.
:-*	Smiley after eating something bitter or sour.
:-&	Smiley is tongue-tied.
:-#	Braces.
:-#|	Smiley face with bushy mustache.
:-%	Smiley banker.
:-< <	Mad or real sad Smiley.
:-=)	Older Smiley with mustache.
:-> >	Hey, hey.
:-|	"Have an ordinary day" Smiley.
:-0	Smiley orator.
:-0	No yelling! (Quiet Lab)
:-1	Smiley bland face.
:-6	Smiley after eating something sour.
:-7	Smiley after a wry statement.

:-8(	Condescending stare.
:-9	Smiley is licking his/her lips.
:-a	Lefty smiley touching tongue to nose.
:-b	Left-pointing tongue Smiley.
:-c	Bummed-out Smiley.
:-C	Smiley is really bummed.
:-d	Lefty Smiley razzing you.
:-D	Smiley is laughing.
:-e	Disappointed Smiley
:-E	Bucktoothed vampire.
:-F	Bucktoothed vampire with one tooth missing.
:-I	Hmm.
:-I	Semi-Smiley.
:-j	Left-smiling Smiley.
:-o	Smiley singing the National Anthem.
:-O	Uh, oh!
:-o	Uh, oh.
:-P	Disgusted or nyah, nyah.
:-p	Smiley sticking its tongue out (at you!).
:-q	Smiley trying to touch its tongue to its nose.
:-Q	Smoker.
:-s	Smiley after a bizarre comment.
:-S	Smiley just made an incoherent statement.
:-t	Cross Smiley.
:-v	Talking head Smiley.
:-x	"My lips are sealed" Smiley.
:-X	Bow tie or emphasized Smiley's lips are sealed.
::-)	Smiley wears normal glasses.
:'-(	Smiley is crying.
:'-)	Smiley is so happy, he or she is crying.
:^)	Smiley with pointy nose (righty). Sometimes used to denote a lie, a myth, or a misconception, as in Pinocchio—or a broken nose. Also seen as :v).
:(	Sad Midget Smiley.
:)	Midget Smiley.
:[	Real downer.

:]	Midget smiley.
:*	Kisses.
:*)	Smiley is drunk.
:<<N	Midget unSmiley.
:<)<N	Smiley is from an Ivy League school.
:=)	Smiley has two noses.
:>>	Midget Smiley.
:D	Laughter.
:I	Hmmm.
:n)	Smiley with funny-looking right nose.
:O	Yelling.
:u)	Smiley with funny-looking left nose.
:v)	Left-pointing nose Smiley, or Smiley has a broken nose.
':-)	Smiley shaved one of his eyebrows off this morning.
,:-)	Same thing, other side.
~~:-(	net.flame.
(-:	Smiley is left-handed.
(:-(	UnSmiley frowning
(:-)	Smiley big face.
(:I	Egghead.
(8-o	It's Mr. Bill!
):-(	UnSmiley big face.
)8-)	Scuba Smiley big face.
[:-)	Smiley is wearing a walkman.
[:]	Smiley is a robot.
[]	Hugs.
{:-)	Smiley with his or her hair parted in the middle.
{:-)	Smiley wears a toupee.
}:-(	Toupee in an updraft.
@@:-)	Smiley is wearing a turban.
@@:I	Turban variation.
@@=	Smiley is pro-nuclear war.
*:o)	Bozo the Clown!
%-)	Smiley has been staring at a green screen for 15 hours straight.
%-6	Smiley is brain-dead.

+ -:-)	Smiley is the Pope or holds some other religious office.
+ :-)	Smiley priest.
< :- <	Smiley is a dunce.
=)	Teenage Smiley.
> > :-I	net.startrek.
|-)	Hee, hee.
|-D	Ho, ho.
|-I	Smiley is asleep.
|-O	Smiley is yawning/snoring.
|-P	Yuk.
|^o	Snoring.
|I	Asleep.
0-)	Smiley Cyclops (scuba diver?).
3:[	Mean pet Smiley.
3:]	Pet Smiley.
3:o[	Net.pets.
8 :-)	Smiley is a wizard.
8 :-I	Net.unix-wizards.
8-)	Glasses.
8-)	Smiley swimmer.
8-)	Smiley is wearing sunglasses.
8:-)	Glasses on forehead.
8:-)	Smiley is a little girl.
B-)	Horn-rims.
B:-)	Sunglasses on head.
C = :-)	Smiley is a chef.
E-:-)	Smiley is a Ham radio operator.
E-:-I	Net.ham-radio.
g-)	Smiley with pince-nez glasses.
K:P	Smiley is a little kid with a propeller beanie.
O :-)	Smiley is an angel (at heart, at least).
O |-)	Net.religion.
O-)	Megaton Man On Patrol! (or else the user is a scuba diver).
X-(	Smiley just died.

Message and Chat Shorthand

If you see...	The chatter means...
Afk	Away from keyboard.
Y	Why?
U	You.
C	See.
BRB	Be right back.
<g>	Grin.
<bg>	Big grin.
<vbg>	Very big grin.
BTW	By the way.
CUL	See you later.
CWYL	Chat with you later.
FUBAR	Fouled up beyond all recognition.
FWIW	For what it's worth.
GIWIST	Gee, I wish I'd said that!
HHOK	Ha, ha! Only kidding!
HTH	Hope this helps.
HTHBE	Hope this has been enlightening.
IMHO	In my humble opinion.
IMNSHO	In my not so humble opinion.
IOW	In other words.
IRL	In real life.
ITRW	In the real world.
JK	Just kidding.
LOL	Laughing out loud.
OTP	On the phone.
OTF	On the floor.
OIC	Oh! I see!
OTOH	On the other hand.
POV	Point of view.
RL	Real life.
ROTFL	Rolling on the floor laughing.
RTFM	Read the fine manual (or help file).
TTFN	Ta, ta for now.
TTYL	Talk to you later.
WRT	With regard to.

Index

N

INTERNATIONAL CONTACT INFORMATION

AUSTRALIA
McGraw-Hill Book Company Australia Pty. Ltd.
TEL +61-2-9900-1800
FAX +61-2-9878-8881
http://www.mcgraw-hill.com.au
books-it_sydney@mcgraw-hill.com

CANADA
McGraw-Hill Ryerson Ltd.
TEL +905-430-5000
FAX +905-430-5020
http://www.mcgraw-hill.ca

**GREECE, MIDDLE EAST, & AFRICA
(Excluding South Africa)**
McGraw-Hill Hellas
TEL +30-210-6560-990
TEL +30-210-6560-993
TEL +30-210-6560-994
FAX +30-210-6545-525

MEXICO (Also serving Latin America)
McGraw-Hill Interamericana Editores S.A. de C.V.
TEL +525-117-1583
FAX +525-117-1589
http://www.mcgraw-hill.com.mx
fernando_castellanos@mcgraw-hill.com

SINGAPORE (Serving Asia)
McGraw-Hill Book Company
TEL +65-6863-1580
FAX +65-6862-3354
http://www.mcgraw-hill.com.sg
mghasia@mcgraw-hill.com

SOUTH AFRICA
McGraw-Hill South Africa
TEL +27-11-622-7512
FAX +27-11-622-9045
robyn_swanepoel@mcgraw-hill.com

SPAIN
McGraw-Hill/Interamericana de España, S.A.U.
TEL +34-91-180-3000
FAX +34-91-372-8513
http://www.mcgraw-hill.es
professional@mcgraw-hill.es

**UNITED KINGDOM, NORTHERN,
EASTERN, & CENTRAL EUROPE**
McGraw-Hill Education Europe
TEL +44-1-628-502500
FAX +44-1-628-770224
http://www.mcgraw-hill.co.uk
computing_europe@mcgraw-hill.com

ALL OTHER INQUIRIES Contact:
McGraw-Hill/Osborne
TEL +1-510-420-7700
FAX +1-510-420-7703
http://www.osborne.com
omg_international@mcgraw-hill.com

Sound Off!

Visit us at **www.osborne.com/bookregistration** and let us know what you thought of this book. While you're online you'll have the opportunity to register for newsletters and special offers from McGraw-Hill/Osborne Media.

We want to hear from you!

Sneak Peek

Visit us today at **www.betabooks.com** and see what's coming from McGraw-Hill/Osborne Media tomorrow!

Based on the successful software paradigm, Bet@Books™ allows computing professionals to view partial and sometimes complete text versions of selected titles online. Bet@Books™ viewing is free, invites comments and feedback, and allows you to "test drive" books in progress on the subjects that interest you the most.